PEEING ON HOT COALS

A Searing Memoir

PAT MONTANDON

To

Sean Patrick Wilsey

Owen Taylor Wilsey

Mira Annapurna Wilsey

You are my heart.

Also By Pat Montandon

Books

How to be a Party Girl

The Intruders

Making Friends (the first Soviet/American co-publication)

Celebrities and Their Angels

Oh The Hell Of It All (hardback)

Whispers from God; A Life Beyond Imaginings (Paper back of Hell)

Peeing On Hot Coals

Plays

Patience Patient

Them Oklahoma Hills

Family Album

Dreams Notwithstanding

Poetry

Black Silence

Testosterone Drums

Tiananmen Square

DMZ

American Dream

Children of Chernobyl

Ghosts

Truth

Contents

Acknowledgements

Darlin', if I tried to thank all the people who helped me with *Peeing*, you would be bored half to death. Listing all my Facebook friends would be a book in itself. Laugh if you will, but my FB friends have become true and treasured supporters in good times and in sad times. I am more than grateful to them.

Team Montandon, or Pat's Angels, as they call themselves, have grown wings strong enough to carry me right on up to heaven, bypassing Saint Peter and all the angel guards. As if in a Botticelli painting, you will recognize the beatific Christine Owner and Katie Lou Ellison, Darwin Bell, Chris Castro, Matthew DeCoster, David Landis, Sean Dowdell, Huntington Sharp, and Leonardo Perillo (ask him how we met!), by the golden halo about their heads.

And where would I be without Dan McKinley and Anthony Duran who, at the last minute saved my literary time frame? I'm sending them virtual kisses and big hugs. Smack!

A heartfelt thank you to Ken Burns, whose documentary *The Dust Bowl* ignited recollections that pushed me to record my images of that frightful time. And how do I express thanks to Bill Newcomer for the gift of bookmarks from his BNC printing company? Maybe platters of my specialty Oklahoma style fried chicken! Bill Greenleaf, my erudite editor, deserves a big shout-out for his meticulous attention to detail. And thanks to designer Brian Burchfield, who created a delightful dust-jacket for Peeing On Hot Coals featuring Rat Dog.

Xiomara Reyes, Madame X as I call her, a lovely young woman who cooks delicious low-calorie meals for me, is one of my best readers alongside Jane Robb, Janie Mae, a longtime friend. And how about Buddy Hatton? That amazing and talented friend drove six hours all the way from his home in northern California to set up a little studio so I could record Peeing. Hallelujah!

I am beyond grateful to all the writers who so generously read *Peeing* and made (really good!) comments about it. You will recognize the names: David Sheff (*Beautiful Boy*), Armistead Maupin (*Tales of the City*), Julia Scheeres (*Jesus Land*), Alev Lytle Croutier (*Harem: The World Behind the Veil*), Mel White (*Religion Gone Bad*), Merla Zellerbach (*Secrets in Time*), and Sean Wilsey, my son (*Oh the Glory of It All*). Sean saw me safely through an ever-changing river of words. He encouraged me when the stream was clogged and offered solace during a tsunami of remembering. I am grateful.

The family. We were a strange little band of characters trudging through life sharing diseases and toothpaste, coveting one another's desserts, hiding shampoo, borrowing money, locking each other out of our rooms, inflicting pain and kissing to heal it in the same instant, loving, laughing, defending, and trying to figure out the common thread that bound us all together.

Erma Bombeck

"Between the earth and that sky I felt erased, blotted out."

Willa Cather

Preface

These days, when I look into a mirror, I hardly recognize the silver-haired woman staring back at me. Wrinkles? Where did *they* come from? At least my eyes are still blue and my mind seems to work, although from time to time, I have trouble calling up a name.

In my old age, I've wondered if I dreamed up my incredible past. Did I actually burn down our house when I was fifteen? I sometimes look at picture albums trying to be sure I didn't fantasize events and people, like my kindhearted but volatile preacher-father who scared the daylights out of me when he talked about hellfire and brimstone. He also taught me to have faith, a belief in myself that kept me going through events that could have killed me: death threats from the Russian mafia; a cruel husband or two—men who caused me to shrink into myself, to become small so they could feel large, when all I wanted was to be loved and treated with respect. I'm sure I remember that correctly.

And did my stern mother exist, or did I imagine her, as well as my eight siblings, several lovers, and those three and a half husbands—not one of whom as I recall, could be classified a lover?

When I toss in my bed at night in a vain attempt to hit upon comfort I search for a glimmer of the girl I once was, when my family, imagined or real, was as alive as you are right now. Was I ever considered a great beauty, a "jet set queen," as news reporters called me? That always caused me to laugh, because I couldn't afford a ticket across town, much less a seat on a jet plane. Later they dubbed me a socialite, an equally absurd title that made me howl with delight. Ha! Me, a socialite. In time, I'm sure I became a feminist and a divorcee and a peace activist and a mother, though seldom was I called a writer. San Francisco reporters didn't want to give an uneducated, curvy, blond-headed Okie girl credit for having brains. They wanted me to remain as they labeled me—a socialite—whatever that meant. And that was that. During my years in Russia and China, some tagged me as a Red. "You aren't becoming a Red, are you?" asked a friend who should have known better. Even when I was given the United Nations Peace Messenger Award and was nominated for a Nobel Peace Prize, San Francisco reporters scoffed. I pretended I didn't care what they thought, but my heart trembled.

For my roundtable luncheons, I entertained folks as diverse as Harvey Milk and Dianne Feinstein and Alex Haley, folksinger Joan Baez and Black Panther Eldridge Cleaver, and my childhood idol, Shirley Temple. At my request, Andy Warhol climbed up on my bed for an iconic picture with my arms around him. His orange-and-navy bow tie was skewed sideways, giving him a decidedly Howdy Doody look. When Merla Zellerbach, a longtime friend, wrote in her *Chronicle* news column that at a roundtable luncheon I had talked about being on welfare as a child, my oldest sister, Nina, called Merla and told her it wasn't true—that we had not, not, not been on welfare. Nina considered the truth to be shameful, and she wanted a retraction. Could that memory be a hallucination? I don't think so.

The Ken Burns documentary *The Dust Bowl* aroused in me reactionary emotions that I thought were entombed in my cerebellum forever. But no, after viewing that biopic and suffering through Black Sunday dust storms, parching drought, and the worst environmental disaster known, I awakened in the dark of night coughing. I could hardly breathe from the dirt blowing through the corridors of my mind as if I lay in a rusted iron bed beside my sister, Poor Little Glendora, in the Oklahoma Panhandle while a ferocious dust storm tried to smother us to death. That telling documentary brought back memories of the dust storms that defined my childhood, dust storms that killed my toddler sister, Bettie Ruth, eleven months before I was born.

The pain of having lived in grinding poverty, suffering through those terrifying storms, and enduring deprivation during the Great Depression ignites within me such compassion for kids that I once took a diamond watch off my wrist and gave it to a hungry child to pawn. And while staying in an ashram in India, I bought brand-new saris for all the young girls living in squalor just

outside the blue-and-pink gates. The children looked like madcap butterflies, joyful and giggling as they twirled in the dirt, the hems of their filmy red, gold, and yellow saris swiftly becoming as gray as their bare feet.

But most of all—yes, most of all—for the first time in my adult life, little by little the horrific event that happened to me when I was seven seeped into my awareness. Perhaps the subconscious, with its own eccentric logic, insists on knowing the truth, even if the truth has shocking and costly emotional consequence. Although peeing on hot coals dramatically affected my life, I hadn't recognized the impact of that agonizing and searing accident until I began writing this book and in the process spontaneously decided to consult a gynecologist.

Before the doctor examined me, I read aloud from my manuscript so she could better understand why I was there. Dr. Collins sat on a chair while I perched on the end of the crinkly paper-covered examining table in a blue hospital gown. Clearing my throat, I began to read, but the tremor in my voice betrayed the roiling emotions hidden in the purgatorial folds of my brain, making a blood smear of the black type as I sobbed.

Dr. Collins cried with me, and then, after wiping her tears, she gently examined me. Afterward, and with wet eyes, she said, in the kindest way she could, that there was evidence that I had suffered a type of genital mutilation from the accidental burns I had received as a child. Waves of grief swept over me. The implications of her finding devastated me.

I was a fetus bathed in the fluid of my mother's grief after the death of my two-year-old sister. I was a baby delivered at home on an iron bedstead by a neighbor lady. I was an infant brought forth into an indifferent world crying out with quavering wails for Home, that watery bath of safety.

And now, after many starts and stops along the way, those events and the dreamed-up characters of my life call out to me in plaintive cries, so I add kindling to the fire around which they gather. Every night, when at last I sleep, they lie down beside me, soothing me, crooning stories to me as if to a child, reinforcing memories in dreams . . . and nightmares.

Chapter 1
The Holy Poltergeist

The old yellow bus, its rusty bumper dragging, kids pressed against the smeared windows, huffed and puffed from the curb in front of the school before I could reach it. "Wait!" I hollered as loud as I could, and ran panting after it on my skinny legs, blond pigtails flying, until my sides hurt so bad I couldn't run anymore. But the bus snorted on, stirring up choking black exhaust and whirligigs of dust, even though snotty J. T. stuck his white-coated tongue out at me from the back window and could have told the driver to stop. "You're stupid, J. T!" I yelled, hoping he could hear me above the noise of the bus and the wind. Placing my grimy hands on either side of my mouth, I continued to bellow at the retreating bus. "J. T, y'all got a big ol' *F* on your papers, and it serves you right for making fun of me for being a new second grader." The howling wind blew the words right out of my mouth and across the rough schoolyard all the way to the cracked teeter-totter.

The bus rattled on down the road and was lost from sight. Oh, no, now I would have to find my way home on that long red dirt road by following fence posts buried in sand up to their jagged tops. My knees quivered at the thought of the Devil or an angry God skulking in the scrub, ready to fling me into Hell for filching half a leftover bologna sandwich from Pansy Jean's red lunch box. Daddy preached about the sin of stealing, so I knew better than to take something that didn't belong to me, even when my stomach growled with hunger. *Mama says everyone is hungry these days, so I should be used to it by now.*

I shivered and coughed and hoped I wasn't coming down with the dust pneumonia like a church member had done. She'd up and died from it. And Daddy talked about how cattle croaked from the dirt that flew across their nostrils and onto the thistles they ate. One time Daddy let me go with him when he helped a farmer whose cow had tipped over and expired from eating too much dirt. I sat in our Model A Ford and watched as Daddy and

11

Mr. Johnson got ready to open up the dead cow and empty the dirt out of her four stomachs. They took sharp butcher knives and cut that poor dead cow from under her stiff brown tail and up over her bloated belly all the way to her neck. And then, phew-ee, a stink like Little Jimmy's diapers, times two, diseased the hot air like a fetid slaughterhouse. I pinched my nose closed, but it didn't help much.

"Jist look at that, Reverend," the man said to Daddy. "She's as full of dirt as these here worn-out fields." He wiped his sweating face with the rag he had hanging out his back pocket and then squatted down in the dirt.

Daddy patted the man's shoulder. "Mr. Johnson, maybe y'all can get a little meat off her even though she is poor. And the hide looks all right."

"Preacher," Farmer Johnson said, all hunched over, his pants covered in bloody innards, his straw hat raggedy looking. "This is the last of my livestock. The very last." He looked up at the burning sun. The sky was as blue as a number two Crayola. Not even a cloud fluffed around up there. It was just a haze of dust and all that unearthly blue. "Sir," he addressed my father. "Sir, I feel like Job, in the Bible. My wheat crop jist shriveled clean up and blew away, the chickens up and died, the cattle died, our new baby girl, Little May Beth, is sick. Preacher," he said, and then, worn out with talking I guessed, he gave out a long sigh, wiped his face with the grimy-looking cloth, took off his hat and put his sunburned head in his claw like hands, and pulled his fingers through his sandy hair. "Preacher, I ain't got nothin' left to take care of the wife and five little ones with." The man began to belch out loud sobs, his shoulders shaking like he was sick with a chill.

Daddy shed tears, too, and said he would try to get help from church members for him, making me wonder if he knew a rich church member I hadn't heard about.

"Reverend . . . " Farmer Johnson heaved a sigh. "Don't bother yourself none. I've 'bout decided to head toward Californie like Farmer Bates, and Charlie Martin, and all them other fellers. Maybe I can pick fruit.

Anythin' is better than jist a'sittin' here a'waitin' to die." The man stood up, but quickly squatted down again, like his legs were too weak to hold him up. "But, Reverend," he said, "I 'preciate your offer, I sure enough do, sir."

Daddy knelt down next to Farmer Johnson, put his big hands on the man's head, and talked to God for a few minutes. Then Daddy stood up and brushed the sand off the knees of his only pair of suit pants and walked to the car. He started the engine, hit the horn twice—*uga-uga*—waved goodbye, and drove off, bouncing over swellings of sand and leaving Poor Farmer Johnson hunkered down in the dirt beside his opened-up dead cow.

"Chick-a-lick," Daddy said, using his nickname for me. "Chick-a-lick, these are hard times here on the High Plains. There's an out-of-control catastrophe going on all around us." He pointed toward a weathered farmhouse and a falling-over barn where good church members had once lived. "That's an example." he said. "Pretty soon we won't have any parishioners left if they keep on dying off or moving away because of the drought and these sandstorms." Daddy took his soiled handkerchief and wiped the tears streaming down his face. "Poor Farmer Johnson," Daddy muttered over and over again. "Poor Farmer Johnson."

I thought about Poor Farmer Johnson now as I walked home past fields full of red sand where golden wheat had once grown. Cow skeletons were scattered here and there, ribs sticking up through drifts of dirt with bits of fur attached to the bones like raggedy flags. It seemed like a cow cemetery.

Home . . . I had to get home to safety before a dust storm decided to take out after me. I looked around, hoping to see a living human being out there in all that dirt. But there wasn't a house or a tree or a bush or a cow or a sheep or a shack, except for one that had sand spilling from its busted-out windows. Not one living thing grew along that road. The land was flat except for wind-whipped sand dunes as far as the eye could see and filled with dust devils. All that forsaken space made me wonder if I was the only thing alive in the whole wide world. Maybe Jesus had come and the Rapture had happened and I missed it and now I was a Left Behind. I glanced around trying to spot danger so I could hide in a ditch. Leaning over, I pulled up my sagging stockings and wiped my runny nose on the sleeve of my brown coat that had once belonged to my sister, Poor Little Glendora, struggling to get over my scaredness. Maybe I should pray. Grit clawed into my skin as I knelt down on the road and addressed the Almighty.

"Please forgive me, God in Heaven, for stealing from that mean girl, Pansy Jean, even though she had more than enough to share and could have offered me her leftover sandwich," I prayed. "Get me home safely, and I promise never to steal again." My squinted-up eyes dripped tears while my nose ran, fusing with the dirt that blew in swirls around me. "And dear God, save me from going to Hell like that preacher man said would happen to me."

Wiping gravel off the knees of my long gray stockings with my coat sleeve, I tied on the yellow rag Mama had given me to cover my nose and mouth against the needling dust, making it hard to breathe. Then I heaved a sigh and started walking, leaning into the wind that zoomed around me. This place was nothing like our old home, which had trees and Bermuda grass. At least there weren't many nettles here. I'd never forget the day I learned about those. Flushed with excitement when I saw a red *A* on my first-grade report card, eager to spill the news to my parents, I'd run unheedingly through a nest of stinging nettles and ended up in pain and sobbing. It was my first memory of mingled emotions. On one hand I was happy, but my legs stung and bled from sticker picks.

"That's a lesson, Patsy Lou," Mama allowed in her Take-No-Prisoners voice. "Pride goeth before a fall."

She knew what she was talking about, because the next day, a church deacon reared up on his white high horse and told my daddy we had to vacate the parsonage, even though Daddy had built it himself, hung flowered wallpaper, sanded floors, and we had scrimped to pay for everything. Mama cried and begged Daddy to stand up to Brother Williams, but Daddy said he followed the will of God, so we moved on.

Now we lived in a dilapidated parsonage with pitted white paint and a front porch so off-kilter I once slid off it and landed on a pile of dirt clods at the end of the overhang. The house, set on the lip of this same narrow road two miles east of Addington, Oklahoma, was bounded by a ditch full of parched bushes stabbing twigs out in a wasted hunt for water.

One of my pigtails had lost its red ribbon, and my hair blew against my face and across my eyes as I lowered my head and trudged along, wondering how many hobos would be hanging out on our back steps when I reached home. It was 1935, and Daddy said we were going through a depression. "Patsy Lou and Charles," he said to my big brother and me one day, "y'all need to know how good y'all have it, even though you're hungry at times. Do y'all know that some of those fellows riding the rails are kids no more than fourteen?"

"No, sir, I didn't know that," Charles answered.

"They look grown up to me, wearing overhalls and stuff." I chimed in. "They wear nice caps, too."

"Patsy Lou, those boys sleep on top of boxcars, starved and worn out, looking for a way to make a living in these hard times. And its overalls, not overhauls."

"Well, they flock to our steps like squirrels to a feeder." My teenage brother hee-hawed, "They slurp up Mama's watered-down soup like I don't know what."

Daddy frowned at my brother. "Son, everyone's hungry nowadays. Hungry men trying to find work, having to leave families behind, trying to get to California and a job. These sandstorms have just about killed us all. We're sure enough living in the middle of a dust bowl."

Mama thought the hobos and bums used a secret sign carved on fence posts leading them straight to our doorstep for a bowl of soup—and if we had the fixings, cold biscuits, too. "When we don't hardly have enough food for our own," Mama said.

Sometimes a wanderer would spend several days at our house sleeping on a back porch pallet and tinkering with stuff that Daddy didn't know how to fix. One man repaired Daddy's car and then drove off in it and didn't come back. Mama was fit to be tied.

"Charlie," she said to my father, "I told you not to be so trusting!"

Daddy wiped his face with a white handkerchief and then tucked it back into his pocket and gave out a long, heavy sigh before answering Mama. "Myrtle," he said, staring up at the sky, "I reckon that feller needs our car more than we do."

Daddy's words made Mama explode like a Fourth of July firecracker. She ran into the house, slamming doors and yelling, "Cain't imagine anyone needin' anythin' more than we do." She shouted until Daddy told her to be quiet and put supper on the table. I was relieved when she simmered down and didn't start World War number one hundred fifty-five thousand with Daddy.

As I looked down the forever road that stretched out ahead, I distracted myself by talking to my sister, Dead Bettie Ruth. She died a few months before I was born, and I never heard the end of it from my older siblings. Bettie Ruth was everything I was not. She had dark curly hair and was beautiful and smart even though she was only a toddler when she died from dust pneumonia. I didn't tell my family that ever since we had visited her grave over a year ago, Dead Bettie Ruth had become my best friend.

On one of our moves into the unknown, we had made a side journey into the familiar—at least to Mama, Daddy, Charles, and Poor Little Glendora—but not to me. It was to the town of my birth, Merkel, Texas, in the hard-hit Texas panhandle, and the cemetery where Little Bettie Ruth had been laid to rest six years earlier.

The air was heavy and silent, except for flashes of lightning and occasional rolls of thunder that suddenly came sweeping across the plains, foretelling rain.

"It's going to rain, I do believe," Daddy shouted, like he had just gotten religion. "Rain, I'm sure of it," he said, hitting his fist on the steering wheel. Sure enough, two fat drops of water hit the car windshield—*splat*— smearing the dusty glass so bad that Daddy had to pull off to the side of the road and take a rag to clean it so he could see to drive.

"Halleluiah! Glory to God!" Mama strangled out a cry, apparently unable to contain her excitement over seeing two drops of rain after five years of drought.

"Hooray!" I yelled from the backseat, but then I cowered down because the rain had stopped and we were approaching the cemetery where Little Bettie Ruth lay in a white casket wearing a white batiste dress, I was told, with a lace cap embroidered in pink roses over her black curls and new white baby socks. An electric current of anxiety circulated between us from Mama to Daddy and Poor Little Glendora and Charles and then to me. Mama held a white lace handkerchief—a friend had gifted it to her at a shower for the new baby that was in her belly—up to her mouth as her cobalt eyes scrutinized the mounded graves that rose up ahead of us.

Daddy parked the car, and we all piled out quietly and reverently like we were going to meet Reverend Billy Sunday and his wife, Ma Sunday. Mama sprinted on ahead of us, her blue flowered dress whipping in the wind that had suddenly sprung up and was blowing tumbleweeds and sand across the graves and banking up against the tombstones. Mama pushed several crinkly weeds off a tiny grave, and then she lay down sideways on that pocket-sized burial place and sobbed. Daddy wiped his eyes with his hands, and then he lay down next to Mama on the mounded dirt and put an arm around her. Not wanting to be left out, I threw myself on top of Daddy. Poor Little Glendora and Charles joined me. We piled on top of our parents on the red dirt grave of our sister, weeping. We were a mound of heartache, our sorrow filtering down through the red earth in a delicate stream, giving Dead

17

Bettie Ruth the sweet taste of our tears where she lay sleeping in her pristine dress and cap with the pink roses on it, and her little white socks, her curly head resting on a pink satin pillow, as fierce wind blew silky red ribbons and shriveled carnations across that desolate cemetery in the panhandle of Texas.

After a few minutes of lying on top of each other all tumbled together like that, and after Mama stopped crying, Daddy told us to get up. There was work to be done.

"Y'all get up now and help your mama and me get these tumbleweeds off of little Bettie Ruth's resting place," he said, already stacking up a pile of crunchy weeds that had congregated around the headstone that he, himself, had carved with his hands and a chisel.

"Look here, y'all," Mama said, holding out a miniscule cup and saucer and a tiny pot to match. "Somebody put these play pretties on Bettie Ruth's grave. Isn't that sweet? Patsy Lou, you want to take them home to play with?"

"No, they belong to Dead Bettie Ruth," I said. I took the toys from Mama's earth-soiled hands and wedged the tiny white porcelain dishes back into the ground that roofed my sister.

Since that day in the cemetery, if I felt scared or lonesome or worried, I talked to Dead Bettie Ruth. "Dead Bettie Ruth," I would say to my sister, "what's going to happen if one of us gets sick? Where will the money for medicine come from?" My sister didn't talk much, and sometimes she disappeared in the middle of a conversation, but this time she shook her dark curls and smiled. Then I knew that everything would be okay. "Bettie Ruth," I continued, "Do y'all think we'll ever have our very own house again? And what if Daddy makes a church member mad by inviting darkies to services like he did at the last place? Will we have to move again?"

My dead sister didn't answer, having disappeared back to Heaven. I decided to talk to God.

"God," I said, my words muffled by the cloth tied over my nose and mouth, "Are you going to make Daddy up and take us off to New Mexico or some other foreign place?"

God was as silent as Dead Bettie Ruth.

Whenever Daddy heard the call of the Lord—and the Lord called often—we loaded up everything we owned and moved. Did the Almighty have a telephone nailed to a cloud just so he could call Daddy? If God did have a telephone, did he have an operator like Lucille, who listened in on our party line? Our phone was a wooden box hooked to a wall in the kitchen. We turned a handle on the side of it until Lucille said, "Operator, what number, please?"

Once in a while, Charles, his Robin Hood features and mischievous blue eyes smiling, quietly lifted the receiver while I stood on a kitchen chair to listen to neighbors gossip, until Lucille said, "Get off the line, y'all kids. I know y'all are a-listenin' in."

Charles crashed the receiver back on the hook, and we giggled like fools. Anyway, if Almighty God had a phone, I wished he would stop calling Daddy so I could catch up at school. Maybe I would answer the phone the next time God called. I imagined the phone ringing and Lucille saying, "Hold on now, sir. Reverend Montandon, God is calling."

I would say, "God?" And a voice like an explosion of thunder from out of a purple cloud, the kind of worrying sound we had when it rained, would spark and boom through those tiny electric wires strung on posts at the front of our house, like it could hardly fit. **"HELLO, PATSY LOU. THIS IS GOD ALMIGHTY, CREATOR OF HEAVEN AND EARTH, THE GOD OF ISRAEL, JEHOVAH, THE SAVIOR, THE EVERLASTING FATHER, THE ALMIGHTY GOD. HOW ARE YOU TODAY?"**

Just imagining such a thing made me fearful of being struck down dead as a doornail. "Sorry, God," I muttered.

As the newest student in my class, it was hard to make friends. During recess at my latest school, I asked some girls if I could play hopscotch with them, but they shook their heads no.

"Y'all are probably a crybaby," Pansy Jean said, her dirty-blond hair done up in fat Shirley Temple curls, making me jealous because my hair was stick straight, and worse, my nose zigzagged a little from a car wreck I was in on the way to my oldest brother's wedding in Pilot Point, Texas, when I was five. I was sitting on Daddy's lap in the front seat when the man driving us in his car hit a telephone pole. *Wham!* I slammed headlong into the dashboard. Blood gushed from my nose like I was Jesus on the cross. It hurt, too. But I was more worried about my new white dress getting ruined, the only new dress I could ever remember owning, than about my broken nose. I held my head way out over the road and watched my glistening cherry-colored blood run into pavement cracks instead of onto my pretty dress.

Church members said my smile was nice, though, and that I had straight teeth. I should hope so. When my baby teeth needed to come out, Mama sat on top of me with her rolled stockings around her ankles, hair undone, a face full of intent, and with kitchen scissors in her rough hands she zigzagged across my gums until she pried the teeth out as I bled. "Y'all are not going to have crooked teeth like Poor Little Glendora," she said, although I wiggled and hollered and tried to get away. Nothing stopped my mother from her appointed rounds.

Thinking about how Mama had dug out my baby teeth, I kicked a rock and watched it tumble into the ditch. This dusty ol' road seemed to go on forever. Heavy, wintry shadows hiding in the leafless trees leaped out to sop up the daylight, making me afraid Brother Webber would skitter out from the dead bushes and snatch me by my pigtails.

Brother Webber had paid us a visit once when Daddy was away water-witching for a dried-out farmer. I lay on the horsehair couch, my tonsils swollen together and dotted with white spots. Mama went to the kitchen for a minute, leaving me alone with Brother Webber.

Mama said to always be polite to my elders, so when he'd asked me

20

to sit on his lap, I obediently perched on the knees of his olive drab suit, hoping he would push me off. But the old man pulled me higher up onto his knees, and before I knew what was happening, he deposited his freckled hands on my chest and rubbed round and round, real hard. "Y'all like that, little girl?" he said. A sour smell churned from his fish mouth.

When I tried to squirm away, he tightened his grip on me until Mama suddenly appeared in the doorway. In a startlingly swift motion, the old man pushed me across his bumpy trousers and off his sharp lap. *Plop!* My bottom splayed onto the icy linoleum floor.

"Patsy Lou," Mama said in a stern voice, "get up from there right this minute and go see about your baby brother. *Brother* Webber will excuse you." Mama sounded mad, and when Mama was mad, she could knock you off your feet with one glance from her penetrating eyes. I even forgot about my inflamed tonsils.

"Yes, yes." Brother Webber hopped out of his chair and skidded across the room. He jammed his brown felt hat with the little green feather in the band down on his head so far it about covered his tiny green eyes. "I need to be getting on home."

"That's a real good idea, *Mister* Webber." Mama opened the door, allowing in a whisk of cold air, and ushered him out. He scurried away real fast, like he expected our lazy old dog Red to fly from under the house and take out after him. *Wham*, the screen door banged back, and Mama slammed the inside door with so much force the glass insets trembled. She didn't even say, "Goodbye, Brother Webber. It was so nice of you to visit."

Lingering against the doorjamb, I had waited to see what was going to happen next, but Mama spotted me without even looking in my direction. As soon as the door thundered shut, she said, "Patsy Lou, come here right this minute." Sweating in the frigid air, she fanned herself with a copy of *The Herald of Holiness*. I sat on the couch, swinging my legs, wondering what kind of trouble I was in. "Patsy Lou, you be careful of Brother Webber,"

Mama said, her words wafting through the pages of *The Herald*. "Do not go into a culvert with Brother Webber, even if he asks you to, and *never ever* go in his house." Mama closed *The Herald of Holiness,* showing she was serious. "Even if that man says he'll give you a fried pie. Understand?"

"Not even a fried *apple* pie, Mama?"

"Not any kind of pie, Patsy Lou, or cake or *anything*."

"Not even if he says I can sit at that little table he made, the one with little chairs?"

"No, Patsy Lou, not even if he says he will *give* you that table set. Now don't be aggravating."

I knew to shut up. Mama's face was so red I was afraid she might bust a blood vessel.

"Never go near that man again, or you'll get a whipping you'll never forget. I'm going to tell your daddy, too. You hear me? Brother Webber is not a nice man."

"I don't like Brother Webber, anyway. He smells funny."

"That's denture powder, Patsy Lou. The man has false teeth. He dyes his hair, too."

"Ugh," I said, holding my nose. "Mama, is Brother Webber a sinner?" Daddy sometimes preached about the Hoors of Babylon who dyed their hair and ended up burning in the fires of Hell.

"We should never cast the first stone, you know that. But I don't think Brother Webber's a Christian, even though he goes to church twice on Sunday and once during the week," Mama concluded, her impaling eyes piercing the veil into the hereafter.

The instant Daddy came home, I heard Mama tell him about Brother Webber rubbing my chest the way he did. Well, Daddy slammed out of the house, started the car, and zipped off down the road like he was a house afire. Mama wrung her hands and paced the floor, asking God to keep Daddy from killing Brother Webber.

About an hour later, with dirt flying around the car, Daddy skidded into the yard, very nearly hitting the porch. One sleeve of his black suit coat was torn from the armhole, and he rubbed his right hand.

"Charlie, whatever happened?" Mama asked, helping Daddy take off his ripped coat. Then she made him sit down in our cracked leather armchair while she washed his face and hands with a cold washrag and put Blue Star ointment on his knuckles. All that time, Daddy didn't utter a word. After Mama insisted he go to bed, I listened at the door—the only way I could find out things, since nothing that didn't involve Heaven or Hell was ever discussed in our family.

Daddy said, "I declare, Mama, I tried to pray with that man, but he just glared at me, his eyes sending out sparks like a fiend. I told him never to touch my girls or any other child, or I would call the police on him! Y'all know what he said? He said, 'Reverend, do y'all think the po-lice would arrest me? Naw, I donate to them. I'm a member of the church, an upstanding Christian, and I have money.'" Daddy let out a sigh I could hear all the way through the door. "Mama, that man is crazy as a hoot owl. He's strong, too— why, he grabbed my arm and hung on. I pulled away, and he plumb tore my sleeve off. I'm sorry to say it, but I boxed that old *reprobate's* ears real good."

Well, I very nearly fainted dead away. *Reprobate!* That was a bad word, I was sure, although I didn't know what it meant. Could Daddy go to Hell for using it? I must not have heard right. My daddy would never, ever use a bad word. Yes, I'd misunderstood, I decided.

I thought about Brother Webber as I trudged toward home, glancing over my shoulder every once in a while to be sure the road was clear. A noise from the bushes startled me. A scissor-tailed flycatcher zoomed up out of the brambles and did a dance in the sky. Mesmerized, I watched and watched, wishing I was a bird and I could fly away to a place with flowers and grass and trees. Daddy said poachers caught scissortails for their long feathers.

"Hide!" I shouted to the bird. "Don't let them catch you." He must

23

have heard me, because he coasted back into the undergrowth and was lost from sight.

Lordy, I looked way down the road, but still no house. I put my schoolbooks on the ground and sat down on a big rock to pour out the sand that had gotten through the raggedy soles of my shoes. Then I dragged myself up and started walking again, hoping the Holy Poltergeist that Mama was always reading about wasn't following me.

Mama wrote poetry. When I was five, she taught me to memorize long poems to recite in church. "Somebody's Mother" was her favorite: "The woman was old and ragged and gray / and bent with the chill of a winter's day . . ." It went on and on. But Mama's tutelage sometimes backfired.

"Patsy Lou," she would say, "get that head of yours out of a book and come help Poor Little Glendora. She's cleaning the house while you gom around."

When she was ten, Poor Little Glendora's appendix had burst. She was operated on at Children's Hospital in Oklahoma City and almost died. That was why we began calling her Poor Little Glendora. At the hospital, a woman gave me the hugest Hershey's chocolate bar I ever saw in my entire life. I hid behind bushes at the hospital and ate the whole thing without once thinking about my sick sister. I didn't tell Mama or Charles or anyone else what I did, and I wasn't at all sorry.

Poor Little Glendora was born before God said she was ready and weighed about a pound, Daddy said. "Why, she fit in the palm of my hand, she was so little." She was five years older than me, but petite, with thin legs that had scars on them and ached all the time. At night Daddy rubbed her legs to help her fall asleep. He said she was having growing pains. With her longish face and dark eyebrows, Poor Little Glendora looked like Daddy, but I looked like myself.

"I was just sixteen and your daddy twenty-three, " Mama often said, "and yet, after the ceremony at your grandpa and grandma's place in Coleman

County, Texas, we left in a covered wagon to spread the Word of God." She always paused at this point, put her hands on her hips, and looked way off into the ancient past. "Why, I remember having one iron frying pan and one kettle to cook with. We slept under the wagon on the hard ground at night. But we could see the stars and it was beautiful."

In their wedding picture that sat on top of Mr. Steinway, our piano. Mama looked soft and sweet and young. Her auburn hair was piled on top of her head and covered in a filmy white scarf. She was smiling and so pretty that I hoped to look just like her someday. When I looked at that picture, I imagined I sat at the top of the tall mulberry tree that grew in my Grandparent's yard, watching the proceedings and stuffing mulberries in my mouth.

Daddy stood next to Mama, with one black high-topped shoe on a large rock and the other foot on the ground. A nifty dresser even then, Daddy wore a white shirt with a stiff high collar, a tie, and a dark suit with matching vest. He looked slender and handsome, with a gentle expression, unlike that of the fervent hellfire-and-brimstone preacher he was now, even though he got the Call to preach when he was fifteen. Daddy was born in Knoxville, Tennessee, after his parents came to the United States from France. They were Huguenots, Daddy said, fleeing religious persecution. He tried to teach us kids French, but my tongue didn't work that way.

Hallelujah! Praise God! Finally our house rose up ahead of me in all its shabby splendor, with tumbleweeds and dirt from sandstorms piled up against the foundation. I broke into a relieved sprint. Lazy Red came loping up to greet me, leaving her puppies under the house where she had birthed them. Her dinners, as Mama called them, almost dragged on the ground from nursing all those puppies. I patted her head, and she wagged her tail so hard her whole body shook.

One afternoon, Charles had crawled underneath the house and found three squirming, squeaking, black-and-white puppies he brought out to the light. "Dibs on the boy," he'd said, picking up a puppy with one black eye, one floppy ear, and black spots scattered all over its furry white body. "Since he's a rat terrier, I'll name him Rat-Dog!"

"That's not a nice name," I'd argued. "How would y'all like to be called Rat-Charles?"

"If I was a dog, I wouldn't give a hoot, s'long as I was fed and had someone pet on me."

"Mama won't let y'all bring him in the house," I said.

"I'll find a way," my brother allowed, returning the puppies to their mama.

Before long, Rat-Dog followed Charles everywhere. After he was taught not to mess in the house, Rat-Dog even slept with him. He was a smart little guy. If anyone dared look cross-eyed at Charles, Rat-Dog showed his tiny white teeth and growled, but his tail wagged like he wasn't real serious.

Now Lazy Red nuzzled my hands, her scrawny body vibrating. She knew that before long, I would sneak a bowl of milk and bread to her, if we had any.

I left Lazy Red to her puppies and hurried across our slanted front porch. As soon as I opened the front door and inhaled the good smells of supper, I felt safe. The scruffy living room with its worn blue linoleum and faded wallpaper was a haven from the road, the dust, and the kids at school. I checked to be sure the paper dolls I had cut out of the Sears-Roebuck catalog were safe inside the piano bench, but before I could say hello to them, Mama yelled at me. "Get yourself in here right now, Patsy Lou. I need help getting supper onto the table."

I threw my schoolbooks under the piano bench and ran as fast as my tired-out legs could carry me. Without a word, Mama handed me a huge bowl of steaming red beans, a big sliced onion, and a pan of cornbread, all stacked on top of each other, to put on the table. Poor Little Glendora poured each of us a glass of Bossy's milk. The family sat down at the scuffed round table, and Daddy said a prayer of gratitude. This was home: where everything was normal, where all my siblings gathered for Thanksgiving and Christmas, even though some of them had to travel miles and miles to get there.

Six of us lived in that drafty old house: Mama, Myrtle Caldonia, a middle name we dared not utter in her presence; Daddy, Reverend Charles Clay Montandon; my fourteen-year-old brother, Charles Clay Jr.; my twelve-year-old sister, Poor Little Glendora; my baby brother, James Taylor, Little Jimmy; and me, Patsy Lou.

Three older siblings were married and living away from home. Carlos Morrison, eighteen years my senior, worked as the youngest superintendent of schools in the state of Oklahoma, and boy did Mama brag on him. He was as handsome as a movie star but as bossy as Jesus with the moneychangers in the Temple. When Carlos was around, he acted like I should obey him without asking one single question. Phooey to that! He wasn't the boss of me. I hardly even knew him or his wife, Marilee.

My oldest sister, Nina, was a sting in the neck. When she visited, she expected us to clean the floors with a toothpick to get dirt out of the cracks. "Mama," she'd say, sighing—she was always sighing, "I'll swan, y'all let these kids get away with murder. This house is so dirty it makes me sick." Nina fanned herself with a pretty, blue, accordion-shaped fan that had a picture of cupid painted on it. She sighed so loud, I'll bet even the saints in Heaven sitting on the right hand of God heard her. Nina sighed over and over: *sigh, sigh, sigh*. Occasionally, she would groan to break the monotony. Mama spoiled Nina, her second born and first daughter, rotten. She wasn't even allow to wash dishes for fear her beautiful hands would be ruined. My next sister in line, Minnie Faye, had to do that chore and she grumbled about it forever and a day and a half. Faye was still upset about it when she was a major adult and after Nina had passed into the great beyond. "Furthermore," Fay would say, her mind back in 1930, "when I was a teenager, Mama bought Nina a dress that I wanted. It was so pretty, pink chiffon with filmy green

27

sleeves and satin ribbons."

I would say, "That happened fifty years ago. Why are you still hanging on to a long-ago grudge?"

Minnie Faye, fourteen years my senior, was less than five feet tall. I was already catching up with her. She claimed she was short because of having to sleep in the backseats of cars when Daddy held revival meetings. Faye was afraid of almost everything. One time she ran about a mile after Charles banged a bunch of pans together, making a terrible racket, when Mama and a farmer lady were canning corn. Minnie Faye thought the pressure cooker had exploded, and she was getting out of there. She and her husband, Cecil, were the sweetest to me of all my family members.

When my talented and beautiful siblings came for Thanksgiving, it was as if Baby Jesus himself was carried in on a sunbeam. Mama killed the old red rooster, for sure, and saved up to make her special cornbread stuffing. After dinner, Carlos would play on Mr. Steinway while Nina and Faye joined him, harmonizing, singing the old family hymns that I could only croak.

"On a hill far away stood an old rugged cross,
The emblem of suffering and shame;
and I love that old cross where the dearest and best
For a world of lost sinners was slain."

My brothers and sisters belonged to a club that wasn't open to me. They talked a lot about Little Bettie Ruth, the most gorgeous baby that ever lived. Bettie Ruth died when she was not quite two, eleven months before I was born and now my invisible friend. I loved her.

As I ate my dinner and slurped my milk, I remembered what Nina had said at the last holiday get-together. "Mama was still crying and grieving while carrying you, and after you got born, too. Little Bettie Ruth had beautiful black curly hair, and you were born bald-headed and so ugly that I covered your face with a blanket when we took you out in public." Nina had the nerve to laugh. My ears pulsated with her sharp attack the way they had when Charles clashed cymbals next to my head once. "Ha-ha-ha-ha." I heard that sound over and over again. "Ha-ha-ha-ha." I put a wad of cotton from Mama's aspirin bottle in my ears, but still I could hear Nina's laughter. "Ha-ha-ha-ha-ha-ha."

My big sister's mean words pinched my insides. In spite of religious teachings, beauty and outward appearances were paramount in my family, and I had failed their test. Façade was central regardless of what was under it. I'd shrugged my shoulders to pretend Nina's words didn't bother me and run off to my retreat, a moldy storage closet. That's where I hid the books and magazines I had spirited into the house. A magazine called *Life* was my favorite. It was a weekly publication that a neighbor lady gave me. I pulled on the string that hung down from the high ceiling, and the overhead lightbulb gave out a dim glow. Then I hunkered down in a rough, musty-smelling patchwork quilt with *Life* magazine open on my lap hoping to learn how to be pretty like my sisters were by seeing what other girls did.

There was a picture story about brain surgery and one about President Roosevelt with lots of men in dark overcoats and felt hats, but I focused on the images of girls in bathing suits sunning themselves on the sand in Miami Beach, Florida, and kicking up their heels for a photographer. They were laughing and having fun even though they were sinning. I scrutinized their makeup, their smiles, their graceful way of standing.

In my hideaway, I covered a wooden box with one of Mama's torn pillowcases and used it as a dresser. A looking glass with a long crack across it was centered on the dressing table. Now I added a worn-down tube of red lipstick that I had filched from Nina's suitcase and a round pot of pink rouge I found in the trash at Faye's house. Mama's old navy-blue straw hat with a red rose on the brim hung on a ten-penny nail I had hammered in the wall. Studying the pictures of beautiful girls in the magazine, I began to experiment. I colored my lips bright red and smiled. Yes, my smile was okay. I used my fingers to add rouge to my cheeks.

I dipped down to one side so as to miss the crack in the mirror, and was pleased by what I saw. I looked like a movie star. Yes! My family would have to admire me now. Situating the navy-blue straw hat with the red rose just so on my head, I tiptoed into Mama's room to find the lapel pin Carlos gave her. It spelled out *Mother* in bright gold letters. I pinned it on my dress, pulled the hat down over one eye like Mama did, and marched happily into the kitchen where everyone was getting ready to sit down for supper.

"Lord have mercy!" Nina sniggered. "A little clown is coming to the supper table. Ha-ha-ha-ha-ha."

Mama spotted me and dropped a pan on the stove with a clatter. "Young lady, take that pin off of your dress right this minute and go wash your face," she ordered with a scary glare. "Carlos gave me that expensive gold pin for my birthday. Take it off right now, or I'll whip your bottom."

With shaking fingers, I unpinned *Mother* from my dress and handed the pin to Mama. I tried not to cry, but then it got worse. Charles came around the table, glaring at me. He reached out and slapped my lips and then wiped his hand across my face, smearing lipstick all the way up to my forehead.

"Wearing lipstick is a sin against the Holy Ghost, Patsy Lou," he said. "Remember Revelation? Jezebel was thrown out a window and eaten by dogs. Better be glad Daddy isn't here."

"Daddy wouldn't let me be eaten by dogs!" I said, and hit his arm with my fist. And then, bawling like a calf looking for its mama, I ran off to bed, not caring that I was hungry. My beautifying efforts had failed, and now Charles thought I was like that sinful Jezebel.

Sitting at the supper table, I hung my head over my steaming bowl of red beans and ate slowly as I recalled that day.

"Patsy, what's gotten into you?" Mama was saying. "Will y'all pass the cornbread?" She and Glendora and Charles stared at me like I was growing horns.

I frowned and scooted the pan of warm cornbread across the table to her. But the memory of my family poking fun at me lingered. I was doomed. I would always be the ugly one in a family of four beautiful sisters. I would never look good enough for my siblings or my folks. I would never belong.

Chapter 2

Peeing on Hot Coals

A few nights later, Charles halfway apologized to me by saying, "Sorry, sis" as we sat in the kitchen doing our homework in the fading winter light. Poor Little Glendora had done her homework at school and gone to bed early so she could have a little peace and quiet, she said.

"I'm not a Jezebel, so don't say I am, Charles! Okay?"

"Okay", he said, pulling my pigtails. "But it's too dark to do homework."

"I'll fix that," I said. "Daddy, will y'all come in here and light the lamp for us?" I hollered.

When our electricity was cut off because we couldn't pay the bill, Daddy had taken two copper pennies and leaned them inside the fuse box. That worked until a fire started from it and almost burned down the house. After that, a man came out from the Light and Power Company and took the whole box out. Now we used coal oil lamps that I was told never to light by myself.

"Chick-a-lick," Daddy yelled back at me, "I didn't hear a 'please' out of that loud mouth that just bellowed at me." He walked into the kitchen, where Charles and I had our school papers spread out on the round dining table.

"Please, Daddy, will you light the lamp? Please, with sugar on it." I smiled up at the overweight man who was my father.

"Okay, Chick-a-lick, that's better." Removing the thin, sooty glass shade from the kerosene lamp, Daddy trimmed the wick, the bottom of which floated snake-like in its bowl of oil. Finished with the trim, he opened a box of Diamond brand matches and lit the wick. "Let there be light," he intoned, like the preacher that he was. "Y'all can't stay up but a half hour more."

I hardly heard him, I was so enthralled by the burning match he still held. It glowed reddish orange, with a blue flame on the very tip, and it was heading for Daddy's fingers.

"Shoot take it!" he said, blowing out the blaze and then putting his scorched fingers in his mouth. "I sure enough burned my fingers. Y'all have to be careful around matches," he advised.

"Shoot take it" was one of the few slang phrases my father allowed himself, although once in a while he would hit his gray felt hat hard against the steering wheel of our black Model A Ford while declaring, "Dagnabbit." One time I dared utter "darn" in his presence. The swat on my behind came before the word had hardly leaped out of my mouth and into Daddy's ears, like a character in the Sunday funnies that I read in secret at my friend Rethie Marie's house. Reading Sunday funnies was considered a sin in my family, as was dyeing one's hair or wearing makeup or jewelry—these were only for hussy women—and so many other things that I lost track.

Daddy's deep voice yanked me back to the present. "Charles, son, the only reason I'm letting you and Patsy Lou stay up after dark is to get your homework done. Don't mess around."

"We won't," we answered.

I dared broach a tender subject. "Daddy, can I go with you to Nigger Town next week? You took Faye to the jail with you once, and Poor Little Glendora and Charles both went to Shanty Town with you, so it's my turn. Pretty please?"

Dragging up a slatted chair, Daddy sat down. The chair creaked with his weight, causing Charles to snigger.

Daddy stood up and glared at my brother. "Y'all are being disrespectful, and I won't stand for it! Do you want me to take my belt to you?" Rat-Dog, who was lying under the table, issued a low growl.

Daddy and Charles always got into it with each other. Charles knew better than to cross Daddy or make fun of him. *Oh, dear Jesus, save us*, I prayed.

"I'm sorry," Charles said. The black curly hair on top of his head sprang up from the sides, which Daddy kept shaved.

Thank you, Jesus.

Daddy sat back down in the creaking chair and launched into a sermon. "Young lady, it's not right to refer to our darker-skinned brethren as niggers, you hear me? That term diminishes their humanity. Just because their skin is a different hue than yours does not mean they are any less than you are." There was a long pause. Daddy shifted in his chair and finally began again, his voice soft. "Children, my mother, your grandma, was killed when she fell out of a wagon back in Tennessee when I was eleven, but when I was a baby, I was suckled by a black mammy. I'm only alive because of her milk. Did you know that?"

"Yes, sir."

"I loved Mammy. I miss her to this day." Daddy pulled a big white handkerchief from the pocket of his overalls and wiped his eyes. He cleared his throat, and after a minute or so, he continued his sermon.

My brother pretended to listen in case Daddy glanced his way. Charles was so bullheaded that I worried about him. One night, he had tiptoed to my bedroom window carrying his shoes and slipped out to go to a basketball game. It was as dark as the insides of the Devil's stomach that night, and Charles stumbled into an open cellar on his way home. His friend got him to a doctor and then brought him home. Charles had a concussion. Mama was more concerned with the odor of cigarette smoke on my brother's jacket than the bandages circling his head. In a fit of religious wrath, Mama hurled Charles's jacket into the yard and said he wasn't fit to come inside. He had to spend the night outside on our cold, slanted porch. My sister and I made him a pallet and got two of Mama's Bayer aspirin for him. Rat-Dog curled up next to him and licked his face.

Thank the Lord. Daddy finally stopped preaching. "Fetch your mama and Poor Little Glendora so we can have evening prayers," he said, "and then you two get on with your homework."

We knelt in front of kitchen chairs, Mama and Daddy, Poor Little Glendora, Charles, and me. Daddy prayed a special prayer for the souls of the Bathing Beauty girls we had seen riding in a truck bed during a rare trip downtown. We kids had crammed into the backseat of our coughing old Model A Ford, watching and listening.

"Mama, look at that!" Daddy had said. "Those girls have on rubber bathing suits!"

Mama clicked her tongue, showing disapproval.

"Why, that's downright sinful," Daddy continued, the back of his neck red like he might have a stroke or something. Leaning across the seat toward Mama, probably thinking we kids couldn't hear him, he said, "Those girls dance in dresses made out of rubber. And I was told they fornicate right on the dance floor."

Charles's eyes almost popped out of his head as he stared at the Bathing Beauties, but his ears took in everything Daddy said. "They're talking about S-E-X," Charles spelled, speaking in a low, smirking voice. Poor Little Glendora kicked him in the shins and giggled.

S-E-X was something not even remotely hinted at in our home. I heard a few distorted rumors of where babies came from, but barely enough to make me curious to know more, and in no way approaching the truth. Mama even had code names for the "forbidden" parts of the body and its functions. Baby Jimmy's penis was called a "peckerwood" or "zipper," and breasts "dinners." If one had to go to the toilet, the word was "treetop," and to urinate was to "zip," although I used the word "pee" to myself. A bowel movement was either "number two" or "big business." Sometimes our family conversations sounded as though we spied for a foreign government.

My friend Rethie Marie talked about people fornicating and "doing it," but she didn't know much about it, either. It probably had to do with a man's peckerwood, but for the life of me I couldn't figure it out. Did the rubber dresses those girls wore have holes in them so the man's peckerwood could go through? Then did he pee? Was that S-E-X? Ugh, I sure didn't want anything to do with *that*!

After prayers, everybody went to bed except for Charles and me. My pugnacious brother was still pretending to do his homework, but I knew he was sneaking looks at drawings of women's underwear in the Sears-Roebuck catalog. I felt a nagging urge to pee, but I was terrified of going to the outhouse after dark. The rickety wooden structure with half moons carved into the sides was located a long way from the house, and not one light led the way. A snake might come up out of the hole and bite my hiney. I decided to ignore my full bladder in the hope that I could hold out till morning.

I commandeered the bench from our black upright Mr. Steinway, a treasured possession, and dragged it to the kitchen to use as a desk. I liked knowing that under the hinged lid of the bench was a tangle of family photographs, hymnals, and a tin of Bayer aspirin that Mama scattered around like chicken feed in case one of her migraines came on. Mr. Steinway was like a member of the family. The scratches and scars it bore attested to its having been hauled across the plains of Texas and Oklahoma every two or three years for as long as anyone could remember, as well as being the playmate for a passel of kids. It was a wonder Mr. Steinway could still be tuned.

With so many mouths to feed, Daddy made sure we always had a cow. Before the drought and sandstorms hit, we grazed her in the overgrown ditches alongside roads in spring and summer and bought feed in the wintertime. "Keep Bossy away from wild onions, or her milk won't be fit to drink," Daddy warned when we headed out with Bossy in early spring. But now Daddy relied on church members to give us feed for Bossy. And I noticed that she was looking as skinny and hungry as I sometimes felt.

Most of the time we still had milk to drink, and Daddy swapped milk for piano lessons. All my older siblings took piano lessons. I was the only exception to the family tradition of playing the piano and singing, and I didn't like it one little bit.

When I was six, a silver-tongued salesman enticed my parents to subscribe to a homeowners insurance policy.

"Charlie," Mama said, "it's a good idea to insure Mr. Steinway. I know it was passed down by your mother, God rest her soul, and it's valuable."

"Mama, who on earth would steal a piano?" Daddy said. "We should insure the cow. She provides for the family better than I can." He turned his pants pocket inside out. "Look at that. Empty. Why, we hardly have enough to eat on. How can we pay for insurance?"

"I'll do without that dress I saved for, the one to replace my old Sunday best. I can wait. We've got to have insurance."

I was hiding behind the big leather rocking chair one of Daddy's church members had given us, listening to their discussion. I was betting on Mama; she always won.

"Well, I suppose I can sell milk to the new schoolteacher," Daddy said. "She asked me about it, and I said she could have the milk for five cents a quart. Enough of this chatter, I've got to go to the church house and write my Sunday sermon." Daddy left, letting the screen slap shut behind him. *Snap! Slam!*

At the supper table that night, we talked about our homeowners insurance like it was the biggest diamond ring ever.

"Mr. Steinway is safe," Mama said, "insured by Capers Farmers. You see their tin signs hanging on fences all over Texas, so we know they're reliable." Mama looked like she had found religion all over again. "They even gave us a metal stamp with our own ID number on it in case anything is stolen. We can stamp the things we want to keep safe. See?" She held up the stamp by its brown handle. "Capers Farmers Insurance Company Number Eighty-nine. I'll pass it around, but be careful, children, those letters are sharp."

Daddy was slurping up a glass of buttermilk with cornbread mashed in it. "Charles," he said with a laugh, "maybe you can stamp Bossy on the side, like ranchers do when they brand cattle."

One day while Mama and Daddy called on a sick parishioner, I crept into their bedroom, opened a bedside drawer, and rummaged around until I found the Capers Farmers stamp. Cautiously, I ran my fingers over the sharp letters and sat down on the floor. I had a plan.

But first I closed my eyes and conjured up a Bible story, the one about Abraham giving Isaac up as a burnt offering. The daddy tied his son's hands and feet and put him on an altar, ready to kill him for God. I sure didn't want that to happen to me, even though at the last minute, a voice said, "Hey there, it's okay. Untie your son. He's safe now."

And in a bush, a sweet little lamb bleated, "Here I am, come and get me."

And the son was safe.

"Dear Jesus," I prayed, "please make me strong the way Isaac was so I don't scream while I make myself insured. Amen."

Taking a deep breath, I stretched my skinny legs out in front of me and drew back with all my might, gathering courage and praying to Jesus. With as much force as I could muster, I whomped down on my thigh with the stamp.

"Oh!" I bit my lip. Unbidden tears streamed down my face. Blood oozed in drops toward the floor. I pulled the hem of my dress down over the flow, hoping the blood would get lost in the pattern of flowers scattered across the fabric. The bleeding didn't last long, but soon angry-looking red marks swelled up like the carbuncles that Daddy had lanced when they sprang up on the back of his neck. But under my wounds, CAPERS FARMERS INSURANCE #89 was engraved into my skin. I would be safe forever. I was *insured.*

After I recovered, I went to the living room where Mr. Steinway lived and in an hour-long binge, stamped CAPERS FARMERS INSURANCE #89 onto its shiny black surfaces. Now, when I was coloring and my Crayola hit a snag on one of the indentations, making my drawings into a scrawl, I thought sheepishly about what I had done.

~~~

Charles was writing on lined notebook paper while I sat on the piano bench, wriggling my feet to ease the growing pressure in my bladder and fiddling around with an arithmetic lesson. I hated arithmetic. Numbers never made sense to me, but I was a good reader and I loved words. Once I wrote an essay about the evils of beer instead of doing the multiplication table and handed that in to the teacher. I got it back with a big red *F* on top of the page, along with a notation: *This has nothing to do with your lesson, Patsy Lou! Are you feebleminded?*

Was I feebleminded? Was something wrong with my brain? When we moved and I started at a new school, I often didn't know what the teacher was talking about. One time I leaned over my desk and tried to copy the answer to a quiz from the girl sitting in front of me. She told the teacher, and I was punished in front of the whole class.

"Class," said Mr. Sullivan, the tongue-chewing teacher, as he tapped a ruler on the edge of his big wooden desk. "What happens if you cheat on a test? Hmmm?"

"We get punished," everyone answered.

Chewing his tongue, Mr. Sullivan scratched his head, and a flurry of snow fell on the shoulders of his brown jacket. My schoolmates giggled.

"Straighten up, children." Chew, chew. "We have a serious matter with which to contend."

"Yes, sir."

"The new girl," he said, pointing at me, "doesn't know the rules. We need to teach her, right?"

"Right!"

If I'd had magic powder, I would have spread it all over myself and disappeared. *Maybe I could plead sick.* I thought of Mama, her headaches, her frowns, her Bayer aspirin, and being sick to her stomach. Frowning, I raised my hand. "Mr. Sullivan, Mr. Sullivan, sir, Mr. Sullivan, I'm sick to my stomach." And in truth I was. My stomach roiled, my bowels rumbled. "I've got a bad sick headache, and I'm going to throw up."

"Artie," Mr. Sullivan barked, "on the double, get the wastebasket for that girl. Hurry it up." Mr. Sullivan chewed his tongue frantically. He looked green. After I threw up a little bit, Artie walked me to the nurse's office, where a wet cloth was put on my head and I was given a Bayer aspirin. Artie hung around as if he didn't know the answers to the test, either.

"Don't pay no attention to Crazy Sullivan," he said. "He drinks."

"Beer?" I whispered, hardly daring to say the word out loud.

"No, whiskey, my pa says."

"My daddy says they put rats in bottles of whiskey!"

"Well, that's what Crazy Sullivan drinks."

After that, I feigned a headache during Crazy Sullivan's classes. The school nurse, Bettie, let me read her movie magazines and gave me a tube of Tangee lipstick so I could learn how to put it on. This time I did a better job of it than I had while looking in the cracked looking glass in the storage closet. I made sure to scrub it off before I headed home. The ads in *Screen Gems* magazine fascinated me. Kotex? What on earth? Ads for Ponds Face Cream, Evening in Paris perfume, and pictures of movie stars in tight rubber bathing suits appeared glamorous, not sinful at all.

Once in a while we didn't have enough food for my school lunch. "Everybody is poor these days, Chick-a-lick," Daddy said, blotting his tears with the white handkerchief he always carried. "These sandstorms are killing farmers. Poor folks, they hardly have enough food for themselves, much less for poundings." Church members paid Daddy every few months with a pounding: a pound of sugar, a pound of flour, or potatoes, or beans, or whatever they had. Parishioners placed their offerings on the altar, and then the congregation prayed, giving thanks. Lately, there wasn't much of anything on the altar, but still Daddy gave thanks. "It's the Depression," he explained. "We may have to sell our piano. A man offered fifteen dollars for him. That would help out a lot."

"No, Daddy, no, no, no," I protested. "I'll get a job. Please, please, please don't sell Mr. Steinway. I pulled weeds for Mr. Anderson. I worked all day long, and it was hard work."

"He didn't have the decency to give you even one cent, now, did he? Y'all are too young to get a paying job, Chick-a-lick, even though you're a good hard worker."

At school that day, my friend Rethie Marie had raised her hand in class and turned me in. I had spent the lunch hour in the restroom so no one would see me, and now to think, my best friend had ratted on me. Rethie waved her hand in the air like a flyswatter. "Teacher, Teacher," she bellowed.

"What is it, Rethie Marie?" Miss Trumball asked. "You're supposed to be studying."

"Teacher, Patsy Lou didn't eat any lunch today."

"Rethie, get back to studying," Miss Trumball said, going on about her business.

I was immersed in reading *Heidi* when I looked up and saw my pretty teacher standing by my desk, her auburn hair fluffed up on her shoulders, her green eyes shining. "Patsy Lou," she said softly, "will you please come up to my desk?"

At Miss Trumball's desk I stood quaking, waiting to hear what I had done wrong.

Her soft hands, with their glossy red nails, patted my grubby ones.

"Patsy Lou, honey, did you have lunch today?" she asked.

I tried to swallow, but couldn't. All of a sudden I understood what adults meant when they said they had a lump in their throat. "Uh, no, ma'am."

"Why didn't you go to the soup kitchen?"

"That's for poor kids." I hung my head so she couldn't see the tears on my eyelashes.

"Patsy, I haven't had my lunch either, so why don't we have a bowl of soup together?"

I walked down the hall toward the kitchen, Miss Trumball holding my hand, the smell of her perfume enveloping me like roses in summer, the skirt of her flowered dress brushing against my legs. I was so happy I wanted to jump up and down and yell, "Wheee, wheee!"

While we ate together, Miss Trumball talked to me. "Patsy, you are a smart little girl. Now to stay smart, you need to eat well. There's nothing wrong in coming to the soup kitchen. Okay?"

"Okay, thank you," I said, starstruck. From then on, I ate lunch every school day.

~~~

Charles threw a pencil at me. "Stop daydreaming, Patsy Lou. We've gotta get our homework done."

"Charles, please, please take me to the outhouse," I begged. "I've got to go, and I'm afraid of the dark."

"Scaredy-cat. There's nothing to be scared of, so get on out there by yourself. Grow up."

"Where's your dog? He'll go with me."

"Little Rat-Dog is under the house with his mama tonight."

Dagnabbit! I had to pee real bad. I crossed and recrossed my legs, trying to stop the flow, but I couldn't hold it much longer. If I wet my underpants, Mama would give me a tongue-lashing, maybe even a spanking. I glanced out the window. Now it was real dark outside, as dark as the souls of sinners that Daddy prayed for every Sunday. Even the moon and stars hid tonight. I bounced on one foot and then the other, holding myself in an effort

42

to keep the urine from leaking down my legs.

Finally, I ventured as far as the screened-in back porch, trying to get up the courage to run to the outhouse. The privy was only a dark outline against a clump of cottonwood trees. Was that Brother Webber hiding out there in the bushes, or was it a werewolf? Whatever it was, I was not going outside, even if I busted wide open.

Maybe I could pee in a glass, I thought, but quickly discarded such a notion. Mama would half kill me to death if she found out I did such a thing. Maybe there was an empty can or even a slop jar among the stuff stacked on the porch. I did a fast survey: Mama's wringer washing machine, a heaping pile of baby Jimmy's stinky diapers, a bar of Fels-Naptha soap, a bucket of ashes . . . ashes . . . in a galvanized bucket that Daddy had scooped out of our heating stove, sitting there on the screened-in porch, waiting for me to pee on them. Hooray! The urine would disappear into the ashes, and Mama would never, ever know.

I hurried to the bucket, my hands holding my genitalia as I tried not to wet my underpants before I got there. Trembling from the strain of holding in my urine, I swiftly pulled off my homemade plaid cotton panties and the attached slip. With frenzied swiftness I straddled the bucket, my bare feet on either side of the warm metal, and let go.

Ah, relief, I thought, discharging a robust stream of urine. As if in slow motion, the liquid from my body rained down in a fall of water that quickly became a torrent hitting the ashes with force and an ominous sound that echoed like bacon fat Mama cooked on the stove—*sssssiiiiizzzzellll*—and released the nether realm of the devil and demons in which the damned suffer everlasting punishment. The earth's crust opened, and a scalding volcanic Hell hit me full force. Magma spewed forth and lye-laced vapor blistered up into the air, where burning rubble penetrated the most delicate tissues of my young body.

I was burning in place, unable to move, as I stood there mesmerized, my bare body and my bare feet, like a statue of Job suspended over the yawning pit of the underworld on that screened-in porch, as fire and brimstone spewed up in a terrifying sermon of fulfilled prophecy, until I fell over backward. My feet hit Satan's bucket, scattering burning embers that seared my left foot as urine dribbled from my tortured body. An animal scream tried to push past my tonsils, but no sound emerged.

Weakened and dazed, I crawled toward the kitchen in a blur of pain, across the worn threshold from the screened in porch, not feeling the splinters that pierced my knees, and onto the kitchen floor linoleum.

On the counter where our supper dishes soaked in the dishpan, I pulled myself to standing, blindly found a glass, filled it with water, and threw it on myself. Then I fell back on the kitchen floor, writhing in agony. "Eieee, eieee, eieeeee," I screamed. "Help me! Help, help!" Over and over, I shrieked.

Mama bolted into the room, eyes bulging, her hair standing on end. Daddy followed at a fast clip.

"Lord have mercy! Patsy is dying," Mama yelled. "She's burned half to death. I can smell her flesh cooking!"

Daddy skidded in the water I had poured on myself, bringing him to his knees on the floor next to me in his long-handled underwear. He put his big hands under my head. "What happened, Patsy Lou?" he asked, reaching for a dishtowel with which to cover me.

"I had to pee," I whimpered.

Charles and Poor Little Glendora watched, their eyes bugging out. Poor Little Glendora leaned against Charles, causing tangled black curls to cover her face. I caught those images in a smudge as I rocked back and forth on the blue linoleum.

"Pray for me, Daddy," I moaned. "Pray that God won't let me die for peeing on the ashes. Oh, it hurts, it hurts bad *Down There*. Eieee, eieee, eieee! I don't want to go to Hell."

"Oh Lord, help us," Mama said over and over. "She's burned herself real bad." Mama lifted up the cup towel. "Blisters are rising on her private parts like yeast in dough. Charles, get the Unguentine right now. Hurry up!"

Pain shot through me in blaring hisses of sound. I screamed and screamed until no sound was left in my body. Then I died. I was dead for three days. "Like Jesus," Daddy said when I finally opened my eyes.

Hearing his words, I screamed again. "Fan me, fan me *Down There*," I demanded. "I'm burning to death," I shrieked.

I lay on our brown horsehair sofa, my legs opened wide. Gauze covered me like a diaper. Poor Little Glendora, five years my senior, moved the air back and forth across my private parts with a copy of *The Herald of Holiness*.

"I've fanned her for two weeks, Mama. I'm tired of this," she whined. "I don't even like her, anyhow."

"Poor Little Glendora, your sister is bad hurt, so do your part to help. I've got a baby to look after."

My sister was unmoved. "You stabbed me with a pencil once, Patsy Lou, and now you want me to stand here and fan you until my arm drops off. Look, I still have the lead in my arm. See." Poor Little Glendora pulled up her sleeve to show a gray dot in her upper arm where I had, indeed, stabbed her with a number two pencil.

Sibling rivalry roused me from my bed. "Poor Little Glendora," I shouted, "you had it coming. You told me I was ugly as a mud fence. Tell Mama what you said to me." I collapsed back onto my bed of pain, too sick and miserable to sustain anger, crying to be fanned. "Please, Poor Little Glendora, fan me and I'll be your slave forever," I pleaded. "I hurt, hurt, hurt, hrrrrrt."

Tears splashed sideways down my face and into my hair. Water leaking from my eyes was so copious that Mama kept a towel over the pillowcase and changed it several times a day.

"You are mighty blistered *Down There*, Patsy Lou," she said, applying Unguentine ointment to the afflicted area. "You should never have done number one over live hot coals."

"Mama, please fan me. Please, please, please."

Sometimes when I slipped in and out of consciousness, I saw white clouds of sweet angels hovering over me, comforting me and giving me the will to cope with the unbroken pain of my injury.

Neighbors came by to offer wilted gladiolas or meat pies as I lay there, spread-eagled and hobbled. I could not look anyone in the eyes. *Mortified* was a new word I soon learned.

"Why, Sister Montandon," a church member said, "this is mortifying."

I would lie there trying to act normal, but I kept thinking about how my school friends would shame me so much that I wouldn't hardly be able to hold my head up.

To cope with these chaotic feelings, I closed my eyes and imagined I was famous and, *click, click*, having my picture taken with Shirley Temple. Oh, how I longed to see a sinful Shirley Temple movie. I didn't have the five cents to go to one, anyway. Pansy Jean owned a big Shirley Temple doll and tap shoes. When she came to school in black patent leather shoes with silver taps on the toes, wearing a red polka-dotted organdy Shirley Temple dress, I was full of envy. Pansy stood on Miss Trumball's desk and tapped while the rest of us sang, "On the Good Ship Lollipop, it's a sweet trip to the candy shop . . ." Pansy's legs swung back and forth, *tap, tap, tap*, back and forth, *tap, tap, tap*, while the red polka-dotted dress and ruffled white petticoats frilled out above her stout legs. I wished with all my might that I was the one up on the desk tap dancing.

When the church choir came to sing and pray for me, Mama covered me up with an ecru lace tablecloth so I would be more presentable. I snuck a look at the choir and then pretended to be asleep. Their maroon robes billowed around them as they stood in a semicircle near my couch-bed, their

46

faces long and serious. Holding their hymnals high to block their view, I noticed that a few still peered around the pages to try to lay eyes on my wounds.

With vases of gladiolas and red zinnias on every table, Mama banging away on Mr. Steinway, the choir tuning up, and lace covering my prone body, I wondered if I was dead; I knew a funeral when I saw one. "Hummmm," the choir sang. "Hummmm." Had I slipped this mortal coil and floated off into Heaven without knowing it? But where was Daddy? He wouldn't miss my funeral. In fact, I'd bet he would even say a few words about me.

When the choir swung into a high-spirited rendition of "Amazing Grace," I halfway sat up, one end of the lace tablecloth hanging over my face. I was alive!

The singers felt the Spirit and lifted their voices to God with gusto. When they shifted into "I'll Fly Away," I thought they just might fly away. "I'll fly away, oh glory, I'll fly away. When I die, hallelujah by and by . . ." But when they segued into "There Is a River Filled with Blood," I felt sick to my stomach. The image of a thick, bloody river caused bile to rise in my throat. My mouth filled, and before I knew what was happening, I threw up onto Mama's lace tablecloth.

Whang! A jarring chord announced that the singing was over, and Mama abandoned her piano-playing duties. "Glendora, go get a towel and a pan of water, right this minute," she shouted to my sister, who was hanging over the back of the couch. Mama ministered to me as the stricken choristers hastily gathered up their things and left.

But I felt sick all over again when a stranger nicely dressed in a seersucker suit and wearing a boater-style straw hat came to talk to Daddy. I was alarmed to hear the man say he had come for Mr. Steinway.

"You know, Mr. Ryan, that thing weighs about six hundred pounds," Daddy said. "You'll need strong ropes to keep it on your truck."

Soon, four workmen, grunting and pushing, finally got Mr. Steinway out the door, and groaning louder still, loaded it on an open truck and tied it down. Draping the now-clean tablecloth around me, I shuffled to the front porch where our family had gathered, weeping. It was as if someone had died. Daddy hugged us and said, his voice choking, "It was necessary." Then, abruptly, "Y'all get on inside. I see a sandstorm coming up. Could be a doozy."

I gazed upward. The sky had turned purplish black. A huge cloud of dirt boiled across distant fields, heading in our direction. "Daddy," I wailed, "is this the End of the World?" The legs I hadn't stood up on in several weeks trembled. "It's the End of the World, isn't it? Isn't it?" I shrieked. "Am I a sinner, Daddy? Will I go to Hell?" I pulled on Daddy's pants pocket to get his attention.

"Patsy Lou, settle down. It's a black blizzard coming our way, and that's scary enough. Cover up your nose and mouth and get inside."

Daddy and a church friend had talked about this being the Dust Bowl, brought on by a long drought and too much farming. These "black blizzards" rolled into town now and then, filling up houses and threatening to choke the eyes and lungs of every living thing with that terrible, fine brown dust. I was more scared than ever 'cause a friend had died from the last one, and several church members had lost their entire corn crop and were hungry all the time now.

"Children, didn't y'all hear me? Get on inside the house now, right this minute," Daddy shouted in his deep preacher voice so as to be heard above the squall. We kids skittered off the porch and slammed inside the quaking old parsonage. Outside, Daddy yanked the brim of his brown felt hat down over his head and turned his back to the wind to button up his suit jacket. My siblings and I huddled close together against the torn screen door like a jamboree of flies with their wings cut off, fluttering and scared. With my hands over my face, I looked between spread fingers as the bruised sky sent sprinkles of sand blowing through the screen. The lace tablecloth flapped

48

around my ankles.

"I've gotta go take care of my flock," Daddy hollered, "Go on, y'all, git on way inside the house and slam the door tight right now!" We watched as he headed for Homer, our ol' car, rocking back and forth in the wind. Daddy's words rode the wind as he bellowed, "I . . . I . . . I . . . won't . . . beeee . . . gone . . . longer thaaan it taaaakes to swing a caaat by the taaail."

Suddenly, like a shot from a BB gun, Mama detonated off the porch, jumped across a hillock of dirt, and began slamming her right hand into the driver's side of Daddy's car. *Bang, bang, bang!* Her undone hair flew around her head like she was a crazy ol' crow, and her coattail rose up so high behind her that I thought she might sail right on up into Heaven. Mama was flying off the handle at Daddy, screaming at him and having a pure hissy fit. Although her words weren't clear, I pretty much knew what she was saying.

"Charlie, you come on back here and take care of your own flock. I just know y'all are going to go see about those darkies down by the dry riverbank, Hattie and her grandson, Gideon, who came by last night and asked you to drive them to see a doctor in Oklahoma City tomorrow."

Daddy ignored Mama, a death-defying strategy, and kept on cranking the car, trying to get the engine started. After several turns and coughs, the carburetor or the engine or something or other took hold, and the car sat muttering and shaking while Mama continued to hit the door with her hand. We watched, bug-eyed, wondering what was going to happen next. Daddy got in the car from the passenger side, slid across the seat, and rolled down the window. Mama looked like she was ready to punch him. Daddy leaned way out the window and into Mama's face. He reached out with his right hand and pulled her close, and then—wow—he kissed her smack dab on her lips! Then he rolled up the car window and took off like he was having a hydrophobia fit, dirt fogging everywhere.

Mama frowned and wiped her mouth with the sleeve of her old gray coat, but she smiled a little, too. I had never, ever seen such a sight. Daddy kissing Mama on her lips—now that was something to have witnessed in my lifetime.

We kids pushed together to get the door closed against the menacing wind that seemed intent on shoving us to the floor. Poor Little Glendora held Little Jimmy, and they were both bawling. "I-I-I h-h-hope Daddy doesn't have a wreck and kill hisself," moaned Poor Little Glendora.

"Mama's the one that might kill Daddy for running off like that," said Charles. "She don't much like niggers, anyhow." He sniggered. "Y'all heard ol' Hattie trying to get Daddy to drive them all the way to Oklahoma City last night, saying, 'Can't y'all see how pale this child is?'"

"Gideon's skin is too dark to tell he's pale," I said, getting my two cents into the mix.

"That's the point, stupid."

"Call me stupid and I won't read *David Copperfield* for your book report, Charles."

The back door busted open with a crash, causing me to almost jump out of my skin. Mama careened into the house like she was drunk or something, yelling orders as she came. "Patsy Lou, you have no business being up and off the couch. Get yourself back up there right now and open your legs before you rub your wound raw again, y'all hear me? We have a norther homing in on us, and your daddy's off helping darkies. Land's sake, I have to do everything around here. We'll be lucky if the house don't fall down. If y'all want to keep on breathing, do what I tell you to do and fast, or I'll jerk a knot in your tail."

"Yes, ma'am," we said in unison.

"Mama," Charles said, apparently not caring if Mama jerked a knot in his tail, "Daddy kissed you!"

Right then I prayed the house would collapse so Charles wouldn't get a belt to his behind for being impudent. But all Mama said was, "Son, it's time to act like you've had some raisin', you hear me?"

"Yes, ma'am."

"That storm is almost full upon us, so no dilly-dallying, children." Mama used her fingers to enumerate the things we needed to do. "Poor Little Glendora, hurry and collect all our rags and start stuffing them in the cracks. I'll get sheets and towels to wet and hang over the doors and windows. Charles, you get that galvanized washtub on the screened-in porch and fill it with water to dump the towels and shee—" A sound like a lightning bolt hit the roof, causing Mama to jump straight up. Sand began sifting down in a thin stream from a hole that opened up in the ceiling. "Lord in Heaven, save us," Mama shouted. "Patsy Lou, go get your slop jar and slide it under that hole before sand gets tracked all over the house."

Hopping to it, I pushed the white porcelain slop jar with pink Cecile Brunner roses painted on it across the worn-out blue linoleum until it was under the trickle of sand.

Mama was rattled but still in charge. "Poor Little Glendora, put Little Jimmy on the floor so he can crawl around," she wheezed. "Patsy Lou, get in your bed and see to it that Little Jimmy doesn't put anything in his mouth."

Everyone scurried around like ants in a maze to do Mama's bidding. The yowling wind screeched in my ears like Ebenezer Scrooge's ghost, and Little Jimmy crawled on the floor, tasting anything he could put in his mouth.

My brother had just dragged our tin tub filled with water into the front room when we heard an explosion of wind, accompanied by a flurry of debris that sailed in whirligigs around the space. In staggered Daddy, with scrawny little Gideon in his arms and Grandma Hattie trailing along behind. She seemed lost in Daddy's shadow. Her gray hair was hidden under a red knit cap pulled way down over her ears. Her baggy gray cotton dress—a color that matched her wrinkled skin—hung from her slight body. Both Grandma Hattie and little Gideon looked scared half to death and as pale as it was possible for them to be covered as they were with dust.

Mama expressed her displeasure by standing with her hands on her hips and muttering "My heavenly days," under her breath without giving even a glance to our colored guests. Daddy pretended not to notice and began imparting directives. "That storm out there is like a serpent of the Devil," he said, "and it's almost full upon us. Better light a lamp in here; it's pitch-dark already." He coughed up a dust ball and spit it into his once white handkerchief.

I lay on my bed, quivering at the thought of a devil snake curling around in the clouds of dirt, lying in wait to bite me on my hiney.

"Mama," Daddy said, "Grandma Hattie and I are going back out there to put a tarp over the car, or it'll be buried in sand by morning time and we may never be able to start it again." Daddy dumped Gideon on my couch bed, and he and Grandma Hattie whooshed out the door. The kid sat staring at me like he was a four-year-old zombie, his hair and skin coated with fine dust.

"Hi, Gideon," I ventured.

He looked at me all wrapped up in my lace tablecloth and began to cry. Tears wore clean tracks down his face and dribbled onto his patched overalls. Poor kid, he was worn out. I handed him my glass of water, and he drank it in one long swallow, all the while keeping his brown eyes tuned in to my face. I thought to give him one of Mama's big ol' cold biscuits from a stash of food I kept under my pillow. That boy grabbed that biscuit out of my hand and gobbled it down faster than a jackrabbit full of lightning. Then, without saying a word, the kid toppled over on my bed, put his thumb in his mouth, and was out like a light with dust fanning so thick around him he could hardly breathe. Meanwhile, the house was bombarded by what sounded like devil's chains.

After a while, Daddy and Grandma Hattie struggled back inside, bringing with them blasts of thudding wind. "Lord help us," Mama fretted, while Daddy and Grandma Hattie immediately began hanging wet sheets over the doors. Grandma's cap had blown off, and her corrugated white hair was now muddy looking and sawtoothed out from her head. Mama yelled orders at us kids. "Patsy Lou, stay on the couch. You're not well yet. Poor Little Glendora, get Little Jimmy off the floor and cover him up with damp diapers so he won't breathe in dust. Charles, soak the towels and hang them over windows. Hurry! There's not much time. And someone cover that black baby up with something damp so he doesn't choke to death."

Grandma Hattie quickly wrung the water out of a thin rag and placed it gently over her grandson's face. Gideon could have been dead except for the rising and falling of that rag with each breath. "That baby's sick and afflicted, and plumb tuckered out, sho 'nuff," Grandma said to no one in particular.

Charles had quickly splashed more water into the big washtub and piled a bunch of raggedy towels and rags in it. Then Mama remembered Bossy and our four hens and the rooster.

"Charles, stop what you're doing and get Bossy," she said. "Your daddy hasn't finished building her shed yet, and we can't afford to lose our cow, or the chickens, either."

"I can't do everything at once," Charles yelled.

"There's no time to waste. Put Bossy and the chickens on the screened-in back porch. Poor Little Glendora, take Little Jimmy to Patsy Lou, and y'all hang up the wet towels."

My brother slammed out the back door into the howling wind. Papers flew off tables, and chairs blew over.

"Children, cover your noses and mouths with damp rags," Mama ordered. "Don't breathe this stuff!"

Daddy wore his canvas carpenter's apron, the one he put on when he wallpapered. Sopping-wet bed sheets irrigated the floor as they hung crookedly over doors and walls. Poor Little Glendora struggled with waterlogged towels. Daddy got a tack hammer from his canvas apron, fished nails from the pocket, and abracadabra, nailed the raggedy towels over the rattling windows. The house shuddered as the brutal wind shrieked and screeched. Water dribbled off sheets and towels. Mama prayed, "Lord help us." Daddy worked to catch his breath like his heart hurt. Poor Little Glendora wept, Gideon slept, and I huddled under the lace tablecloth, holding Little Jimmy tight while he cried. Grandma Hattie sang an odd-sounding spiritual halfway under her breath.

Pew-ee, Little Jimmy needed his diaper changed! "Mama, Mama, Mama, Little Jimmy has a load of number two in his diaper!" I yelled.

"Lord help us," Mama said.

Grandma Hattie took over with Little Jimmy, changing his diaper and singing another spiritual we all knew. Soon, Daddy's baritone joined Grandma's exuberant soprano, and even Mama's sweet alto joined my off-key enthusiasm. "Swing low, sweet chariot, coming for to carry me home. Swing low, sweet chariot, coming for to carry me home."

Grandma Hattie shuffled her bare feet in time with the music and the wind. With every thud assaulting the house, Grandma Hattie shouted, "Hallelujah!" and raised her hands high in the air. "Well, I looked over Jordan," she sang, "and what did I see, comin' fo' to carry me home? Hallelujah! A band of sweet angels comin' fo' me, comin' fo' to carry me home."

After several rounds, we wound down and sat listening to the storm battering our world and hoping for a chariot—at least, I did.

The whole parsonage—all five rooms, the porch, and my storage closet—shook like it might take off and fly through the air. What if an earthquake happened, I wondered? A neighbor had been to California, and she often talked about earthquakes—how a big hole opened up in the earth and we could fall into it, and then the earth would close and we would never know what hit us. All night I monitored the amount of daylight at the top of the bedroom window to be sure our house hadn't fallen into a big earthquake hole.

A deafening bang assaulted the south side of the house, scaring the pee right out of me. "Daddy, is this the Apocalypse?" I blubbered. I worried a lot about the End of the World that Daddy preached about all the time. "Are the seven horsemen on their way with the Antichrist?"

"We never know the place or the hour, but I don't think this is it," Daddy allowed between gasps for breath.

The back door crashed open, and a hurricane wind came barreling through, bringing a haze of whirling, choking dust with it. Furniture flew. Charles yelled for help as he tried to pull a recalcitrant Bossy onto the screened-in back porch. Bossy wanted no part of whatever was happening. "Moo, moo," she complained, casting wild eyes up toward Heaven. Daddy and Mama ran to help Charles. One of the hens squawked and got away, her feathers turned inside out by the wind. But Charles still held three hens and our ol' rooster, Errol, by their feet. I could hear the commotion even over the noise of the wind. With all the clucking, scratching, squawking, mooing, wheezing, and howling, it was like a zoo.

Mama, Daddy, Grandma Hattie, and Charles—who looked like he was made out of dirt—eventually got Bossy and the chickens settled and the door bolted. Dust blew through cracks. The whole house rattled.

"Don't let those animals get into the kitchen," Mama warned. "They'll do their business all over the place." With that, Bossy let loose.

"Oh, puke," Charles said, looking down at his splattered feet.

"Tarnation," Daddy roared. "I'm taking myself off to bed. I can hardly breathe."

"Me too, Charlie," said Mama. "I'm simply all fagged out. Let me know if the house blows over." She kinda laughed and headed off to bed with Little Jimmy in her arms, leaving us to fend for ourselves.

Grandma Hattie nestled down on the foot of my bed next to Gideon, who hadn't stirred in spite of the commotion going on around him. Hugging the slight little fellow to her, Grandma Hattie began snoring almost as loud as the storm.

After a stretched-out sleepless night, and after the sandstorm finally subsided, Daddy took off for Oklahoma City with Grandma Hattie and Gideon. Before the rest of us could shovel the dirt out of the house, there was a knock on the door. It was one of Mr. Steinway's loading men. He held a piano leg and a handful of ivory keys in his big, rough hands. He said Mr. Steinway had blown out of the truck and scattered his bones all across Highway 177, stopping traffic in both directions. It was a sight! The man laughed and then seemed to think better of it.

"Thought y'all might like to have some of them remains," he said, handing the leg and ivory keys to Mama.

I was teary-eyed. "Oh, goodness. Mr. Steinway killed himself. He didn't want to leave us."

"We'll have a nice funeral when you get well, Patsy Lou," said Mama with unaccustomed gentleness.

But that wasn't the end of what happened during that doom-filled dark when the land was throwing up all over itself and flinging itself over pastures, digging them up and burying towns and houses in sand and trying to kill everyone as dead as Mr. Steinway was. It turned out that scrawny little Gideon had a wicked case of measles that I inherited, soon followed by mumps and chicken pox and whooping cough. I was so shrunk up from all those ailments that my rib bones protruded out of my skin. Poor Little Glendora said I looked like a stringy chicken, and then laughed and gave me a piece of ice chipped from a big block that Daddy had bought us as a treat. Then she hugged me. Later I wondered if I'd had a fever dream. It was beyond my comprehension that my sister had actually hugged me.

~~~

As I slowly began to heal, a deep itch inside of me mingled with the pain. It was an itch I couldn't reach. I was lying with Mama and Daddy in their big iron bedstead. "Mama, itch me, itch me," I begged. "Please itch me.

I've got a sticker way up inside me."

Mama gingerly put her finger into the rim of my vagina a bit, trying to get to the source of my itch. Daddy whispered some Mama. She smiled and blushed. A secret transmission that had something to do with my itch took place between them. Then I was lost in the urgency of my pain and the sticker inside of me. But still, I heard Daddy whisper that married life might be very hard for me. "Patsy just might be disfigured from that burn," he whispered to Mama.

I suffered nightmares, talking in my sleep and walking in my sleep, too. Poor Little Glendora said she couldn't get her beauty rest because I kicked and screamed so much. Sometimes I dreamed the Devil blew fire at me and I couldn't get away. Other times I dreamed that God and his angels were plotting to take me to Heaven with them, but I told them I didn't want to go. One night Mama came to the bedroom nursing Little Jimmy to try to soothe my inner war. "I'm moving," Poor Little Glendora said, making a pallet for herself on the living room floor.

One morning Mama told me I had walked in my sleep the previous night and had even left the house. "Land's sake, Patsy Lou, y'all gave us a big scare," she said, bleary-eyed. "We've been up half the night looking for you."

I grew so fearful I would hurt myself that every night I stayed awake as long as I could keep my eyes open. When I was able to be up and about, I walked cautiously, like a cowboy, Charles said. Poor Little Glendora said I was bowlegged and would always be that way. Although embarrassed, Charles carried pillows for me to sit on when we went to church or visited church members. I was powerfully ashamed.

Months later when I squatted to pee, viscous ropes of yellow mucus poured out of me. It was so thick that I wound it around a twig I found on the ground to pull it out of me. Did this have to do with the disfigurement Daddy had talked about?

I didn't understand what it meant to be disfigured. Somehow, I

,ught I had sinned. I worried, but I didn't talk about my fears to anyone—not to Mama, Daddy, my sisters, my best friend, or even to myself. Such topics were not discussed in my family. The scars that affected my life were locked within delicate folds of pink tissue and complex coils of gray matter. Terrifying memories of a burning clitoris and injured vagina disappeared as cleanly as if a gunman's bullet had sliced through my skull, severing the most complex biological structure known: memory. Decades would pass before recollections of that time began to reemerge.

Chapter 3

Dog Days

After three years in Addington, Oklahoma, we were on the move again, heading to Chillicothe, Texas, where Daddy would pastor the Church of the Nazarene. Daddy seemed down in the mouth, not his usual singing and joking self. I wondered if it had to do with Brother Webber. The last Sunday in Addington, church members stood to sing "God Be With You Till We Meet Again" when Brother Webber came busting in the door in his olive drab suit but without shoes or socks. In a high, scratchy voice he hollered, "I'm Jesus, I'm Jesus!" and began dancing around. Then he swore. "Fuck God," he yelled.

The congregation was as mummified as if Halley's Comet had come out of the dust soaked sky and smacked into the church, killing them all dead, immobilizing them in place. Only two people were left, Brother Webber and Daddy.

Daddy quoted scripture in a voice as deep as a trombone: "Satan has gotten into y'all, Brother Webber. Revelation 22:15 says, 'Outside are the dogs and sorcerers and the sexually immoral and murderers and idolaters, and . . .'"

Brother Webber put one of his fingers up in the air and hightailed it back outside.

Resuscitated, church members pushed and shoved to get to the front door so they could see what was going to happen next. What happened next was that Brother Webber danced over a bed of stinging nettles the way Jesus walked on water, seeming to not even notice the stickers. Daddy scampered to try to catch him but fell into the nettle bed and got barbs in his hands like you wouldn't believe. Brother Webber's screech sounded like a tire rim on pavement: "Reverend Mountaintop is the Devil!" Then he hotfooted it off down the street.

Mama tended Daddy's wounds, Little Jimmy clinging to her rayon skirt. Stunned, Charles was trying to help Mama when Brother Webber came back and circled the church twice, all the time declaring the preacher was Satan. "Reverend Mountaintop is the Devil incarnate!"

I was mighty relieved when the police arrived, sirens bleating against my eardrums, and dragged him away—to an insane asylum, we were told. Church members shook their heads, holding their hands over their mouths to hide smiles, or giggled self-consciously. Others were scandalized. All I can say is that it sure put a damper on our going-away celebration.

"Mama, what does 'fuck' mean?" I asked on our way home.

Mama hauled off and smacked me on the face. "Don't let me ever hear tell of you saying that nasty word again, Patsy Lou."

I was so taken aback I didn't even cry.

Having to leave my friend Rethie Marie and Teacher made me so miserable that I holed up in my secret reading place, the musty-smelling storage closet, for two days, with a stash of books, hard cheese, saltine crackers, and a glass of Bossy's milk, bawling. When I finally showed my puffy red face, no one seemed to notice that I hadn't been around. Mama just said for me to help her pack up our things, and no dillydallying. Her face was also puffy and her spirits seemed low, but she pretended to like a change of scenery.

"We have to go where God calls so we can further the Kingdom," she said.

Assorted church brethren and two of Daddy's black friends helped drag, push, and shove our worldly goods onto the trailer. In no time at all, it was piled high with blackened pots and pans; dishes, both chipped and not; a tangle of iron bedsteads; a cardboard box of clothes; six of Grandma Taylor's quilts; one hope chest; one chest of drawers; one worn-out horsehair couch, used for a bed when I was burned; two torn but still useable armchairs; one scuffed-up dining table and eight chairs, one broken; one broken-down wringer washing machine; two galvanized washtubs, one with a small hole in its side where Charles had hammered in a nail; one wooden crate Daddy had built to carry the chickens and the rooster in, now under a tarp at the back of the trailer, with the chickens cackling away; and in a special compartment to hold her steady, our cow Bossy, with her tail hanging outside the slats. Right away, a load of manure started streaking down.

Like a banana split with a cherry on top, the whole conglomeration was topped with bedsprings and mattresses. The rest of our belongings were stashed in the backseat of the Model A Ford. Mama's blue enameled coffeepot with a chip on the spout protruded from a cardboard carton, and a bunch of Bibles, hymnals, and a zillion copies of *The Herald of Holiness* stashed wherever they would fit were the sum of our earthly possessions. But as we sang in church, our treasures were laid up somewhere beyond the blue. I sure hoped so.

Squirreled down in a nest of quilts and sustained by a messy stash of dry soda crackers, rat cheese, and a Mason jar of water was Poor Little Glendora next to the window on one side, with three-year-old Little Jimmy on her lap. Charles sat on the other side. And there I was, scrunched in the middle with my blue-haired cat, Bluie, nested on my lap. Charles had smuggled Rat-Dog aboard and was feeding him our cheese and letting him lap water from the communal water jar.

"Charles," Daddy said before we left, "we can't take that dog with us. He's to be given to Brother Riser to kill his rats." Daddy attempted to soften the blow. "Son, I'm sorry to have to do this, but we have all we can handle. You'll find another dog when we get to Chillicothe."

"Rat-Dog could never kill anything," Charles said, his chin wobbling like a flat tire on the highway. "Besides, I don't want a different dog. I want Rat-Dog."

"Son, this is a hard time for our family. Don't make it any harder."

Now here we were, packed like sardines, Mama said, not knowing the half of it.

"Patsy Lou," my brother whispered, "keep your cat away from Rat-Dog." Rat-Dog's black ear perked up at the sound of his name. The other ear, his white one, couldn't perk all the way, but he was listening; I could tell by the light in his golden-brown eyes. That little guy was as intelligent as all get out. He seemed to understand Oklahoma English and then some. After Rat-Dog heard all he wanted to hear, he lay down on the floorboard of the hot car, his long pink tongue lolling out, and laid his head on his paws and slept.

"You keep Rat-Dog away from my cat," I snapped.

"Keep your voice down, Patsy, or Daddy will hear."

"Stop the ruckus," Daddy yelled, straining to be heard above the clatter of our fourth-hand Model A. "If y'all start acting up, I'll stop the car at the side of the road and take a switch to y'all."

We sailed along in peace for a while, although *sail* isn't exactly the word. We bucked along. The only sounds were the rattling car, the squeaking and jerking of the trailer, Bluie hissing at Rat-Dog, Rat-Dog snoozing, and Mama singing, "Amazing grace . . . how sweet the sound . . ."

The car and trailer seemed to be lurching across the dividing line uncommonly often. I heard snoring. Oh no! Daddy was falling asleep. "Mama! Wash Daddy's face," I yelled, "quick!"

Mama grabbed the wet rags she kept with which to help Daddy wake up. He had a sleeping sickness and often started snoozing while driving. Traveling with Daddy was like being tied to a railroad track and hoping the trains had stopped running. Our automobile adventures vied with *The Perils of Pauline* as Daddy careened perilously close to open ditches, fences, trees, and cows, all the while declaring he couldn't understand what all the screams and hollers were about. It was downright damaging to my nervous system.

When he came fully awake, Daddy sniffed the sour air. It was permeated with the odors of melting cheese, expelled gas, Little Jimmy's pee, and dog. Charles and Poor Little Glendora rolled down their windows about halfway, and we were being whipped by a torrent of dusty wind against our faces and blustering cracker crumbs all around. Bluie dug her claws into my leg, hanging on, while Rat-Dog tried to stick his head out the window, but Charles made him stay on the hot floorboard so Daddy couldn't see him.

"I smell a dog," Daddy shouted over the windstorm barreling through the car. "Charles, is Rat-Dog in this car?"

"N-n-no, sir."

"Don't lie to me, son."

"Yessir."

"Dagnabbit, I told y'all that y'all couldn't bring that terrier!" Daddy was almost foaming at the mouth.

"It's okay, Charlie. Let Charles keep him. I don't mind," Mama said, surprising the pants off me.

"Mama, we hardly have enough money and food to get us to Chillicothe, much less feed a dog."

"I need to go to the bathroom!" I wailed, hoping to divert attention.

"We're almost at a filling station, so hold on, Patsy Lou, and don't go on the ashes," Daddy said.

Laughter broke the tension, but I didn't think it was funny. I still suffered from my burns, not being able to get rid of the sticker I often felt deep inside of me. It was such an uncomfortable sensation that sometimes I would sneak away from prying eyes to try to scratch the sticker. I could never reach it.

Daddy was fixated on Rat-Dog. "When we stop, y'all walk that dog so he doesn't make a mess in the car. Y'all hear me, Charles?"

The next dusty little town we came to was Lone Grove. Daddy jockeyed the car and trailer to the curb in front of a flying red horse filling station. We piled out and ran to the nasty restroom, glad to stretch our legs and relieve ourselves. Afterward, we walked down Main Street looking at boarded-up store windows, most with dust piled up to the windowsills, while Charles helped Daddy. Little Jimmy was slung on Mama's hip, sucking on a sugar tit, when she started talking to us in a serious tone.

"Girls," she said, "y'all know many of our friends and relatives had to leave Oklahoma and Texas in their old rattletrap cars to get away from the dust storms and feed their families." There were tears in Mama's eyes. "Off to California they went. They had to give up this good red earth and the prairie where they were born so they could survive." This was not the mother I knew. Usually she was as stern as a hanging judge. "Poor Little Glendora and Patsy Lou, turn around and look me in the eyes."

We obeyed, of course. When didn't we?

"Y'all don't know it yet, but y'all have gained moral fiber by learning to handle adversity, all the moving around, the hard times, without complaining. Y'all know Daddy isn't well, so I'm counting on y'all." Mama wiped her eyes with one end of the hankie with the sugar tit tied to it. She sighed. "Well, time to get going," she said, just as Daddy gave a loud shout to come on, we needed to get on the road.

We wobbled along at about forty miles an hour, staring out at tired-looking mesquite trees and mournful, white-faced cows clustered against post and barbed wire fences. *I'll bet they wish they were grazing in a green pasture*, I thought, feeling sorry for them. I felt sorry for Bossy, too, riding along by herself under a tacked-on roof with her tail swishing over the side. At least Charles gave her fresh water and hay whenever we stopped and would milk her every day.

"I don't hear Rat-Dog snuffling around on the floorboard," Daddy said. "Where is he, son?"

My brother could hardly talk. He coughed several times and then blurted out the story. "I"—sniff—"gave"—sniff—"Rat-Dog away." Putting his head down on his knees, Charles burst into full-blown howls. "Boohoo," he sobbed. He had a long string of snot running out his nose. Eventually, after blowing his nose, he calmed down a bit and, between sobs, told us what had happened. "Y'all told me to get rid of him, and there was a man sitting on the curb whittling, and he said, 'Son, how much do you want for that cute dog?' 'He's not for sale,' I told the man, 'but I have to give him away, so I'll give him to y'all.'" At the end of his tale, Charles once again erupted in loud-pitched howls of grief. "I miss Rat-Dog," he sobbed.

Poor Little Glendora and Little Jimmy joined in the wailing. I brought up the rear. "We want Rat-Dog, we want Rat-Dog, we want Rat-Dog." The commotion we made steamed up the windows of the already hot car. "Lord help us," was Mama's contribution to the chorus.

Daddy pulled off the highway and got out, Mama following. Digging around on the floorboard where Mama sat, Daddy lifted a big watermelon out of a cardboard box.

"Come on, children, look what I bought back there. Watermelon, yum-yum. It's still cold, too."

"We don't want watermelon. We want Rat-Dog." Tears streaked our dusty faces. We weren't about to be bribed, although I did consider it. Watermelon sounded mighty good to me.

Mama opened the car door and pulled Charles out. She patted his back and told him she was sorry. It wouldn't have seemed natural for her to hug Charles. Our parents seldom hugged us and never said they loved us. Once, when I asked Mama if she loved me, she said, "I gave birth to you, didn't I?"

The watermelon treat was a dud, so we got in the car and Daddy pulled back out onto the two-lane road. An unnatural silence reigned. Our misery deepened. Hunger and fatigue were accentuated by the thought of losing Rat-Dog. In the next town, Daddy found a filling station and must have been feeling remorseful and a little ashamed, because he gave us each a nickel, something I could never ever remember happening before. We hotfooted it to the RC Cola bin and pulled out bottles of Orange Crush and RC from the melting ice. Mama must have been too tired to care how she looked, because usually outer appearances were important to her. Even without funds, she made sure we were fairly clean and our clothes looked okay. But here she was, sitting on the curb with us, swigging a bottle of Dr Pepper with her navy-blue dress hiked up, showing her tiny ankles and her stockings knotted just below her knees. She never showed her legs, which Daddy called "shapely."

When the high-pitched car warning signal, *uga-uga uga-uga*, sounded, it was time to be on our way. We sullenly clambered into our allotted spaces. I said my usual prayer that the car would start. More often than not, it didn't. Several times, I burned my hands trying to help push a car that had been sitting in the sizzling sun. It made me scared when Daddy cussed in his arcane vocabulary while trying to fix the car. I vowed when I grew up I would have an automobile that always started. Well, thanks be to Jesus, this time our old Ford started right off.

"Charlie! You're heading the wrong way," Mama shouted in a sharp voice. "Are you asleep?"

"I can't stand all that crying and carrying on," Daddy said. "I'm heading on back to the flying red horse filling station to find Rat-Dog, that's where I'm heading." He worked up a sweat trying to get the car and trailer turned around. We were crossways on the highway, and our Gypsy rig was causing a ruckus.

After a few minutes of driving back and forth and getting nowhere, Daddy leaned out the window, and using his preacher voice, introduced himself to an impatient motorist. "Howdy, brother," he said. "I'm Reverend Montandon, and I need to get turned around here. I'd appreciate it mightily if y'all could give me a hand." The man looked annoyed but carefully removed his white suit jacket and straw boater hat, shut the motor of his shiny new Studebaker off, and frowning, took up the chore of directing traffic for our raggedy caravan.

"This is downright embarrassing," Poor Little Glendora said, sinking down into the quilts. "I don't want anyone to see me."

Charles took up the battle against self-centeredness. "What's the matter with y'all? No one knows y'all. Stop being paranoid."

When we were finally on our way again, our spirits brightened. We began singing "She'll Be Coming 'Round the Mountain." Charles wept with joy, Little Jimmy wanted watermelon, Bluie purred, I ate cheese, Daddy sweated, Mama sang, and Poor Little Glendora declared her independence. "Stop calling me Poor Little Glendora. I'm almost grown," she said. "I'm Glendora, just plain, beautiful Glendora!"

"Ha-ha," I retorted. "Y'all think you're something on a stick!"

My sister picked up my Heidi book, ripped out two pages, and flung them out the window. "I *am* something on a stick."

Well, the fat was in the fire. I grabbed Mama's coffeepot and hit my sister over her curly-haired head. Her shrieks were so loud, they could be heard all the way to darkest Africa, where our missionaries taught Heathens to wear clothes and love Baby Jesus. Mama's head spun in our direction faster than you could say Jack Robinson. She was mad as an old wet hen.

"Girls, stop that fighting right this minute. Y'all hear me? I mean it. Patsy Lou, stop picking on Poor Little Glendora, or I'll have your daddy turn Bluie loose in these fields."

"That's right," Daddy said. "Quit the bickering or suffer the consequences."

"It's okay, Daddy," Poor Little Glendora simpered, while twisting the skin on my arm into a purple knot. "I forgive her the way Jesus forgave Judas." I pretended to accept her sugarcoated forgiveness.

Outside the flying red horse filling station, a man with skimpy white hair and a sad lack of teeth who, nevertheless, chawed down on a wad of tobacco, sat in a seedy-looking armchair that had the stuffing falling out of it. He allowed as how he saw us pull out with our piled-up trailer. "Couldn't hardly miss a trailer with a cow tail a-hangin' off the back end nohow. Hee-hee." Said he saw our dog, too. "Some ol' feller had a rope 'round about his neck and was a-tryin' to lead him off, like, but that there dog—hee-hee—bucked up such a fuss, barkin' and bitin', that the feller let go a' the rope and—hee-hee—that li'l ol' dog took off a-flyin', like. I never in all my borned days seed nothin' like hit, I'm tellin' y'all. Why, thet li'l rat terrier went off a-runnin' like a turpentine kitty on the plains of Texas, ran down that there road right there, he did, tryin' to catch that trailer of yurn. Yesiree, that li'l feller was a-goin' and a-goin'."

The man stored snuff in his jaw, waiting to get to the end of his story before spitting it into the coffee can he held. He missed the can, and a long stream of slimy brown snuff landed on the dust near our feet, where it rolled into a ball. *Splat.*

"Disgusting," Mama whispered. For once I agreed with her.

"Thank y'all for your help, brother. May God bless you," Daddy said. "It's come on me to say a prayer for y'all."
The fellow looked bewildered. "Don't see as how it'll hurt or help anythin'. I s'pose hits yore bounden duty, so iffen hit makes y'all feel better, Mr. Preacher Man, y'all go on ahead. I ain't no Christian, though. Hee-hee."

After Daddy finished a long prayer, and after the toothless fellow had spat again, we took off to find Charles's dog. Daddy drove slowly down the highway, peering in ditches and scanning the road ahead, hoping to see Rat-Dog. Charles walked in front of the car. Every few steps he would veer into the weeds growing rankly on either side of the road and call for Rat-Dog. Poor Lit—Glendora and I got out of the car to help. We called over and over, "Here Rat-Dog, here doggie, here Rat-Dog."

Honking cars zoomed past, kids staring. When a Highway Patrol car came up behind us and stopped, I thought for sure we were in trouble. Daddy pulled off the road under a mesquite, the only tree in sight, and hauled himself out of the car. Instantly he transformed into preacher mode.

"Howdy, brother, I'm Reverend Montandon. We're dawdling along because we're looking for a little rat terrier dog that belongs to my son up there . . ." Daddy's eyes welled up. "It's my fault he lost his dog, Rat-Dog . . ." Daddy couldn't continue.

The Highway Patrol officer looked uncomfortable at such an unbridled display of emotion. His long, pale face turned rosy right up to his hairline. He put a finger under his white shirt collar and tugged on it. When he swallowed, his Adam's apple bobbed up and down while his khaki tie rode the wave. The man wore an official highway patrolman's jacket and trousers with high leather boots and a billed cap, which must have been hot as fire.

"Reverend, I'm Officer Wellington, sir, and the old feller back at the flyin' red horse fillin' station told me about y'all and your dog. I came to help y'all. I'll stop traffic and ask people to be on the lookout for your little dog. Rat-Dog, right?"

I thought he might say, "Hee-hee," but he didn't.

After that, other drivers gave us thumbs-up as they passed, even though their kids crossed their eyes and stuck out their tongues. I stuck my tongue out at them, too, until Mama told me to stop.

About two hours later, when the shadows of the lone tree we sat under were as long as a cow's tongue, Charles let out a loud whoop. Lying in a bed of weeds and sand at the side of the road, panting like all get out, was Rat-Dog.

"Son, don't pick him up until we know if he's okay or not," Daddy said. While they were ministering to Rat-Dog, I got our Mason jar of water and carried it out to him so he could have a drink. He lapped up almost the whole jar of water. Turned out his right front leg was broken, it looked like, and his paws were raw. A car must have hit him, but he wagged his short little tail anyway. Being careful of his wounds, Charles carried Rat-Dog to the car, where he gave him more water to drink and the last piece of cheese.

Daddy found his toolbox and got out a knife. Slivering off two pieces of wood from one of the trailer rails, he took a sheet of sandpaper from his toolbox and smoothed the wood into a splint for Rat-Dog's broken leg.

Folding his white cotton handkerchief over several times, with Mama's help Daddy gently wrapped the wood nice and tight around Rat-Dog's broken leg and tied it with butcher's string.

"That should do it, Charles," Daddy said. "He won't walk on it till it's healed. Dogs are smart that way."

Poor little Rat-Dog, son of Lazy Red, without a daddy, took it all in and beat his tail hard against the car seat, whimpering a little.

Mama put Blue Star Ointment on Rat-Dog's paws, then broke out a package of bologna and sneaked a few pieces to a hungry dog before putting together our biscuit sandwiches. She'd kept the meat from spoiling with a small block of ice in a bucket. Charles was busy with Rat-Dog, so Daddy, with the help of Mr. Wellington, managed to get Bossy out of the trailer, staked her to graze, milked her, and fed the cooped-up chickens. We had half a bucket of warm, foamy fresh milk to go with our sandwiches.

"Thank you, Bossy," I said into her big, hairy black ear. She flicked her ear like I was a fly, letting me know she appreciated my consideration. Bossy was a Jersey and matched Rat-Dog in that they were both black and white.

Glendora and I spread a quilt over the crunchy weeds at the side of the road to use as a table and another quilt for us to sit on. The sun was low on the horizon, casting us in a golden Jesus glow: Mama, Daddy, Little Jimmy, Poor Little Glendora, Charles, Rat-Dog, Bluie, and Mr. Wellington, who removed his high leather boots to reveal a pair of once-white socks with holes in the heels. Then there was Bossy and me. Daddy gave a blessedly short blessing. After we ate our sandwiches, Daddy cut big juicy slices of warm watermelon for each of us. Delish, as my sister Faye would have said.

But we weren't through with the day yet. Charles had an announcement. "Uh, y'all, Daddy, thanks for looking for my dog . . ." He began to cry, so I patted his hand. "I'm changing his name to Hero-Dog," he added. "Because he sure enough is."

"Charles," I said, "he'll forever be Rat-Dog to me." And that's the name that stuck, hero though he was. The same thing was true of Glendora, who forever after and always was called Poor Little Glendora.

It had taken us the whole day to go thirty-five miles. Now it was getting on toward dark and we had no place to sleep that night. Mama and Daddy prayed about it, and soon Daddy felt called on by the Lord to knock on the door of a worn-out looking farmhouse in the distance off a dirt side road. This was not an unusual occurrence. We often stayed in the homes of strangers.

Daddy straightened his tie, put on his black suit coat, tucked his white shirttail into his trousers, and picked up his black leather-covered Bible. With the confident stride of a Man of God, he walked up to the door of the farmhouse and knocked. A fellow wearing Farmer John style overalls answered. Daddy introduced himself. After a few pleasantries, he told our story and asked if we could come in. The farmer—Brother Lively was his name, he said—opened his door wide and invited us in. In fact, just as Daddy knew would happen, Mr. Lively and his wife, Mrs. Lively, said we should stay for supper and spend the night.

"Reverend Mountain, we been prayin' for a Man of God to pray with us," said Farmer Lively. "Our hearts are heavy, so we'd 'preciate a blessin' of the spirit."

"Amen, brother," Daddy said. "Praise God. I got a message from on high to come up to your house. We'll have service with y'all tonight and pray that God lifts your problems right off your shoulders. Hallelujah!"

"Glory to God," said Farmer Lively. "Amen."

We enjoyed a supper of red beans, onions, cornbread, and chow-chow. Mama helped Mrs. Lively, a taciturn woman, make pallets for us to sleep on. Rat-Dog was not allowed in the house, so Charles slept in the car with his pet. Bossy and the chickens shared space in the barn.

My pallet was next to a Philco radio. "If you chillun want to listen to the radio, it's okay," Mrs. Lively said, talking real loud. "We'uns halfway deaf, so noise don't bother us none."

When the praying was done and after I heard snoring, I turned the radio's round dial to *On* and stumbled onto a station with music. Leaning my head against the mesh speaker, I was instantly transported. The most poignant sounds I ever heard in my entire life waterfalled out of the speaker in a silvery torrent. A deep-voiced announcer, sounding like God himself, said, "You are listening to the NBC Symphony Orchestra with Arturo Toscanini conducting Symphony Number Nine in D Minor 'Choral': *Allegro ma non . . .*" I couldn't understand the name of the symphony, but I understood something more important. All I had to do was close my eyes, and there I was in the audience with people I heard clapping. My soul soared. I grew wings.

Someday, I decided, I would have my own bed to sleep in with a Philco radio next to it, so I could listen to beautiful music all night long. I was enraptured. That transcendent melody touched a chord inside of me, a wellspring of my spirit, and caused soft tears to thread down my cheeks and drop onto the top of my slip. I drowned in the music. That healing symphony sustained me during the rest of our haphazard journey, plagued by flat tires, bickering, hunger, and exhaustion.

Chapter 4

Herding Flies

The parsonage in Chillicothe was so beautiful and big and white that I almost couldn't believe it. Mama said it was a Victorian house. Furthermore, we had a yard with grass and flowers and one bent-over cedar tree that looked like an old man with green hair. Other places we lived had boasted only hard-packed earth for a yard. In the summertime, when it was sweltering hot, the hard little yards were sprinkled with water to settle the dust. The aroma of water on parched earth is the sweetest smell ever. But now we had a beautiful house and a yard full of orange-colored flowers and a crooked-old-man cedar tree.

The modest wooden church sat next door to the parsonage. We could keep an eye on things, Daddy wouldn't have to drive a long distance, and Mama wouldn't have to worry about him. But before we were even halfway moved in, two skinny men wearing shiny black suits and carrying Bibles showed up.

"We're deacons of the church," they announced, looking like they'd eaten sour persimmons. With pursed mouths, dark eyebrows bracketed by furrowed frown lines, brown hair indented by the black felt hats they'd just taken off, and small, mean-looking eyes, they made me fearful.

"Reverend Montandon, we think y'all should know we don't allow colored folks to come to our church. We've been a-hearing rumors that y'all let Negras attend your services. Brother Justice and I, Brother Price, are here to welcome y'all. But also to let y'all know Negras have their own place of worship in this town and are not allowed at our services."

Daddy bristled, but Mama smiled and held him back. This did not bode well for a solid and happy beginning. Before Daddy could utter "dagnabbit," or "shoot take it," or try to show them the error of their ways, Brother Price and Brother Justice got down on their knees right there on the Bermuda grass, said a prayer, gave us tight smiles, and left.

"Let's us go inside the house," Daddy said. "We've got to pray about this. Those two aren't the only deacons on this beach. You kids, come and pray, too, and make your minds focus on what this is all about. It's about power and trying to push your father around so I don't get in the way of their agenda. They are bigots and don't want to have to cope with anyone different from themselves. But children . . ." Daddy paused to catch his breath before continuing. "Children, God is no respecter of persons. He cares only about a pure heart. We'll pray until we get an answer about what to do. Now kneel down, close your eyes, and bow your heads."

I sure hoped God sent his answer right away; otherwise, it would be a long night. Apparently, Daddy got his answer, because two Sundays later, six polished-looking black men, friends Daddy had made, sat on the last row at the back of the church, turning identical brown felt hats round and round in their hands, staring at the floor, not looking at anyone. Church members acted like they didn't see the black folks, but you bet your bottom dollar they saw them, all right. And how. There was so much buzzing and whispering and sideways glances and turned-down mouths, it was like being in a hive of angry bees.

One Sunday about two weeks later, we were rushing around trying to get ready for church, knowing the members—especially Brother Justice and Brother Price—would be timing us with their gold pocket watches to see if we were on time. Mama looked frazzled. Strands of gray interlaced with brown escaped their usual bun and were flying around her face. Since it was considered a sin of vanity to adorn oneself, she didn't wear a wedding band or a touch of makeup. Her florid complexion and deep blue eyes betrayed Irish ancestry.

"Before I married your papa, I was Myrtle Taylor," she said. "Don't you children ever forget it." Mama firmly believed in the power of God and her own interpretation of the Bible. Even the way she walked emphasized her beliefs. Her steps were forceful, determined. Mama was a power to be reckoned with, having survived twelve pregnancies, eight live births, three miscarriages, and one baby dead inside of her for two months. "Now don't you children give me any grief. We've got to get to the church house on time or the members will be upset," she said. "Be on your best behavior, too. Remember, y'all are the preacher's kids and subject to scrutiny."

Our small living room assumed its normal air of disorder as gawky and now partially deaf Charles Clay and Poor Little Glendora pushed and shoved in an effort to be first out the door. Slung over Mama's right hip was Little Jimmy, who still sucked his thumb and was recovering from the croup. The pungent aroma of Vicks VapoRub radiated off his chest. "I'm not going to lose another baby, the way I lost little Bettie Ruth," Mama said, rubbing Little Jimmy down with the almighty power of Mr. Vicks.

We walked along in single file toward the church house. The powdery Texas dust drifting up with each footstep encompassed us in a russet halo. When we reached the white clapboard chapel, I quickly pulled away from my family to sit on one of the rough slatted benches with my new friend, Sudie Lynn. Mama had said I would never amount to a hill of beans if I didn't stop playing pretend all the time. I sure didn't want to sit next to her.

The sparse congregation was filing in and taking their usual places. Fat Sister Kookin's rocking chair blocked the center aisle, but no one dared protest. Her loud "ah-ah-mens" and "praise-the-Lords" accompanied a slow descent into the chair's cushions. The church service could not begin until she was ready, as she was a deacon of the church and had money, we were told. "Jesus help us!" she exclaimed, rolling her brown horse eyes toward the ceiling. After worship, Sister Kookin's Model A Ford would be pushed down the little hillock where she parked in order to get it started. The whole congregation would help push Sister Kookin's car and then wave to her after the car coughed and snorted and finally started, scattering half the animal population of Chillicothe, Texas.

Now everyone was quiet except for a baby in the row behind me. He made greedy smacking sounds as his mother nursed him from ample breasts, first the right and then the left. I took guilty peeks at the woman. Her titty was only partly covered by a blue handkerchief edged in purple tatting. I watched until the baby stopped sucking and pulled away. Then the woman's huge brown nipple was exposed with one drop of milk suspended from it.

"Disgusting," Mama said. "The very idea of putting her dinner right out there for the whole world to see! Charlie Clay Montandon," she said to my father, "y'all ought not to let her do that in the House of Worship."

"Mama," he said, "that woman is just feeding her baby."

"She's nothing but a hussy, if you ask me," Mama snapped her apron for emphasis. "I've had a passel of kids, and never, not once, did I show off my dinners in public."

I always tuned out during Daddy's sermons about hellfire and damnation. I didn't want to think about all those poor sinners burning in Hell's fire. When I burned myself peeing on hot coals, it hurt so much that I thought about Hell and sinners and vowed never to play cards or do any of that other stuff, either. I wasn't exactly sure what that other stuff was, but Rethie Marie said it was fornication. Maybe so; Daddy often preached about the fornicators.

"Hallelujah! Glory to God!" someone shouted. Daddy was through preaching, and everyone was rising for the final hymn and altar call. The sermon always ended the same way. I could recite it by heart. There would be sad music and then Daddy beseeching sinners to come to the altar and let go of their evil ways. I could have preached Daddy's sermons myself.

"Please turn your songbooks to page forty-five," Daddy said. I started whispering the words he would say ahead of him. "Now, folks," I said, "as we sing the last song, remember, this may be your final hour on earth. You had better think about that, brothers and sisters. You had better march up here and give your hearts and souls to God. This could be your last

76

opportunity to make things right with your Maker."

As our emotional pitch for Heaven became more intense, Daddy's voice and mine became thunderous—too loud, actually. I got a stern look from those sitting near me, and one from Daddy, too.

"Mother, while you play," I continued, whispering real soft now, indicating the black upright piano, "and the choir sings, I want those of you who are burdened with sin to come forward . . ." Mama banged away on the piano as the choir, wearing the mournful expressions of career saints, tuned up.

I leaned over and whispered in Sudie Lynn's ear. "Bet you a copper penny they'll sing 'Softly and Tenderly.'" She ignored me. But I wasn't one to give up easily. "That song always makes people cry. Y'all just watch."

When the choir launched into "Softly and tenderly Jesus is calling, calling for you and for me . . .Come home, Come home, o-o-o-h sinner, Come h-o-o-me," Sudie Lynn grinned and handed me the penny tied in the corner of her hankie and meant to go in the collection plate.

The problem was that I fell for that song every Sunday and went trailing up to the altar to confess my sins. What if I were to die today? Would I be saved? No, I would go straight to Hell for making fun of Daddy and his preaching and mocking God's songs. "Ooooh," I moaned, tears of fear coursing down my face. "I don't want to die a sinner."

At the first *O-o-o-h*, several of the devout enveloped me as if they had found a genuine diamond on a kid's treasure hunt. They propelled me to the mourner's bench, where I fell on my knees sobbing. "Here's little Patsy Lou, Lord Jesus, a sinner," intoned the supplicants. "Only you know what dark deeds she has done, what evil thoughts she's had."

Others were shouting, "I've got religion!" My mind wandered from my own sins long enough to peek and see if Brother Cantrell was going to throw a songbook like he sometimes did when spiritual enthusiasm overwhelmed him. Sure enough, I could see him winding up. Daddy ducked as the book sailed through the air, its pages fluttering in the breeze.

"That was a good meeting," Daddy said at the supper table that night. "Lots of people prayed through to victory, and folks didn't even seem to mind my new friends, the black-skinned brethren, being there."

"Ha-ha," Charles offered. "They minded, all right. There were lots of ruffled feathers. Most of the people looked the way our chickens did in that sandstorm when their feathers got turned inside out. Did you take a look at Brother Price and Brother Justice? They were so mad they looked like Rat-Dog does when someone gives me a bad time. I expected them to bare their teeth and growl."

"Well, now, don't be hasty, Charles. I had a good long talk with Sister Kookin, and she seemed okay with, as she said, Negras attending our services. Said she would pray for them, even. Now that's enlightenment and what Christianity should be about. Praise God," Daddy said. "Now let's go to bed. But before we go, Patsy Lou, I have something I want y'all to hear." Pulling his gold-rimmed spectacles down on his nose, he caught me dead center in his gaze. "Chick-a-lick, since y'all keep reciting my sermon in church, I'm going to call on y'all to stand at the pulpit next Sunday and deliver the sermon." He smiled and reached out to pat my cheek. "I mean it, child."
I ran off to bed, knowing I would sure have to do some fast studying of the Bible.

Something awoke me from the velvety blackness of sleep. Was Glendora still in the bed? I probed for her with my foot.

"Stop kicking me," she hissed.

"There's somethin' wrong . . ." Before I could get the words out of my mouth, a scream, as if Satan had poked a transgressor with his pitchfork, numbed them in my mind. It was Mama.

"The church is on fire!" she shouted. "Help! Help! The church is on fire!"

My sister and I stumbled to the window. Next door, the small wooden chapel was alive with flames. The whole neighborhood was lit up. Daddy struggled with a garden hose. Charles headed straight into the inferno.

Mama yelled, "Come back here, Charles. Y'all be killed." We watched in fascinated horror as our brother disappeared into the wide black mouth of the church.

"Oh, Lordy, he'll be incinerated," I cried, using a word I had just learned.

When he finally stumbled out of the blaze with a stack of hymnals in his arms, he collapsed on the ground near our window. His hair was frizzled to a nub. His face was grunged with soot. Rat-Dog, uh, Hero, limped over and licked Charles's face, wagging his little tail.

"The piano, the piano," Mama wailed as folks materialized from nowhere and began to pry the side door of the church off its hinges. Soon, the monster upright, its keys covered with soot like some out-of-place comic in a minstrel show, was pushed out the door. In thirty minutes, it was over. The church was a blackened, smoldering ruin. And our lives, too, lay in shambles, having been consumed by the same conflagration.

We had to move from our beautiful Victorian parsonage to a tumbledown house on the outskirts of town. My heart cried big bloody tears as I packed up my treasured books: *The Magic Garden*, *The Golden Touch*, *Gulliver's Travels*.

Our rented house was funny looking, not funny ha-ha, but funny peculiar. So many of the faded blue shingles had long ago been blown off by whirlwinds whipping it to pieces, the place looked like a checkerboard sitting there on a weedy lot without an iota of greenery for company. The house seemed lonesome inside, too, where wind leaked through rattling window frames and left lacy traces of dust across the splintery floors and in our clothes and hair and food. We made do with four rooms so small that when we walked past them, our chairs banged together, as if grumbling about the further reduction of our circumstances. The thing I longed for most was our yard. I missed our green lawn like my friend Sarah Ann must have missed her hair, which had fallen out after she had scarlet fever. I pined for the fragrance of Pinks and Moss roses, the glory of red and gold and lavender zinnias, and the Indian blankets with their black-eyed centers and brilliant orange petals resembling the skirt of a squaw dancing by firelight.

Daddy was bad sick, and we didn't have any money at all, not one penny. We even had to sell Bossy since there was no one to milk or graze her now. Mama sent Poor Little Glendora to Oklahoma City to live with my big sister Nina and her husband, Harold, for a while. Charles was going off to college. He had three jobs to work his way through Oklahoma A&M. Carlos helped a little, and Faye and Cecil helped, too, but they weren't exactly on easy street with a new baby, Linda Faye, and a bunch of hungry white-faced cows mooing all the time. We were forced to go on Relief, a new office set up by President Roosevelt to help the poor. We were humiliated.

"We've got to trust in the Lord and keep on going forward," Daddy said, his voice breaking. "We inherited strong pioneer spirit and we're good folks, so just know that the Lord will provide."

"As soon as we can, we'll move back to Waurika," Mama said. "We still have lots of good friends there from the time Daddy was pastor of the church."

Waurika was in Oklahoma near the Texas border, where the storied Red River meandered, and where they had a rattlesnake roundup every year, and where Daddy baptized his flock. The women being dunked to wash away their sins wore dresses for the sake of modesty, but their white garments filled with air and ballooned to the surface of the water, revealing all. When Daddy put one hand behind the person's head and the other on their forehead, an assistant would hold their nose as they were immersed into water that harbored water moccasins and rattlesnakes. Daddy intoned in his God-on-a-sunbeam voice, "I baptize thee in the name of the Father, the Son, and the Holy Spirit."

Glub, glub.

If they survived, the saved person was doused two more times. They came out of the water hoping not to encounter a rattler, shivering and crying, looking like half-drowned rats dressed up in white water soaked garments.

You know what's funny? I was never baptized. Can you imagine that? My parents were so tuckered out, they must have forgotten about me. Which is just as well, because they couldn't have hogtied me into going into that river.

~~~

Before we could make it back to Waurika and the Red River, I was sent to live with family friends on a farm about ten miles from Waurika. Their last name was Hammer, and their three sons had the unlikely names of Jack, Claw, and Tack. Honest. The Hammer boys gave me my first introduction of sorts to S-E-X.

The Hammer family's unpainted two-story rambling farmhouse was set high on a hill. They didn't have a lawn, but they did have a yard full of dusty yellow sunflowers. They also had a windmill, a tilting off its foundation barn, chickens, pigs, cows, plenty of wholesome food, and three sons. I thought they were rich. The Hammer boys were never referred to by their first names alone. It was always, "Come right here this minute, Mr. Claw Hammer," or 'Now, Mr. Jack Hammer, don't you forget to fetch in the wood." It made me giggle, as that was exactly the way black people addressed white folks.

They were gentle folks. Neither parent being a minister, there was no need for them to set an example or expect me to. And they were kind, as well. They listened to what their children had to say. Mrs. Hammer frequently held me on her ample lap and talked about God and how Jesus bled and died for our sins. I always felt a burden of guilt after being reminded that Jesus had bled for me. He didn't have to bleed for me; I would never ask anyone to do that, I thought. For all their softer and more loving attitude, I never heard anyone call the Hammers by their given names, whatever they might have

81

been. They were Mr. and Mrs. Hammer to their family, to the world, and to each other. I became Miss Patsy Lou.

What tickled me the most was having a bed of my own. For the first time ever, I did not have to sleep with a family member. But in spite of advantages like this, I was penetrated with sadness, as though I had suddenly grown older before I was ready for it. I ached for my siblings, Charles and Poor Little Glendora, and my daddy, too. But to my surprise, I missed Mama most of all. It was like being separated by death and just as final. It would have been strange and unnatural for us to write each other. Mama had said we couldn't even afford a penny postcard. I grieved in silence and was overwhelmingly homesick. I fought wistfulness by thinking about how happy my family would be when I got back home to Chillicothe. They would smile and hug me, I was sure.

"Okay, Miss Patsy Lou, little girlums, what would you like most in the world?" Mrs. Hammer asked one day while she was doing her morning baking: seven big loaves of bread, two pies, a cake, and a platter full of sugar cookies.

To go home, back to Mama and Daddy, I thought. But knowing that could not be, and knowing it would hurt Mrs. Hammer's feelings for me to say so, I blurted out, "Piano lessons."

"Well now," Mrs. Hammer said, dusting the flour off her hands, "I'll see if we can arrange that."

I was stunned; I couldn't believe it. Piano lessons, just like that! I could learn to play like Mama and Carlos Morrison and Nina Aileen and Poor Little Glendora. Oh, oh, oh! For years I had begged Mama to give me piano lessons, but she said she was too worn out to fiddle with another child learning the scale.

"But Mama," I had pleaded, "trade lessons for milk from Bossy, like you did for Poor Little Glendora."

"No, and I don't want to hear another word about it, Patsy Lou, and

82

that's final," Mama said.

But now Mrs. Hammer was answering my prayer to be able to play the piano.

"You can take lessons from Miss Irene and practice there, too," Mrs. Hammer said. "She'll be mighty pleased, I'm sure."

My fingers itched to get started.

Piano lessons began two days later. I was always right on time and tried to stay past the appointed hour. It wasn't long before I could perform simple pieces like Beethoven's *Minuet in G* or MacDowell's "To a Wild Rose."

"Patsy Lou, honey, you're going to be a great pianist someday," Miss Irene said as she patiently listened to me practice.

No one had ever been so kind to me. It was the first time anyone, except for Teacher, had called me "honey" or given me a compliment. My efforts at mastering the piano doubled in order to facilitate the prediction.

Of the three boys, Mr. Jack, the youngest Hammer, was the nearest to me in age. He had a moon face covered with freckles, haystack blond hair, and a mischievous air. He became my friend, protector, and teacher. Jack also gave me my first introduction to sex.

Sex was something that had not been even remotely hinted at in our home. I had heard a few distorted rumors about where babies came from, but barely enough to make me curious to know more, and in no way approaching the truth. As you know, I thought the code names Mama taught us for "forbidden" parts of the body and its functions were Christian and therefore correct. With terms like "treetop" for toilet and "zip" for pee, it was a shock to hear Mrs. Hammer boldly refer to bodily functions without genteel circumlocutions. I could hardly look her in the eye when she asked if I needed to go to the toilet. It set up confusion in my mind. I knew Mrs. Hammer was not a "bad" woman, and yet here she was saying things for which I would have been walloped at home.

One hot Sunday, Mrs. Hammer announced there was going to be an all-day meeting with dinner-on-the-ground that very Sabbath. Dinner-on-the-ground meant that each lady of the parish was to bring her own food specialty. After the sermon, they would carefully place their offering to the food god on church benches laid outside seat-to-seat to serve as a buffet table. Grownups could lean over the back of the benches to reach the victuals, but we children had to stretch our arms through the slats.

Every woman wanted her dish to be oohed and aahed over and eaten first. That was her accolade, her blue ribbon, her reason for being. Heaping platters of fried chicken and bowls of red beans, coleslaw, mashed potatoes, and collard greens covered the benches, releasing and mingling their aromas in the warm air. But best of all were the desserts: pecan pies, fried pies, sweet potato pies, chocolate cakes, angel food cakes, molasses cakes, cookies, and in the summertime, watermelon. They would have cut down on rations for months to be able to put on this display of bounty. I enjoyed sneaking around and listening to grown-up gossip.

"Law, Sister Beth, that girl over yonder standing next to Alma's boy is as common as pig tracks. And alls she put on this here table is one measly covered dish, a little bitty dish at that. And she acts mean and uppity."

"Now y'all know she ain't got no call to act like that. Why she paraded downtown big as daylights in hardly nothing more than a thin hankie coverin' her titty. And she has the shamelessness to act as happy as a dead hog in the sunshine."

"Law," the woman chuckled, "goodness gracious. We'll pray that God shows her the error of her ways."

While the adults were gossiping and setting up the "tables," us kids enjoyed a blessed freedom from discipline and supervision. It was considered enough to instruct us to base our games on Bible scripture. That was how I came to play "Fornication." Jack Hammer thought up the idea after he got bored playing Judas in "The Last Supper." We perked up at the thought of an entirely new game and waited breathlessly for the rules.

"Y'all have to drink all the water y'all can hold," he told us. We girls trooped dutifully to a barrel of water placed in the meager shade of a salt cedar tree. A rapidly melting block of ice floated on the surface. A big metal dipper hanging by a long string was attached to the side of the barrel. We took turns drinking the cool water. We drank and drank until our stomachs were distended. Shifting from one foot to the other, crossing our legs in discomfort, we ran back to the boys.

The chosen play area was a culvert in the back of the church. "Now wait right here, and don't y'all dare pee until we tell y'all to," Jack said as he and the other boys ran to the barrel to drink their fill. My bladder was stretched to capacity, and pee was slipping down my legs in tiny rivulets. The boys returned. Giggles echoed in the culvert.

"Now, y'all line up over there," Jack said, indicating one side of the culvert. "Now take your bloomers off."

My panties had a hole in them, and by now they were soggy. I didn't want my friends to see, but the other girls were complying, so I, too, bent over and quickly pulled my panties off and hid them behind my back.
"We're the fornicators," Jack whispered conspiratorially, "and we're s'posed to show our 'thing.'"

Fly buttons were undone amid giggles and coughs. Soon four small penises were exposed. With suppressed excitement, knowing this sure wasn't the kind of Bible story the adults had in mind, I was transfixed.
"Now here's what we're to do next." Jack pulled up my dress and rubbed his limp "peckerwood" on my distended stomach. Everyone was sniggering and fumbling clumsily with one another, except for Sally Mae and R. D., who were several years older. Out of the corner of my eye, I saw them leave the culvert.

"Now we're s'posed to pee," Jack announced, leading off first. Giggling uncontrollably, we relieved ourselves in the dirt. Urine splashed onto shoes and dusty legs. Then, as if by word of command, we all ran out of the culvert to find different playmates. Lost in our guilt, we dared not look at one another.

I had just finished eating a dish of homemade vanilla ice cream when I realized something was wrong. Some of the parishioner women were running to Sally Mae's house as if a silent alarm had been sounded. Their faces were masks of pious concern. I ran, too, my wet panties chafing my legs and my patent leather shoes rubbing blisters on my heels. Screams like jagged flashes of lightning pierced the heat. I pressed on through a patch of nettles and stickers. My legs were scratched, and the red ribbons on my pigtails had come untied and brushed my shoulders.

On tiptoe, I peered through a window screen. The grownups were kneeling in a circle, hands clasped tightly in front of them, their eyes closed. Loud entreaties to God rose from open mouths, up to the ceiling, higher and higher, their lamentations rising through the shingles on the roof and up into a dark, clouded sky. Higher and higher the vibrations went, above the Universe and finally, finally, past the sun and the stars directly into the ears of a listening Almighty, or so I imagined. Their jumbled prayers and overlapping words whirl-pooled inside my head, making me dizzy. Crawling across crabgrass, my knees stinging, I reached the back door and crept inside, catching the screen with my foot so it wouldn't slam. A shriek like someone was on fire slashed the prayers like a scythe.

I sidled around the edges of the hullabaloo, crawling still, until I found a slatted rocking chair that was perfect for seeing without being seen. Here I had a clear view of the circle of praying women. In the center of the group, Sally Mae lay on her back, held down by two women. Her legs were being held wide apart, exposing the tender pink flesh of her private parts. Sally Mae was fighting and scratching and crying, trying to get away.

"Come help us, Sister Martin." The woman's scratchy voice matched her stiffly starched print dress. Sally Mae's mother, her long brown hair hanging in her tight face, moved into the circle. She bent over her daughter and mumbled something to her. Sally Mae quieted. Mesmerized, I watched a tall, thin woman hand Sally Mae's mother a bottle of clear liquid. In a high, piercing voice, Sally Mae's mother demanded her daughter to repent of the sin of fornication with R. D. "We caught you in this house, in this very bedroom, Sally Mae, no more than an hour ago. Now you have to be made clean."

With impassioned entreaties to God to cleanse Sally Mae of the sin of fornication, her mother slowly poured the liquid over her daughter's private parts. The familiar smell of rubbing alcohol reached me simultaneously with Sally Mae's unearthly screams, assaulting my ears, nose, and mouth, zigzagging through my brain: hellfire, brimstone, the smell of my own flesh burning.

I ran out of the house as if pursued by demons. My breath, coming in short, painful gasps, burned my throat. My heart pounded so hard, I thought it might explode. I ran and ran until I reached the water barrel, where I sank to the earth. The moisture from spilled water penetrated my clothes and dampened my hair, eventually soothing me.

From my spot on the ground, I saw the women walking slowly away from Sally Mae's house. Their long-sleeved, high-necked dresses seemed scarcely to move as they advanced. One by one, they filed into the church house, and were quickly joined by the men and children. Numbed, I didn't budge until Mr. Hammer came looking for me. Darting quickly ahead of him, I took my place inside. Mechanically, I responded to the hymns, prey to unknown terrors and conscious of my own wickedness. I equated Sally Mae's shame with what I considered my own. I sat in church that day, wondering whether the Devil had entered my soul the way Daddy preached happened to the fornicators. I trembled to think what Mama would do if she ever discovered what I had done in the culvert. *I'm not worthy of the Hammers' kindness*, I thought.

Thereafter, I spoke only when spoken to and assiduously avoided any contact with Mr. Jack Hammer. Mrs. Hammer was convinced that I was sick and put me to bed for two days. I would lie there experiencing constant palpitations of my heart and the rush of blood to my head and wondering if the weakness I felt was normal. *Maybe God is punishing me*, I thought. Finally, Mrs. Hammer gave up and called my sister Faye to come and get me. I needed my family, she said.

Chapter 5

Daddy

When Mrs. Hammer said my sister Faye and her husband, Cecil Antrim, were coming to take me home in a few days, I was made whole again. Talk about a healing! Knowing a family member was coming after me cured all my maladies. The three summer months I had stayed with the Hammer family felt like three years. I was going home to fussing and quarreling and hunger and Daddy snoring and trying to catch his breath; back to Poor Little Glendora giggling with her girlfriends, and now a boyfriend for sure; back to ... I wasn't sure what. Was Daddy still sick? Was he dying? Every single night I said a prayer for him. Surely God or Jesus or Moses or Peter or Paul—one of those Bible folks—would not let him die.

At home, us kids were required to memorize and recite a Bible verse for church every Sunday. A few times I got by with "Jesus wept," the shortest verse in the Bible, but then Mama forced me to move on or get a big black *X* instead of a star on the church calendar. One verse I memorized was Jesus saying, "Take up your bed and walk," after healing someone or other. If he went around healing the sick and afflicted all the time, raising them from the dead even, then it seemed to me that my daddy, who held Jesus's teachings up in front of the congregation every Sunday, deserved to have the favor returned. In my prayers I said as much, but so far Jesus hadn't gotten back to me.

I ached for my family, all of them, all the time, even Carlos and Nina. I experienced my brothers and sisters and Mama and Daddy as being part of a thick rope knotted and twisted together the way I read Siamese twins Chang and Ing were, intertwined and extending outward from my skipping heart. That tie, constructed by birth order, tugged tight around my chest and neck, choking me sometimes, but as much a part of me as the hair on my head: Carlos Morrison, Nina Aileen, Minnie Faye, Charles Clay, Poor Little

Glendora, Dead Bettie Ruth, Little Jimmy, Mama and Daddy. My siblings were paragons of all that was superior. I loved them, admired them, envied them, felt inferior to them, and missed them more than anything on earth.

Still hoping to measure up, I studied beauty magazines that Mrs. Moore, a sweet-faced neighbor, saved for me along with *The Saturday Evening Post*, *Life*, *Look*, *National Geographic*, *Liberty*, and *House and Garden*. Even though most everyone on the pages had smoke curling out their mouths from Chesterfield cigarettes and were therefore sinners, I devoured these links to an unfamiliar world and waited on Mrs. Moore's porch every week to collect the reading material. I read and reread articles about how to improve myself. Not only did I learn about makeup, hairstyles, skin care, and good posture, but about efficiency.

In the magazine story I read, a pretty housewife was pictured being efficient. She wore a frilly white apron and smiled a big white smile while standing in a polished kitchen with everything she needed to bake a chocolate cake right there at her fingertips. In that dirt-free kitchen, I felt sure the knives, forks, and spoons weren't tumbled upside down along with balls of string, stubby pencils, Bayer aspirin, and dead bugs. Nor were the dishes chipped or the pans blackened like ours were.

The day after I got the news that I would be going home, I was cooling off in the Hammers' slimy, stinky water tank, hanging onto the sides, frogs underfoot, pretending to be baptized, when Mrs. Hammer's soft voice brought me back to earth—or to water.

"Miss Patsy Lou, little girlums, we need to have us a fly roundup before you go home." Having participated in several fly roundups, I understood what Mrs. Hammer was talking about. "Kindly dry yourself off," she urged. "We've gotta git rid of them flies. Mr. Jack Hammer, Mr. Claw Hammer, and Mr. Tack Hammer are all here, so we'll have us a reg'lar army."

In my mind's eye I saw the Hammer boys and myself in crisp white uniforms with glittering gold-and-red trim, marching in step and carrying a rippling flag with a great big green fly painted on it.

Inside the rambling old house, flies buzzed and struggled against their fate, stuck as some were on strips of gluey flypaper that hung down from the ceilings in long curls. Still, about ten million swarmed the room, careening off windows, dive-bombing bread, stalking across the tabletop, and humming an alarm about the upcoming battle. The windows were spotted black by their presence. They gave off a rotten egg smell that fogged the air, making me cough.

"We've gotta have us a strategy meetin'," Mr. Claw Hammer said, his flushed face and bright eyes replacing his usual apathetic appearance as he herded us into a football-style huddle. "Now, this is how we're gonna take 'em," he whispered, like he thought the flies buzzing about were enemy spies and understood English. "Miss Patsy Lou, y'all be at the kitchen winders. Mr. Jack Hammer, y'all take the back room winders. Mr. Tack Hammer, y'all have two rooms to guard, Ma and Pa's room and the sun porch. I'm the commandin' officer, so I'll oversee."
Claw enjoyed plotting fly warfare. "I even got us a record for the Victrola," he said, holding up a black disc. After winding up the Victrola, Claw put a fresh needle in the arm, all set to drop onto the record when our marching orders came through.

Mrs. Hammer interrupted. "Mr. Claw Hammer, I declare, son, I'm impressed by your plannin', but y'all are gettin' carried away. I'll oversee. But music is a good idea and kinda fun. Hurry on now. I need to get supper a-goin'. It's almost three o'clock."

Mr. Claw Hammer continued with our battle plan. "After y'all take positions, Ma'll blow this here whistle or shout, 'Attack.'" He showed us a silvery whistle. "Reveal your weapons," he said.

We held up the white flour-sack dishrags Mrs. Hammer had given us.

"Take your positions, and we'll sang our fly song."

I sprinted to my post at the kitchen window, dishtowel ready, standing at attention as I awaited my orders. I was a soldier, and this was all out war.

"And now, to the tune of 'My Country, 'Tis of Thee,' get ready, set . . . sang!'" Mr. Claw Hammer led off.

> "There are no green flies on me,
>
> There may be one or two,
>
> Great big green flies on you,
>
> But there are noooooo green flies on me!"

"Attack!"

The Victrola scratched out, "Onward Christian soldiers, marching as to war . . . ," as we advanced on the enemy. We flailed away as flies careened crazily across rooms, butted against windows, and hung out on the ceiling, the icebox, and the top of the wood cookstove. We flapped our weapons, running and shouting, "Shoo fly, shoo fly, shoo fly," outflanking adversaries, driving them toward the door Mrs. Hammer held open. Giggling, hysterical, we fell down, got up, laughed, fell down again, overjoyed by gory combat, as loony as the flies. Murdering flies was so much fun, we didn't want to stop.

The fly population was reduced, but enemy forces still droned at the windows, searching for an exit strategy. That's when Mrs. Hammer took out after them with a swatter cut from a piece of old screen door nailed to a stick. The flies retreated, crawling up walls, discharging black bombs on window glass. One green horsefly daredevil opened fire on my hair, but with one swipe of my hand I ripped off his wings and crushed him like the enemy combatant that he was. Then, flying in formation, with Mrs. Hammer hot on their tails, came fighter pilots, their transparent wings fluttering, bidding farewell to fallen comrades and trying to escape. It was too late. Finally, they waved a white flag of surrender, gave up, were smashed, and went off to bug heaven.

I was worn out from the battle, but a jolt of energy shocked through me when Faye and Cecil showed up to take me home. Cecil was driving a silver pickup truck that looked to me like one of God's chariots, situated as it was against the dried-up landscape. I was overjoyed to see them and about hugged their necks off. Cecil was like a brother to me. I loved his sandy hair, sunburned face, shy grin, slow way of talking, and the way he teased me. He was a generous and kind man.

Cecil supplemented his meager farm income with a line of penny gumball and peanut machines. Inside the round apparatus holding colored gumballs was the added inducement of miniature ceramic pots and doll furniture. He kept these gifts and goodies in a spare bedroom at the farm. Babysitting my chubby niece, Linda Faye, one day, I gorged on so many gumballs and peanuts that a tormenting stomachache kept me sitting on the toilet all night long and half the next day. Cecil laughed and said he'd thought that might happen, but now he was sure his inventory was safe from one thieving relative.

Cecil had come courting Faye when I was almost six and we lived in Waurika, Oklahoma. They were seniors in high school, ready to graduate and go off to college if they could find jobs to pay for it. Cecil Antrim was a star high jumper with lots of medals and trophies in the shape of tiny silver track shoes. Daddy said Cecil was so bashful that he stared holes in the floor when he had to wait for Faye, and he always had to wait, so we had a holey floor for sure. One time, Cecil scooped me up and took me for a ride in his Ford V8 with a rumble seat sticking out the back. He drove to the drugstore and bought me a vanilla ice cream cone. After that, I went around singing a song I heard on the radio:

"Give me a date and a Ford V8
With a rumble seat built for two
And let me wahoo, wahoo, wahoo."

Cecil and his older brother Homer lived with his father and grandpa in a house on a dirt road way out in the country. After their mother died, they were brought up by their father and grandfather without female interference, Cecil said.

I was nested down behind a big easy chair eavesdropping, as I was prone to do, when Cecil and Faye thought they were alone one Sunday afternoon. They sat on the couch kinda close to each other. Faye was gussied up in a floaty white dress with flapper spit curls pasted over her ears and wearing orange-colored Tangee lipstick that made her look like she had eaten a Halloween pumpkin. The two of them hemmed and hawed awhile until Cecil gave Faye a peck on her pumpkin lips. Fay giggled and wiped her mouth with the back of her hand, all the while gazing up at Cecil like he was the Second Coming of Christ our Lord. When he started talking to Faye in kind of a serious way, I thought for sure he was going to propose. But no, he was getting up the courage to talk about his mother dying. He was having a hard time, it sounded like, almost as if he wasn't certain he wanted to talk at all.

"Homer and I were just little kids," he said, gazing down at his shoes, working to get the story out. "We were doing our chores. I guess we started helping out almost from the day we were born, it feels like." He laughed, a forced sound with no fun in it. "Well"—he hesitated—"well, mother died just a little while before, but still, cows had to be milked and chickens fed and watered. There are always chores on the farm."

Faye spoke up. "Oh, how awful. Y'all want to go to a movie?" My sister frequently said things that didn't make sense, filling any quiet space with words.

"Faye, I suppose I need to tell you this, uh, well, since we're getting kinda serious." Cecil unfolded his lanky body and started pacing the floor, back and forth, back and forth, making a path. "Well, as I said, Homer and I were at the barn." He cleared his throat. "Well, the fella who came, uh, to, well, take care of Mama, you know, to ready her for buryin', came outside to where Homer and us was standing. The man had a white enamel bucket in his hands."

"The dickens," Faye said. She didn't seem to actually be listening to what Cecil said.

"Yes, well, it was hard. Uh, well, that man, the mortician, saw Homer and me and, uh, said, 'Hello, boys, how y'all doin'?' Like it was a reg'lar kind of day." Tears oozed from Cecil's eyes. He dabbed at them with a handkerchief and blew his nose.

"Cecil, that's the dickens. Well, I say . . ." Faye seemed addled.

"Well, okay, uh, that mortician fella, well, you know, he emptied that bucket he was carryin', and . . . and . . ." He couldn't continue. But he had Faye's attention. Mine, too.

"Cecil, I say, what on earth?"

"I reckon I'll always be haunted by what that man did." Cecil sat down next to Faye, blew his nose again, stared at the floor, and in a rush of words like air going out of a balloon, continued. "My mother's blood was in that bucket, blood that man poured on the ground right in front of us. 'Bout broke my heart in two."

For the only time I ever knew tell of, my sister didn't say anything. After a long silence, Cecil cleared his throat and asked Faye if she would like to go get a Coke. Yes, she surely would, she said. I wondered if I should pray for Cecil's mother, who had died and left him alone until he found Faye.

At prayer meeting service one Wednesday evening, I had nodded off, hypnotized by the droning, bee-like prayers and holding my pee so I could put out Hell's fire should the Devil appear, dreaming in that funny state of half-here and half-there, when all of a sudden the church door busted open and my sister Faye appeared like an apparition, looking so distraught she could hardly talk. Her eyes were ginormous, her hair standing straight up on her head as she screamed and sobbed, "Help! Jesus is coming, Jesus is coming! Help! I saw him, I saw him, I saw him."

There were eleven at the prayer meeting that night, and every one of the Saved looked terrified. I was scared so much I couldn't move at first, but quickly leached courage from Daddy by clinging to his pant leg.

"Will Jesus send me to Hell?" I sobbed. No one answered, so I joined the Faithful, hoping to fool my way into his good graces. Stampeding to the church house door, the prayer meeting folks fell on their knees, staring up at the clear, midnight-blue sky, a sky full of a gargantuan, blood-red moon shining down, lighting up the land, a visitation from the Holy Spirit.

Daddy's voice boomed, "Revelation 6:12—'And I beheld when he had opened the sixth seal, and, lo, there was a great earthquake; and the sun became black as sackcloth of hair, and the moon became as blood.'"

Lamentations began, crying and beating of chests, prayers for forgiveness, until Daddy had the gumption to ask Faye where she had seen Jesus.

"On the screen door," she said. A multicolored Christian cross, that symbol of suffering and shame, had manifested on the screen door to our kitchen with Jesus inside it, Faye explained.

That was a good enough reason for the prayer meeting folks to strike out for our house. Brother Dean, his eyes as large and shiny as the moon, pushed Faye, our visionary, forward, and Daddy carried me in his arms as we followed a luminous path to the parsonage. Most parishioners sobbed out strangled praises to God: "Praise the Lord! Praise God in his sanctuary; praise him in his mighty heavens! Praise him for his mighty deeds." Through a field of dried corn we trooped, across a ravine, took a shortcut through a culvert, ran up a gravel path, and finally arrived out of breath at our screen door, the door that held the manifestation revealed to my sister.

Yes, there it was! Tristimulus values had created a large iridescent cross on the screen door of a humble preacher that broadcast as powerfully to

Faye as Christian radio stations in Del Rio, Texas. The imposing harvest moon had cast an abundance of heavenly light that refracted off the screen, shattering the mesh into a rainbow-colored cross, at the center of which were golden rays that Faye interpreted as Jesus. A cross, that Christian symbol of suffering and resurrection—along with the Seven Men of the Apocalypse, the Mark of the Beast, and the book of Revelation—were so ingrained into Faye, as they were in me, that the fear she swallowed with Mama's milk now overflowed into a wall-eyed fit of anxiety.

That cross on the screen door shimmered across Faye's eyeballs in prismatic, fanatical fervor, igniting her long-held fear of Armageddon, the End of the World. Was she saved? Would she be caught up into Heaven, or left to tough it out during a time of tribulation, skirmishing with the Antichrist, maybe to be thrown into a lake of fire? Faye was twenty years old, but even so, the horrifying scenarios taught from the pulpit had sent her thrashing through a field of dry corn and into the church house, yelling, "Jesus is coming! Jesus is coming! Help! Help!"

If reminded of what she had done on that Wednesday evening, Faye looked sheepish and changed the subject. She was good at changing the subject. But my sister was always present for any family member in need of help. She was especially kind to me.

~~~

The day Faye and Cecil picked me up at the Hammer place, they had been married five years and continued to live on the Antrim farm in Waurika in the same house in which Cecil grew up and where his mother's blood had pooled on the ground. About half an hour after leaving the Hammers, riding along in the silver pickup, I asked Faye if Daddy was still sick.

"He's not doing very good, Patsy," Faye said, tearing up. "He's not going to make it." Emotional clouds rolled through the cab of the silver pickup and let go with a shower of weeping. Light sprinkles, followed by torrential precipitation, created tributaries that flooded into an ocean of salty tears, nigh near drowning us. Linda Faye, a toddler now, followed her mother's example by loudly boohooing, I joined in, sobbing so hard that the yoke of my dress got sopping wet. Cecil, who could have used windshield wipers on his face, bumped the pickup over to the edge of the narrow road and parked until we collected ourselves. We sat there blubbering, the four of us, noses running, wallowing in future grief.

When I dried out enough to talk, I asked Faye if she was sure that Daddy was dying. "Faye, you can't be sure, can you, not really sure? Only God knows for sure."

"That's right, Patsy Lou," Cecil answered, since Faye was still sobbing. "Only God knows for sure, and your daddy is a strong man. People in churches all over the state are praying for him, churches he built, wood and all, with a hammer and nails and his own two hands."

"Then he could get well." My fingers were crossed for good luck. Now I was desperate to get on home fast so I could see Daddy.

When we pulled up to the house in Chillicothe, I jumped out before Cecil even shut off the motor to the silver pickup. Everything looked run-down. Inside, Daddy sat in a rocking chair with a quilt over his legs, looking thinner than I remembered him.

"Chick-a-lick! Come on over here and give your daddy a hug. Look at you. Why, you're half grown already."

"Oh, Daddy." I buried my face on his chest, bawling.

"It's okay, Chick-a-lick, it's okay," he said, patting my head over and over again.

"I ... was ... afraid I wouldn't ever see you again. I love you so much."

"Well, I guess my Maker isn't ready for me yet. Maybe he wanted me to see my baby girl once more. Chick-a-lick, I'm glad to see you have a sensitive soul."

We were interrupted by a cacophonous sound announcing the arrival of

Mama, Poor Little Glendora, and Little Jimmy.

"Mama," I yelled, running to the door. "Oh Mama, I'm home!"

"I can see that," Mama said, busily unloading a bag of groceries from a neighbor lady's car. "Take these to the kitchen and help Poor Little Glendora out. She's had to do all the chores since you've been gone."

"Are you Patsy Lou?" Little Jimmy asked, hanging back. I reached out to hug him, but he pulled away and ran outside to play. Rat-Dog followed him, tail wagging.

"We missed you," Poor Little Glendora said as she put the canned goods away. "Since Charles went off to college and I came home from Nina's, it's just been Little Jimmy and me. Seems strange for it to be so quiet."

Mama bustled into the kitchen, not even seeing me, preoccupied by bigger things. "Girls, we're moving back to Waurika next week. Charles is coming home from school to drive us, and Carlos is helping out, too."

"But Mama, I just got home."

"Patsy Lou, your daddy is mighty sick, so we need to live near friends we can count on. Besides, Carlos, Nina, Faye, and Cecil all kicked in money to buy us a house in Waurika. Five hundred dollars! It's near the Beaver Creek and floods from time to time, but at least we have a home of our own."

Our own house! My dreams were coming true, floods or not.

~~~

Waurika had a population of one thousand souls, all huddled in the middle of nothing. I'm not exaggerating. The landscape was flat, without a hill or barely a green thing growing. I could see for about one hundred miles ahead to the next mesquite tree. The sight filled me with despair, especially when Daddy took the wheel. The straight-as-a-string highway lulled him to sleep faster than a lullaby. But once we were settled in Waurika, he had a resurrection of sorts. The Nazarene church deacons asked him to be their preacher every other Sunday, and Daddy revived. Mama seemed to cool down, too. Her ridged frown lines softened, and she sang hymns around the house, instead of yelling at me all the time. Sometimes, when Daddy wasn't able, Mama did the preaching. It put me out to say so, but her stories were more entertaining than Daddy's and not as scary, either.

I was going on fourteen and a junior in high school, having been triple-promoted due to confusion about my scholastic record. We moved so often that my records were either lost or inextricably mixed up. As a result, I was the youngest pupil in high school and had my usual hard time keeping up. Now even recess was a misery. The constricted feeling in my chest kept me from running and playing outside. I wondered about my classmates. Did their knees ever turn to jelly and their hearts flip-flop scarily in their chests?

Poor Little Glendora was a beauty, everyone said, and ol' boys, as Mama described them, followed her around like hound dogs—especially Edgar Woods, a church member whose widowed mother was a pillar of the church. Poor Little Glendora was my role model, in spite of Mama's constant comparing of us, which was upsetting as all get out. Poor Little Glendora was everything I wasn't: helpful, good-natured, industrious, and cooperative. She was olive-skinned, while I was fair; she was petite, while I was tall; she had small feet, while my feet were big and flat. Why had God ordained these differences? It wasn't fair. Happily, though, I could still fit into Glendora's clothes, and that was a big bonus. Lucky Poor Little Glendora had a job as the receptionist and bookkeeper for the Waurika Light and Power Company, earning enough to buy angora sweaters and soft pastel skirts. After she left for work one day and before the school bus came, I sneaked one of her sweaters to show off in at school.

Poor Little Glendora missed the pink sweater I had filched and came storming into the schoolhouse to get it. She caught me in the restroom and removed the garment, an active scene but heavy with silence. The rest of the day I slumped around in a ratty old coat, pretending I was cold, even though the red mercury in a big thermometer located in the school hallway showed it was about a zillion degrees. My schoolmates, most shouting Christians, weren't fooled. A poster quickly appeared on a bulletin board with a caricature of me in a coat with drops of sweat running down my face. I knew the artist was J. V., a good-looking senior the guys said was a queer, whatever that was. Queer or not, he could really draw. Ripping the picture off the bulletin board, I walked home all the way across the bridge spanning Beaver Creek.

Daddy stayed in bed most of the time now, always cold, breathing heavily. One day, I overheard Mama and Daddy talking about Glendora and Edgar Woods. Daddy said, "Poor Little Glendora set her cap for Edgar, and she got him. She's made her bed, so now she'll have to lie in it."

Cap? What cap? Poor Little Glendora didn't wear a cap. What were they talking about? She might have made a bed, but what did that have to do with Edgar Woods? I was bumfuzzled. When Mama told me Glendora and Edgar had run off and gotten married, I cried like a two-year-old. How could she do that? She had promised me I could be her bridesmaid and wear a frilly pink dress when she was declared Mrs. Married! How could she have done such a thing? When I tried to find out more, Mama snapped at me, saying they were living in the country with Edgar's widowed mother, and that was all she knew.

I decided to find out for myself about Mrs. Edgar Woods, and trudged out to the isolated farm where they lived. One reason to traipse two miles on a hot day was to see if my sister looked different after "doing it." Off I went on a long, straight road and then up a hill, past the Waurika cemetery and then a mile on to the Red River Bridge. There were rattlesnakes and armadillos in that neck of the river, and I needed to watch out for feral hogs, too. If a seven-hundred-pound feral hog came stomping out of the brush and took out after me, well, let me tell you that would not be fun. About an hour after starting my trek, I was tired out and my feet stung. I couldn't remember why I'd wanted to make such a trip. But finally, down a short dirt road, I spied the

Woods house.

I sat down near a falling-over barbed wire fence to recover my strength before knocking on the door. You better believe me, that old place could sure use a coat of paint. When I pushed open the squeaky wooden gate to the weed-filled yard, two big russet-colored cur dogs came leaping and barking at me, nearly knocking me down.

"Get away, go! Get away from me," I shouted.

Sister Woods appeared. "Stop it, Bowser. Get down, Spot," she ordered without energy. Reluctantly, with a few little barks and growls, the dogs settled down. Sister Woods was a thickset woman wearing a faded print housedress, and with a vinegary face so wrinkled I thought of the witch in the fairy tale "Sleeping Beauty."

"You-uns come to see y'all's sister?" she asked, so tired seeming it was hard for her to push those words out of her mouth.

"Yes, ma'am," I said, wondering if she would offer me a poisoned apple.

"She's round yonder in back, a-doin' wash. Got work to do, don't y'all stay long, hear?"

Bowser and Spot danced in circles around me as I followed a dirt path at the side of the weather-beaten house. I crossed a chicken yard where Rhode Island Reds pecked at the dirt, past a pen holding a big ol' hog wallowing around in mud, until there, under a cottonwood tree, I saw my sister. A large black wash pot was heating over a wood fire. Off to the side of it, Poor Little Glendora was bent over a galvanized washtub scrubbing overalls on a corrugated washboard. Sweat stained her slender back. Her hair was a mass of fuzzy ringlets. She wasn't wearing shoes. That unkempt washer-woman couldn't be my beautiful sister! What had happened to her?

"Hi," I said, feeling like a stranger.

When she saw me, Poor Little Glendora burst out crying. The years of jealousy and sibling rivalry evaporated. Words choked my throat. After what seemed an eternity, she dried her eyes on a corner of her dishtowel apron. "Y'all want a drink of water?" she asked.

I nodded yes and followed her into a mildew-smelling kitchen. My sister motioned me toward an oak water bucket with a metal dipper hanging by a string from its side. "Get yourself a drink of water," she said.

I took my time downing the tepid water, trying to think of something to say to Poor Little Glendora. "Well, I'd best be getting on back home," I murmured after finishing the dipper of water.

"Tell Mama and Daddy and Little Jimmy hello for me," she requested, as if we lived on the other side of the moon.

"Well, bye," I said, and bolted out of the yard, fleeing those symbols of drudgery, the wash pot and scrub board. They chased me. If I didn't hurry, they would catch up. *Oh Lord, save me*, I prayed as I ran, *save me from the wash pot and ironing board.* I shed tears for Poor Little Glendora and her lost dreams and vowed that such a thing would never happen to me. Alongside the road, cows chewed their cuds and mooed in sympathy. Rattlesnakes slithered from my path.

A few weeks later, I was eavesdropping on my parents' conversation when I found out that Poor Little Glendora had gotten an annulment from Edgar Woods. Just how that happened was a mystery to me. My beautiful sister took flight from small town Waurika, the ironing board and wash pot, and went to Corpus Christi, Texas, circumventing the gossip sure to swirl around her like a poisonous tide pool. "That girl must have done something bad to have lost a good man like Edgar Woods," people said, their voices as stern as God banishing a sinner from Heaven. A negative was never uttered about a man no matter what he may have done. Only the woman was ever at fault.

Mama prayed unceasingly for her favorite child. She was mortified that there should be such a thing as a shattered marriage in our family. Thank the Lord, Poor Little Glendora never got a divorce but had an annulment.

Mama was able to forgive her. But the shame was there.

"I can hardly hold my head up," Mama said. "Patsy Lou, if you ever divorce, I'll disown you. Just remember, young lady, if you are lucky enough to marry—it's forever." Mama was just getting wound up, so I tried to sneak out of the room, but it was useless. She grabbed me by my dress, ripping a seam, hauled me back inside, and started quoting Bible scripture, as I knew she would.

"Ruth says in the Bible"—she held up the Good Book—"'Entreat me not to leave thee, or to return from following after thee, for whither thou goest, I will go, and whither thou lodgest, I will lodge. Thy people shall be my people and thy God my God.' Promise me, young lady, you'll never divorce."

"No, Mama, I'll never divorce," I said. I would have promised her anything at the time. Besides, I couldn't imagine letting a boy touch my private parts, as I was told they did, especially since I still had a sticker deep inside me and had started having my period, which came as a huge shock to me. All that blood—and pain! Can you imagine that no one told me this was going to happen? Anyway, the sticker sensation came and went, but it was always there.

My true love was reading. I read everything from Bunyan's *Pilgrim's Progress* to *True Story* magazine, *David Copperfield*, Shakespeare's plays, and movie publications. I was every lovesick heroine, every movie star, and every damsel in distress. Marriage was the last thing I ever wanted—no, no, no! But I did like romance and the idea of being admired by boys.

~~~

Soon, Mama's concern about Poor Little Glendora was superseded by her concern about Charles. Little Jimmy and I were having breakfast when Mama stumbled into the room. "Something has happened to Charles," she said, her eyes wild-looking. "I dreamed two black shadows fell over him and swallowed him up." The words were hardly out of her mouth when the neighbor we relied on for phone service told us we had a long-distance call.

Mama went skidding out the door, knowing it was something serious to merit a long-distance telephone call. When she got back, she said someone from a hospital where Charles went to school had called. Seems that Charles was riding his bicycle when a car came out of nowhere and hit him full on and then sped away. My brother had suffered yet another concussion and was hospitalized. Mama couldn't leave Daddy, so Faye and Cecil went to Oklahoma A&M College in Stillwater to see about him.

Charles recovered in a few weeks, though Mama thought he was never the same after that. But he was smart and even a member of Mensa, his IQ was so high, a fact he never failed to point out. Charles had wanted to fight for his country and felt put out when he was classified 4F because of hearing loss.

At Christmastime, Daddy complained about the cold, and indeed, a thin, slushy snow covered the ground. I gave him a bundle of firewood tied with a red ribbon as a joke Christmas gift. It worried me that there wasn't money to buy a gift for Little Jimmy. I tried to charge a toy for him at the local dry goods store, but they turned me down. There was just no way we were going to have a celebration. Even the cedar branch I pulled off a tree in a neighbor's yard and decorated with tin foil from Lucky Strike cigarette packages didn't make it look like a real holiday. Back in Addington and Chillicothe, Christmas had been special. Now even our decorations had disappeared.

Little Jimmy kept saying he wanted Santy Claus to bring him a scooter. "Jist a scooter," he would say, smiling, showing teeth that were worn down and brown from malnutrition.

Daddy told Little Jimmy to climb up on the bed next to him. "Son," he said, his voice breaking, "I don't think Santy's going to be able to find our house this year, not in the snow."

"Oh yes he will," said Little Jimmy with six-year-old assurance. "Santy loves snow." Nothing could dissuade him.

That night we turned on our RCA radio to listen to a message from

105

President Roosevelt about the progress of the war. After evening prayers, Daddy led us in singing "Silent Night, Holy Night," and then for Little Jimmy, one chorus of "Jingle Bells."

I awoke hesitantly, not wanting to give up my dream. Was it Christmas morning? No, it was still dark. A gleam of light broke into my sleep-fogged mind. Looking out the window, I saw the silver pickup! Cecil and Faye were lifting a small pine tree decorated with icicles and angel's hair out of the truck. In a flash I was outside, oblivious to the snow. Throwing my full weight against Faye, I half strangled her with the exuberance of my embrace. Not only did they bring the sparkling evergreen, but for Little Jimmy, a glittery orange scooter.

"I knew Santy would find us," Little Jimmy yelled on Christmas morning, speeding through the drafty old house on his new scooter. "I knew it all along. Santy would never forget me."

The day after Christmas, December 26, was my fourteenth birthday. I spent it engrossed in *Gone with the Wind* and the life of Scarlett O'Hara, a gift from Carlos and Marilee. In my mind, I lived at Tara. I became Scarlett O'Hara, wearing hoop skirts, giving grand entertainments, and being sought after by admiring males. That life was more real to me than my actual surroundings. My imagination soared, and nothing seemed impossible for me to accomplish as I read.

On December 31, 1942, Daddy said he thought maybe he should go to the hospital. Carlos came as fast as he could drive to take him to the Waurika hospital. The day was cold and dreary. A thin blanket of snow covered the uninviting countryside. We stood worriedly outside the house— Mama, Little Jimmy, and me—to say goodbye to Daddy.

"Mama," he said before climbing into the car, "don't forget to milk the cow." The corners of his mouth raised in a smile at his little joke. We hadn't had a cow for years. "I love y'all," Daddy said. He got in the car, and we waved goodbye.

106

Before Mama could even get herself dressed to go to the hospital, a neighbor lady came running up the road to tell us to call the hospital—there was bad news. It was Carlos. Mama said he was crying, so she knew the news wasn't good. Many times over the next few days and the years to come, Mama related, verbatim, what Carlos told her.

"Mama," Carlos blubbered, "no sooner had I got Daddy to the hospital and helped put him in the hospital bed, than he fell out of the high metal bed and died."

Mama told me later that it was kidney disease, heart trouble, and dropsy that killed him.

All my siblings came home for Daddy's funeral. They went to the funeral home with Mama to select a coffin for Daddy to lay down his head in, and later I got a report. Carlos took charge. Nina selected the color of the coffin. Faye cried. Charles got into a fight with Carlos for being so bossy. Poor Little Glendora acquiesced to whatever Nina wanted. Cecil stayed home with Little Jimmy and me.

The night before daddy's funeral service, our house was a confusion of family members and friends. There wasn't room for me to sleep at home, so I ended up at the house of a church member, alone. Throughout the long night, I alternately sobbed and shivered.

On the day of Daddy's funeral, I was seated with my family near the front of the church. The church was overflowing with relatives and friends from across Oklahoma, Texas, Tennessee, Arkansas, and Georgia. I stared at the man lying in the brown coffin with a white veil shrouding his face, and decided a mistake had been made. That wasn't my daddy. The sickly sweet aroma of gladiolas, carnations, roses, and lilies melded with body heat and emotion, overwhelming me. My head felt light. I was dizzy. Suddenly, I slid to the floor, my lanky arms and legs clattering against the bench. Marilee helped me to my feet amid gawkers and awkwardly steered me outside. As we walked up the aisle toward the door, I was aware that the minister had quieted, and then in a booming voice he said, "God bless Poor Little Glendora."

Shoot take it, I thought. *Poor Little Glendora gets the credit even when I'm the one who faints.*

Daddy's death left me feeling bereft and friendless. Bedtime held horrifying nightmares of the End of the World and sinners burning in Hell. Every night I battled the shakes. I shook so hard, the bedsprings squeaked. The more I tried to relax, the more I shook. I lay in bed alternately shaking and sweating, my heart tumbling around in my chest. I was afraid I was dying. There was no one to whom I could confide. Getting out of bed, I fired up the kerosene heating stove and sat by it for hours on end, shivering, trying to get warm.

Sadness made me feel like my body had been pierced by icicles that penetrated the core of my being. I was lost. So was Little Jimmy. He hung around the house, never leaving Mama's side. Mama became even more severe, never smiling, but frowning and yelling at me for any perceived infraction of her rule. I couldn't please her. Her migraine headaches worsened. She spent days at a stretch with a washcloth over her eyes, consuming Bayer aspirin by the boxful. Finally, Dr. Dillard came to our house and gave her a shot of morphine as a temporary cure.

Mother often repeated the story of her last talk with Daddy. "I talked to your daddy just before he died, Patsy Lou. He told me I would have to bear the burden alone, to bring the children with me when I die. But you are belligerent and mean. When you defy me, your eyes look just like a snake about to strike."

"That's an awful thing to say, Mama." I trained my snake eyes on her.

She hardly paused for breath before continuing. "I have the burden of rearing a seven-year-old boy and a teenage girl alone and with hardly any money."

"I'll go to work, Mama!" *And get away from you,* I thought.

"Then go to work, Patsy Lou. You're fourteen, old enough to pay your own way."

"That's okeydoke with me. Merle and Tyler said I had a job at their café whenever I'm ready. And I'm ready."

With all of Mama's abilities admitted, she remained closed-minded and autocratic. She ruled with the unquestioned authority of one whose direction on all matters came straight from God. I loved her, feared her, and hated her, all at the same time. But more than anything, I wanted my mother's acknowledgment and approval.

~~~

One Saturday afternoon, Brother Dean and Brother McClellan, influential church elders, knocked on our door.

"Just a minute," Mama said, quickly running a comb through her tangled hair and removing her apron, while I threw toys, papers, and general clutter into the nearest closet. The men wore navy-blue Sunday go-to-meeting suits, which made me think something serious was afoot. Once they were seated side by side on our broken-down divan, they got directly to the point. Brother Dean took the lead.

"Sister Montandon, our preacher left us, and we have a proposal to make to y'all."

Mama gave them her full attention.

"We would like for y'all to fill the pulpit until we can find a man." Brother McClellan took over. "We sure enough need you, Sister Montandon, and we can pay you a little somethin', too."

The request was barely out of their mouths before Mama said yes. How could she refuse this answer to her prayers? In this simple fashion, she succeeded to the ministry in Waurika, Oklahoma.

Chapter 6

The Loneliest Night of the Week

World War II was having a good effect on the economy in Waurika. It was as if the town had struck oil. There were soldiers and "fly boys" everywhere. It looked like a battlefield. The fellows came swarming in from Sheppard Field, fifty miles away over the state border in Wichita Falls, Texas. It wasn't that our little town with its dusty Main Street, three cafés, one picture show, four bars, and one pool hall was so exciting, but that beer could be bought there. Most of the surrounding counties were dry, which meant that no alcoholic beverages could be sold, at least not right out in the open for people to see.

Saturday night was *the* night to be seen dragging Main Street decked out in your spiffiest outfit, riding in a boyfriend's car—if you were lucky enough to have a boyfriend, and if he was lucky enough to have a car. A song I heard blaring from jukeboxes on Main Street, "Saturday Night Is the Loneliest Night of the Week," seemed to be exactly the way soldiers must feel so far from their families. The fellows from Sheppard Field were bound and determined to ease that loneliness by imbibing as much beer as their bodies could hold, and all too often, more than their bodies could hold.

When the blistering summer sun crackled against Waurika's pavement on Sunday mornings, the stench of fermented malt regurgitated by Saturday night cowboys and "ninety-day wonders" was enough to make even the most devout not venture out until the streets were hosed down. As I walked along the main drag—the only drag, actually—the sour odor billowing out in a stomach-turning vapor from bars and cafés such as Rattlesnake Bill's, Slim's, and Snake Eyes, caused me, the pious daughter of two Christian ministers, to pull the scarf covering my pin curls off my head and across my nose.

"Patsy Lou," Mama said, "don't y'all ever dare let me hear tell of you going into one of them beer parlor honky-tonks, or I'll thrash you within an inch of your life."

Even though I was ready to graduate from high school and thought I was grown at sixteen, I dared not disobey Mama. The one time I had was so disastrous it made me turn crimson to think about it.

It was a Saturday night, the most important night of the week in Waurika. The town buzzed. In bars and cafés, soldiers downed bottle after bottle of Pabst Blue Ribbon beer and coerced local girls into "putting out"; they were soldiers and might not live long. It was a movie night, too, heaving with possibilities. I pretended to be spending the night with a girlfriend, when in truth I was going to the midnight movie preview with Jeff Washburn, an Air Corps lieutenant I'd met at the café where I worked.

When he asked, I said I was eighteen. At five feet six inches, with 32D dinners, a sixteen-inch waist, and curvy hips, I did appear deceptively mature. Lieutenant Washburn had no reason to doubt that I was eighteen. I had taken to imitating movie stars like Betty Grable and Lana Turner, piling my long auburn hair on top of my head and anchoring it with a white fake gardenia in the latest Hollywood glamour-girl fashion. My face was bronzed with Max Factor Pancake #12, my lips vivid with Pink Lightning, a fashionable new lipstick. This miraculous transformation took place after I left home every day. I kept a stash of dime-store cosmetics at the Waurika bus stop café where I worked. Before going home to face Mama, I removed all incriminating traces of makeup. My striving to be glamorous was not about sexuality but rather the desire for attention, the need to be accepted, or even to be thought of as special in some way. I remained chaste and virginal; the idea of sex scared me half silly.

Jeff had walked me home—well, almost home—one night after work, so in a way, we'd already had a date. Since I wouldn't let him walk me right up to my front door, fearing Mama's wrath, he'd taken me halfway and then bent and kissed me goodnight. My very first kiss! I didn't know how to act. I kept my lips so tightly closed that Jeff laughed and said, "Next time, Patsy, next time, you just wait." You can imagine the goose bumps that gave me.

The picture show always reeked of dirty socks, a smell that was an integral part of movie night. I was so exhilarated by the ninety-day wonder cozying up next to me, my Air Corps lieutenant, that nothing else mattered. Jeff was beyond handsome, a true hepcat, in his dress uniform with two shiny silver bars on each shoulder. And to think he had chosen to take me to the midnight preview, when prettier girls were a dime a dozen in Waurika. Envious glances from my peers soothed my parched ego. I was cooking with gas, I thought, preening self-consciously in a black crepe dress with big shoulder pads and a sweetheart neckline. The dress cost seven months' salary but was worth it. The dress, along with my makeup, I had kept hidden at the café in the employee restroom.

Jeff and I shared a bag of popcorn amid impatient stomps and yells for the movie to start. He was *so* romantic. When he picked up my hand and licked the popcorn butter off my fingers, well, I nearly died. It was all I could do to stay in my seat and not stand up and yell, "Wow!" but I acted like it wasn't a big deal. But when he kissed me and tried to put his tongue in my mouth, I was shocked.

"Stop it!" I said.

Jeff laughed and said that someday I would like it. *No, I won't*, I thought, but decided to keep quiet.

The picture was *To Have and Have Not* with Humphrey Bogart and Lauren Bacall. You can imagine how excited I was. When Jeff put his arm across the back of my seat, it marked another milestone in my romantic life. Feeling daring, I leaned my head against Jeff's broad shoulder.

The audience stirred as if someone had taken a huge wooden cooking spoon and whirled it around the edges of the movie house, creating a vortex. At the center of the current, a loud commotion arose, one that sounded familiar. The hair on my arms was electrified. I bolted upright in my seat.

Mama? Oh no! No, no, no! It *was* Mama! *Lord in Heaven, save me.* I scooted down in the seat, attempting to hide, but alas, it was no use. Mother advanced down the aisle like an avenging angel. Her graying hair had worked loose from its bun, her complexion scarlet. She wore a faded housedress turned wrong side out and a pair of down-at-the-heel furry house slippers. Sparks shot from her eyes. She could have set fire to the whole place by blinking.

Homing in on me, Mama leaned across the startled officer, grabbed me by my Lana Turner pompadour, and yanked me to my feet. She pushed air across her vocal cords like a hellfire-and-brimstone prophet, her voice reaching clear up to the balcony. Though it wouldn't convert anyone waiting for the movie to start, I'm sure it made them certain a crazy woman was in their midst. With stabbing words that eddied across the theater, she addressed the hapless lieutenant: "Do you know this child is only sixteen? Furthermore, it's a sin against the Holy Ghost to attend a picture show."

Jeff's mouth hung open, and he gulped like a landlocked fish.

Titters of laughter and loud coughs followed us as Mama propelled me up the aisle toward the exit, just as the "Star-Spangled Banner" began playing and a picture of a rippling American flag appeared on the screen. Everyone stood up, hands over their hearts, but Mama paid no attention. Her patriotic fervor was focused on me, her wicked daughter.

Outside, my tears were uncontrollable. I could hardly speak. "H-how c-c-could you d-do that to me?" I wailed as we walked the deserted streets toward home.

"Your daddy told me I would have to bear the burden alone," Mama said, her mouth a barometer of displeasure under the yellow streetlights. "To think I would raise a honky-tonk kind of girl who has no more thought for her widowed mother than to go off with some alley-cat boy to an old movie house. It says in the Bible, 'Honor thy father and thy mother that . . .'"

I had heard Mama's speech so many times, I could recite it to her backwards and three times on Sunday. For two miles, up the highway and across the Beaver Creek Bridge, with Mama shuffling along in her house slippers, she didn't stop quoting scripture.

"'Then I saw an angel coming down from heaven, holding in his hand the key to the bottomless pit . . . And he seized the dragon, that ancient serpent, who is the Devil and Satan . . . threw him into the pit . . . shut it and sealed it over him, so that he might not deceive . . .'"

I hate her, I thought. *I'm going to save my money so I can get away. I'll leave and never come back.*

The second I entered the house, a good two blocks ahead of my tormenter, I went directly to the out-of-tune upright piano loaned to us by church members, and began to play and sing a risqué ditty Merle Carter liked to sing:

"Roll me over
In the clover
Roll me over
Lay me down
And do it again."

I *wanted* Mama to hear me.

And indeed, she did. Mama crossed the narrow space from the door in one giant step, looking as if I had conjured up a devil from the Fiery Pit. Simultaneously, she slammed the piano lid down on my hands and slapped me so hard my head snapped. *Whap, whap!*

"Oh my goodness," I screamed, thrusting my stinging hands out for her to see, "you've broken my fingers!"

Mama was not influenced by my allegations of pain. "Your talent isn't to be used for the Devil. 'Vengeance is mine, I will repay, saith the Lord.'"

That night, I was consumed by the shakes. More than ever, I was determined to escape the rigid, fanatical woman I called Mama.

~~~

My boss, Merle Carter, was a thin, pixy-faced woman with short brown hair who was always laughing, always wore red, and was never without a cigarette between her ruby lips. She was fun. I liked her and listened to her.

"Y'all need to apologize to y'all's Mama, Patsy," she advised when I told her what happened. "It ain't good to fight with her, honey."

Although it galled me to do so, I halfway apologized to Mama. "I shoulda told you about the midnight preview, Mama. Sorry."

"Told? *Told* me? You should get on your knees and beg my forgiveness, young lady."

"Okay. Forgive me, okay?"

Mama didn't forgive me, but we began to get along a bit better, so at least I didn't feel like I was being followed by the scary Holy Poltergeist all the time.

~~~

The war concerned us all. Three-quarters of the boys in my senior class volunteered or were drafted to serve Uncle Sam. Most didn't come back. We all wanted to do our part. The Waurika Café where I worked had a contract to make sandwiches and prepare jugs of iced tea for troops transported through town on the *Rock Island Rocket*. Beginning to feel an attraction to and from the opposite sex, I begged Merle and her husband, Tyler, to let me go with them the next time a troop train came through. Merle said no. Tyler said no. *No!*

"No, Patsy, you're too young and green to handle soldier boys," Merle told me.

That's why I was so surprised one day when she said I could help them take lunches to the station that evening. Well, let me tell you, I primped like I was going to be photographed with Clark Gable for *Photoplay* magazine. Several times I had surreptitiously watched troop trains slide into the station, so I knew what Merle meant. Even before the trains stopped, soldier boys were dangling out of the windows, giving out razor-sharp wolf whistles to any female in the vicinity, calling, "Baby doll, throw me a kiss," in plaintive tones that created a tempest in nubile bodies. Hearing the sex cries of the male caused my developing sex hormones to soar as high as the grain elevator, our tallest peak, amidst cascades of giggles as shrill as the wolf whistles.

Sometimes the boys marched up the road and back in tight formation so they could stretch their legs after being cooped up on the train for Lord only knows how long. It was a Big Secret. We sure didn't want the Axis powers to find out those troops had pulled into Waurika. A slip of the lip could sink a ship. On the days the soldiers marched, my friends and I sat at the side of the road wearing filmy, flowered dresses, ankle-strap shoes peeking out from under our skirts, lips vibrant, flirting. The fellows sent sidelong glances our way, encouraging us to throw them our names and addresses we had printed out on slips of paper so they could write to us. Many did.

And now here I was being permitted—no, *requested*—to be on the train platform to deliver boxes of egg salad sandwiches and jugs of iced tea to our boys in the service. Golly, gee whiz!

When I saw the train hooting up the track toward us, I quickly reapplied lipstick, ready for admiring whistles. Merle grinned, her ever-present Camel cigarette jutting from her scarlet mouth. The sandwich boxes were ready, helpers in place.

Looking sly, Merle said, "The train's not gonna be in the station long, they said, so we've gotta move fast." She dropped her cigarette on the platform and ground it out under the toe of her red patent shoe.

"Well, I'm ready," I said, matching Merle's wide smile.

The silver train slowed and slid to a stop. An eerie silence ensued. The train windows were closed. Shades were drawn. There were no whistles. It felt the way it did just before a cyclone struck. Every drop of air, light, and life was sucked from the atmosphere, making it hard to breathe. This must be a funeral train. Then a window shade lifted and a soldier stared out. Merle began to laugh hard. "Ha-ha-ha-ha."

Then I knew what they had done, the reason they had invited me to come with them. The train was a Negro troop train. Those black soldiers knew not to whistle or even look at a white girl, though they risked their lives for us in a segregated war.

I dropped the box of sandwiches, kicked off my high heels, and ran from the depot. I ran from Merle, from Tyler, from the hushed train, and from the poignant face of the black man who stared impassively out from that soundless train. Hot tears rolled down my face.

I wished for Daddy. He would have told Merle and Tyler about honor, equality, and respect, and then he would have prayed for the safety of those soldiers going off to God only knew where—Germany? Japan?—maybe to be killed. It took me a long time to forgive Merle and Tyler the insensitivity they had exhibited toward me and the Negro soldiers.

~~~

A special reprieve came along between Mother and me. Mother was going to Oklahoma City to visit a sick uncle. Hooray!

"Patsy Lou, y'all are in charge," Mama said, anxiously checking her brassiere for the bills she had pinned there with a huge safety pin. Her brassiere was her bank. "Patsy Lou, don't y'all get into any trouble while I'm gone. Little Jimmy, y'all be a good boy, y'all hear? I'll only be gone two days."

Mama was dressed up in her Sunday outfit, a pretty navy-blue rayon dress with red dots on it. Her hair was drawn back into its usual bun, but she had placed a flat, pie-shaped navy-blue straw hat rakishly over one eye. Since it was considered sinful to wear makeup or jewelry, Mama wore neither, not

117

even a wedding band. She would, however, dust a layer of flowery Rachel #2, a face powder approved by the Almighty, over her face, eyebrows, and eyelashes, making her look like an albino I once saw pictured in *Life* magazine.

"Bye," I said as Mama trudged off to the bus station, Daddy's worn Gladstone bag in her hand. Little Jimmy and I waved until she was lost from sight.

Freedom! I danced into the house and started sweeping. I had plans. Tom, a farm boy, and his sister Alice were coming for supper, and I wanted everything to be perfect. I hadn't dared start preparations until Mama left, because she would never have allowed me to have a party. Merle Carter had loaned me three sizzling steak platters, three salad bowls, and a yellow oilcloth tablecloth. They were hidden under my bed along with four thin T-bone steaks Merle had given me.

"Jimbo," I said to my seven-year-old brother, "see if y'all can find me some flowers."

Little Jimmy scurried off, eager to be part of an exciting evening, and returned a few minutes later wearing a big smile. In his hands he held a straggly orange canna lily. I put the flower into a Mason jar of water and centered it on the yellow oilcloth-covered table. I squinted my eyes up real tight to make everything look soft and fuzzy, and surveyed the room. Why, I thought, it looked just like a Hollywood party I'd seen pictures of in a movie magazine.

When Tom and his sister arrived, they brought playing cards and said they would teach me to play hearts. Tom was as skinny as a sliver of wood and about the same color. More often than not, he wore khaki pants and shirts, thus blending into the background like a bird hiding from a predator. His hair was beige, his skin was beige, his eyes were beige, and his fingernails were usually beige from the dirt he failed to clean out from under them. His reedy voice suited his features the way a flute suits the sound it makes. His sister was equally drab, but they both had one great attribute: they liked me.

I fired up the kerosene stove and cooked the T-bones just the way I had learned to at the café, well done without a trace of pink. There was a gratifying sizzle when I served them up on the special metal platters.

"Dee-lish," drawled Tom, smacking his lips. "With rationing, the war and all, I haven't had steak in a coon's age." We ate in silence, chewing the tough meat, dipping white sliced bread into gravy. After supper we sat on the floor and played hearts. Cards were strictly forbidden in our home, so with each shuffle of the deck, a delicious thrill of guilt ran through my body.

Before Mama was due to arrive home the next day, I bustled around to clean up all traces of my foray into wickedness. The old frame house had just been painted inside and out, probably for the first time in thirty years, Mama said. Volunteers from the church had soaked every splinter of the structure with linseed oil and then painted it an angel white. No matter where you stood, inside or outside, the strong smell of paint was present.

"Little Jimmy, help me get the house cleaned up so Mama won't know we had a party, okay?"

"Okay," he replied. "I'll help. Rat-Dog will, too."

I laughed as I watched Rat-Dog snuffling up crumbs from the floor like a vacuum cleaner. Then I looked at my baby brother and laughed again. A glob of paint had dripped into his hair, and the solution was to cut it out. Mama had used clippers to remove the paint along with a big chunk of his blond hair. Now he looked like some poor white-trash kid.

It was cold, so I put Mama's chenille bathrobe on over my slip, went outside, and filled a squat little tank with kerosene for the living room heater. After seating the tank into its slot, I lit the stove so we could get warm. I was in the kitchen drying dishes when Little Jimmy, Rat-Dog at his heels, erupted into the kitchen as if propelled from a slingshot. His blue eyes were as big as our iron skillet.

"Fire! The stove is on fire, Patsy Lou!"

I ran to the living room, but heat radiating from the stove flattened me as soon as I reached the door. Inching into the room, I saw that the sides of the fat kerosene heater were glowing crimson and looked ready to explode. Kerosene dripped a faucet of flame onto the metal surround. Apparently, I hadn't seated the tank properly into its receptacle. Fuel gurgled unimpeded into and over the stove, feeding the fire. Flames were already climbing toward the ceiling. Screaming for Little Jimmy to get out of the house, I bolted toward the door.

"Jimmy, get out, *now!* The stove is going to explode! Run!" We didn't have a phone, so I jogged down to the Miller house, Mama's housecoat flapping around my legs. "Mr. Miller, our house is on fire," I yelled. "Call the fire department!"

In the short time it took me to run to the Miller house and back, a crowd of spectators swarmed at the front of our house as though to bear witness to the demise of a dignitary. In its death throes, our home spewed flames, sparks, and electrical wires. Tongues of fire leaped out windows, igniting nearby trees and weeds.

I fell to my knees right there at the side of the road and began to pray. "Oh dear God, help, help. Stop the fire, please, God. I'll never sass Mama again. Forgive my trespasses . . ."

Where was Little Jimmy? I got to my feet. I didn't see him anywhere. "Jimmy, Jimmy, Jimmy!" I yelled, trying to be heard over the sounds of our groaning, spitting house and the noise of the increasing crowd of onlookers. "Jimmy, Jimmy, Jimmy, Jimmy!" Over and over, I called for him. Could he still be inside the burning house? A bolt of fear jolted me forward. Jumping over downed electrical wires and dodging falling timbers, I pushed toward the flaming structure.

Abruptly, I was halted. A man I recognized as our mailman grabbed me. He laced burly arms across my chest, clasping his hands together at the front of my body to hold me fast. "Patsy, y'all cain't go in there, y'all be killed."

Hysterical, I tried to pull away, to no avail. I shrieked my brother's name again and again. "Jimmy, Jimmy, Jimmy, Jimmy!" Smoke billowed. Our home was an inferno.

The fire department arrived, sirens wailing.

"Help me—my baby brother," I screamed. "He's . . . seven . . . a dog, and, and—help me find him! Jimmy . . ." Breaking away from the postman, with a fireman on my tail, I thrashed through tall Johnson grass and cattails toward the outhouse. "Jimmy, Jimmy, Jimmy!"

Was that a voice? Where? Where?

"Jimmy, Jimmy, Jimmy!" My throat was raw. Smoke filled my lungs. Mama's chenille robe caught on nettles and pigweed, slowing my progress. "Rat-Dog, Rat-Dog! Jimmy!"

"Let me do the lookin', Patsy," the fireman said, trying to catch me.

"No! The fire's my fault. I'll find him," I said, pulling away from the man.

We kept thrashing through the weeds. I looked in the outhouse. Little Jimmy wasn't there. I ran to the west side of the house, screaming Jimmy's name.

"Patsy Lou?"

"Little Jimmy?"

"Patsy Lou."

"Where are you?"

"Here," the fireman said. "Over here in the weeds."

There, hidden in a nest of pigweed, lay Little Jimmy, his face buried in Rat-Dog's belly. They were curled into each other. Sobbing, I dropped to the ground and rounded my body against my baby brother and Rat-Dog, my arms enclosing them both. I kissed them, whimpering, as ashes drifted down in a blizzard of soot, smearing a dark farewell on Rat-Dog's fur and on our tear-streaked faces. There in the weeds, we watched our home take its final breath, heave a sigh, and crash amid snapping, glowing embers.

Rounding us up after the fire was our neighbor, Laura Hensley, a weather-beaten, outdoorsy woman who lived in a log house on an island between two branches of Beaver Creek. With tenderness and consideration, she took Little Jimmy, Rat-Dog, and me to her house, treating us as one of her own. Laura Hensley was the epitome of concern, clucking over us, patting our heads, feeding us. "Never y'all children mind. We'll take care of y'all," she said and drove us to the bus station to pick up Mama, who was due in on the eight o'clock Greyhound bus.

What was I to do? I couldn't possibly tell Mama I had burned our house down. My eyes were so red and swollen I could hardly see. The chenille bathrobe still flapped around my ankles, but someone had given me a too-large black coat to drape over it. My knees trembled. I shook all over.

The silver-and-blue bus pulled into its spot. Brakes squealed. My stomach roiled. I thought I might throw up. How could I find words to tell my mother about the house burning down? *She will kill me*, I thought. *I deserve to be killed.* The bus door swung open. Steps were extended. And there she was, Mama, the first passenger off the bus. I was surprised that she looked the same as when she had left, a hundred years ago, it seemed.

Anxious to rid myself of the bad news, but so scared I could barely utter the words, I ran toward the bus. "Mama," I sobbed, "the house bur . . ." I liquefied into a puddle of pee and could go no further, completely unraveled. It was left for Mrs. Hensley to tell Mama we were homeless.

Mama stared at me with that set look she got, her jaws clenched. "Save us, save us, Jesus help us," she said, all the time twisting a white handkerchief round and round over her index finger. "I declare, Patsy Lou, the minute I turn my back, see what happens. Oh Jesus, help us!" Inside the brightly lit bus terminal, Mama dropped to her knees, instructing Little Jimmy and me to do likewise. "God," she prayed, "y'all know we have no friend but you. We are really in a fix, Lord, and I expect y'all to help. I'm a widow woman without funds, Lord, and . . ." She went on and on.

I glanced up through wet eyelashes and saw that we had attracted a curious but respectful crowd. When Mama finally ended her entreaty to the Almighty, she stood up, straightened her straw hat, picked up her Gladstone bag, and said, "Mrs. Hensley, we'd be grateful if you could put us up for a spell."

Mama took me to the burned-out shell to see if we could salvage anything. We searched dismally through the ruins for anything to reclaim. I was in another part of the charred remains when I heard an unearthly gasp.

"Mama, what's wrong?" I said, rushing to her side.

My mother was holding something at arm's length as if handling a rattlesnake. No, no! She'd found the playing cards Tom had given me. They were hidden under my water-logged mattress, but apparently hadn't burned. Lord in Heaven, help me!

"Oh, dear Jesus," Mama moaned, flinging the sinister pasteboards away from her. "Oh, dear Jesus, to think I would live to see such evil in my own home." She fixed me with a look that pierced my eyeballs, passed through the occipital lobe, zoomed into the parietal lobe, and like an electrical shock you barely survive, lodged in my frontal lobe, where memory is stored. "I have taken a viper to my breast," Mama said flatly.

Well, I guess I don't need to tell you how that scalding terminology made me feel.

But I felt better when I heard both Faye and Charles tell Mama not to blame me for what happened. "It was a terrible accident, Mama," Faye said. "It's not right to blame Patsy Lou. She's feeling guilty anyway, and if you aren't kind, it might scar her for life." I already had plenty of scars.

We only had four hundred dollars in fire insurance, not nearly enough to buy a house. My grown siblings didn't have much money, either, and could hardly help in any real way, although they did the best they could.

Carlos was a remote figure with two children to support. It was all he could do to keep his life on track in such troubling times.

Nina was still bossy and acted superior. She and her husband, Harold, now had two children and another baby on the way—a baby Nina kept saying she didn't want. "I don't want another child," she said. "I'm an interior designer, and I don't have time for a crying baby." She yelled at her husband, "Harold, it's your fault." Mild-mannered Harold tried to placate Nina, saying he would keep doing the housework and would take care of the new baby, too. Nina sniffed. Even after the baby, a girl named Pamela, was born, Nina often said right in front of her daughter that she never wanted her. Now how do you think that made Pamela feel? It made me sad for Pamela, a sickly baby who—well, I'll get around to that later.

Poor Little Glendora had eloped with good-looking C. L. Hendrix, a merchant marine. She now worked as a receptionist for Monsanto Chemical Company in Texas City and loved her job, especially the attention she got from the men who worked there. "They stop by my desk to chat and bring me coffee, flowers, and little gifts," she bragged. I would have bragged, too. Poor Little Glendora sent money to Mama on a regular basis. I had visited her once in Galveston and saw the ocean for the very first time, ate lime sherbet, wore high heels, got a really bad sunburn, and had a great time. Glendora was popular and smart, and Mama never stopped talking about how good she was.

Faye and Cecil were always the most loving and easygoing of the lot. They still lived on the farm about ten miles from town. Faye worked at the local bank. My niece, five-year-old Linda Faye, spent more time with Mrs. Martin, a jolly, overweight woman, than she did with Faye.

Neither Faye nor Cecil gave two hoots about housekeeping. Their house overflowed with things like old saws, worn-out bedspreads, old dresses, and dust, dust, dust. When I babysat, Linda and I cleaned house for them. Let me tell you, it was a big job scrubbing mud off the kitchen floor on my hands and knees. It took several buckets of soapy water to get it clean. Of course, it didn't stay that way long, since everyone—Faye, Cecil, his brother Homer,

Grandpa Antrim, farm workers—all tromped through the kitchen directly from the muddy ground outside the back door.

Charles was now a preacher and married to Sybil Cantwell, the daughter of the district superintendent for the Church of the Nazarene, a powerful position. Apparently, he made life hell for my softhearted brother. Charles and Sybil had two children, Charlo Joyce and James Ray. They moved, as we had, from one impoverished parish to another. But wherever they lived, Charles also went to school, studying for a master's degree. Charles didn't seem to have the Call the way Daddy did. I wondered if he became a preacher because it was expected of him. My heart hurt for my brother. He deserved a better life. With his ongoing education, maybe he would get it yet.

We needed a home, and Mama would find us one. "If God is for me, who can be against me?" she stated unequivocally. Without so much as a backward glance, she set out to secure a proper dwelling for us. When Mama had a purpose, nothing could deflect her. Neither snow, nor rain, nor heat, nor gloom of night could keep her from her appointed rounds. She was more determined than the Postal Service. Mama had the four hundred dollars of insurance money and lots of grit. Housing was scarce even for people who could afford it, much less for a poverty-stricken widow with two children.

Within ten days, we had a new home. Mother discovered an unoccupied two-story house five miles from town. She hunted down the owner and bought it for one hundred fifty dollars. She then proceeded to acquire a choice corner lot in town for two hundred dollars, a lot that everyone thought belonged to someone else. She used the balance of the insurance money to get the house moved and placed securely on the plot of land at 409 East D Street.

Hallelujah, we were moving to our new house! Laura Hensley helped us pile all our stuff, what little we had, into the bed of her Ford truck, and we were on our way. It was like old times, with pasteboard boxes holding a bunch of odds and ends— whatever was salvaged from the fire—but no Bossy or chickens. Loaded up the way we were, I thought we looked like pictures of Polish war refugees I'd seen in the *News-Democrat* almost every day. We were on our way home to a house, but without one stick of furniture.

"God will provide," Mama said with assurance as we headed to East D Street.

Well, you can't guess what happened next. Mama was right. What God didn't provide, the town did. When we walked through the door of our home, I reeled back at the number of people crowded together there. People I didn't know, those I did know, and those I loved, like Merle and Tyler, the postman, and Mrs. Hensley, smiled at us. Some wiped their eyes. We had one surprise after the other. Mama looked stricken. Someone got her a chair to sit on. A church deacon stood up, knocking over his chair in the process. He righted the chair and began to talk.

"Sister Montandon, Patsy Lou, and Little Jimmy," he said, clearing his throat. "Oh, and Rat-Dog, too." Smiling, he reached into his pocket and pulled out a rubber dog bone for an ecstatic Rat-Dog. Everyone laughed. "Now," he said, "we believe in doing unto others as we would have them do unto us. Y'all have a need, and we've tried to help y'all." There was a smattering of applause as three laundry baskets with gifts were dragged across the floor and presented to Mama.

With little cries of joy, she unwrapped package after package, until her fingers must have tingled from the effort. There were cup towels, dishes, flatware, pots and pans, sheets, throw rugs, recipe books, and even a box of bobby pins for me. When I thought we had reached the end, we were taken on a house tour. There was a gas stove, a refrigerator, three beds, and old-fashioned handmade quilts—everything secondhand, to be sure, but beautiful.

Mother tried to keep the quiver from her voice. I had never seen her like that. "Thankee," she said quietly. "I knew the Lord would provide, but not this well."

Peeing On Hot Coals

Covered dishes releasing delicious aromas of home-cooked food were placed on the round kitchen table. In the center of the bounty was a large white sheet cake. Written in blue icing on the white frosting were the words *Welcome Home*. I swallowed. Tears clogged my eyes as I suddenly became aware of small-town love. I gazed around and saw warmth and beauty in faces that previously had seemed closed and stern. I looked at my mother, at the lines creasing her face, the gray in her hair, and for the first time, acknowledged her indomitable spirit.

Chapter 7

A Pretty Girl Is Like a Melody

At last, high school was over, and my red-bordered diploma representing years of struggling achievement was hanging by red string across my bedroom mirror. I knew my education was only beginning, and for me the next step was underway. I was going to be a model, come hell, high water, or Mama. My friend, Good Old Tom, as Mama called him, unaware that he was the one who had given me the "evil" playing cards she'd found after our house burned down, lit this desire—not the kind he hoped to light, I must say—by giving me a book titled *How to Be a Model*.

Mama was at prayer meeting, having allowed Little Jimmy and me to stay at home—praise the Lord—when Good Old Tom came over. It was getting on toward dark, but serious-looking clouds gloomed the landscape, making it seem later than it was.

"Patsy," Tom said, "when I found this book, I thought about y'all being so nice and tall. Y'all should model."

"Really, Tom? Do y'all *really* think so?" I batted my eyelashes at him to ensure a positive reply. Tom swallowed and nodded yes, his fine beige hair like a dead stalk of wheat hanging over his beige eyes. He leaned in to kiss me. No way—I did not want him to put his tongue in my mouth or my ear or anywhere else boys had tried! I whirled around so fast that his puckered up lips landed on my vinegar-rinsed hair.

Tom was unfazed. "When am I gonna get to really kiss y'all?"

"When I go to Dallas to model, y'all can take me to the train station, and I'll kiss you goodbye."

"Y'all know I want more than that, Patsy." He smiled his beige smile, setting off quivers in his slender nostrils. "Say, I have news. My sister Alice who lives in Dallas . . ."

I giggled. "That rhymes. My sister Alice lives in Dall—"

128

Good Old Tom continued as if I hadn't said a word. "Anyhow . . .
Alice said y'all can stay with her until a room's ready at the YWCA."

"Oh, that's wonderful! Tell Alice thank you." I gave him a chaste kiss
on the lips.

"That's a start, Patsy. I'll pick y'all up when you're ready to go to the
Big D."

"When I've saved enough money, I'll go," I said, wondering how I
was going to make that happen. But I was bound and determined to learn how
to model so I could be ready when the time presented itself. *How to Be a
Model* was seldom out of my hands. I studied it with the same intensity
fundamentalist evangelists studied the book of Revelation. After Good Old
Tom left, I shoved my iron bedstead and wooden dresser up tight against the
wall, scraping the bluebonnet-sprigged wallpaper, to make room for a runway.
It was practice time.

How to Do a Model's Pivot
Stand with good posture, your body turned at a slight angle.
Place your left foot in back of you at a right angle to your
body. Bring your right foot in front so the heel of your right
shoe touches the toe of your left. Bend the knee of your right
leg. Now come up on your toes and turn.

Dressed in my teal-blue graduation dress and footed in new black
patent sling-back high heels, I stood like a statue and then began my model
walk. My right hand indicated the collar on my pretend Dior New Look, a
look causing frenzy in the fashion world. Placing one foot in front of the other
the way the book instructed, I glided gracefully across the bedroom floor, or
so I thought, exuding confidence and feeling svelte and glamorous.

Suddenly, the expectant clouds hanging from the sky expelled
rumblings that boogied with lightning and turned my room into an old-time

Charlie Chaplin kind of movie, lit up in jerky blue flashes. I could tell the storm was a fast-moving prairie display, all show but no rain, so I kept right on practicing with no less determination than an athlete trying for an Olympic gold medal. If the tempest outside the window could have illuminated my thoughts, you would know I imagined myself on the cover of *Ladies' Home Journal*, *Redbook*, or even—yes!—*Photoplay*! The snooty girls who hadn't invited me to their graduation parties would sit up and take notice then, for sure.

To the accompanying rumble of thunder and flashes of lightning, I pivoted down an imaginary runway, lapping up appreciative murmurs from an audience of movie stars. Why, there were Bette Davis and Rita Hayworth, Ingrid Bergman, and— *gasp*—Shirley Temple . . . and . . .

"Ohhhh, ouch," I squealed, abruptly cut down like a tree in the forest, sprawled in a graceless heap of arms and legs and illuminated by nature's ice-blue light show. I yelled for my brother. "Little Jimmy, come help me quick. I've twisted my ankle!"

My brother bounced into the room with his pal Rat-Dog, eager to be part of whatever was going on and happy for company during the thunderstorm. Rat-Dog, his little white teeth stretched into a grin, was energized by what he perceived to be a game. With hyper force, he jumped across me three times and then ran in circles around my fallen body, causing eight-year-old Little Jimmy to laugh as he tried in vain to pull me up. I finally managed to crawl to my bed and hoist myself onto it.

"Little Jimmy, will y'all please get me some slivers of ice from the icebox and wrap them in a dishrag? And one of Mama's Bayer aspirin, okay? Don't tell Mama when she gets home, okay?"

"Okay," he said. "Unless she takes out after me with the flyswatter."

My ankle attended to, I lay back on pillows, feeling thwarted and lonesome, though the atmosphere brightened when a ray of sunshine beamed itself onto my bed. "Come keep me company, Little Jimmy, and Rat-Dog, too."

Rat-Dog tried to make a flying leap onto the bed but missed the first time. He tried again and made it. He landed on my face, but quickly apologized by licking my lips. He was ten years old and could live to be eighteen, we learned. He still acted like a puppy. After assessing the situation with his alert golden eyes, he circled the quilt as if a fortuneteller would materialize to tell him where to settle down before finally curling up near Little Jimmy lounging at the foot of the bed.

My skinny kid brother began to crack jokes. He always made me laugh—about our financial circumstances, about how stern Mama was. "Why," he said, big blue eyes sparkling, "remember when Mama chased me around the outside of the house, swatting my behind like I was a bug while the neighbors watched, and me yelling, 'Help, a crazy old woman is trying to kill me with a flyswatter'?" Recalling the incident, he laughed so hard tears rolled down his face. "And then, after a turn around the house, Mama was so out of breath, she collapsed on the ground. When I tried to help her up, she reared back and swatted me on the head so hard that my ears buzzed. Lord have mercy, it stung. All I did was say 'darn' to send her off on that tear."

"There were loose wires on that swatter, too," I said. "I know, 'cause she hit me with it a couple of times. But you and Charles can usually handle Mama. Me, well, I can't do anything right."

"That's because she's afraid y'all get pregnant."

"Pregnant? Me? I'll probably go to my grave untouched by human hands."

"Ha-ha-ha, not if Good Old Tom has his way! Hey, didja know all our siblings and their kids are coming next week?" Little Jimmy began to call the roll: Carlos, Marilee, Nina, Minnie Faye, Charles, Poor Little Glendora, our niece Linda Faye, and Nina and Harold's brood: Pamela (Poor Little Pamela), Harold Don, and Marilyn Kay. Then there were Carlos's two, Jenny Lynn and Buddy. "Big crowd, so get ready to sleep on the floor—or, ha-ha-ha, with

Good Old Tom."

I threw a pillow at my blond-headed baby brother. "Cut that out. That's not funny! Besides, I'll be at work when they're here. I have to make money so I can go to Dallas to be a model."

"You? A model? I've seen pictures of models. I know what they look like, and it ain't like you." Little Jimmy laughed. "Everyone thinks you'll stay right here in Waurika, marry Good Old Tom, and have a bunch of kids."

"Well, I'll show y'all! Just wait and see. Tell that gossiping friend of mine Lucille Tallant that I said so!"

"Better hide the flyswatter, then. Mama will never let you go. She says models sell their bodies and modeling is a sin against the Holy Ghost."

"Y'all know that's not true. Besides, I told Mama if she lets me go to Dallas for the summer, I'll work in a department store to earn money for college."

"Well, good luck, sis. We'll see."

My ankle healed quickly, so I was soon back at the Waurika bus stop café working for Merle and Tyler. My tips were the best of anyone there. I discovered that being efficient, cheerful, and flirty got me bigger tips, especially from soldier boys. The mood was good since our troops were kicking the Axis powers in the tail, Rome was liberated, and D-Day had just happened. The fellows hung around me even though the story of Mama dragging me out of the picture show had been passed on to most everyone, it seemed. Whenever the midnight preview was mentioned to me, I knew that person knew about Mama and was trying to embarrass me. Well, they succeeded. That event would follow me all the rest of the days of my life, even if I dwelt in the house of the Lord forever, amen.

Balancing four heavy white plates of steaming red beans, cornbread, canned corn, grits, and catfish on my arms took concentration, especially since I didn't want to spill food on the dress I wore. I waltzed between tables, my arms laden, while Teresa Brewer belted out on the red Wurlitzer, "I'm a big girl now, I want to be treated like a big girl now," and I mouthed the words along with her. Customers clapped when I "sang," and my tips elevated by a dollar or two. After I badgered Merle to prime the jukebox so it would repeat that song, she finally gave in. I needed those tips. The idea of making it to the Big D, Dallas, conjured up a hymn Daddy sang: "I know the Lord will make a way for me, if I live a holy life, shun the wrong and do the right . . ." Well, so much for that. Y'all know that I back-talked Mama and sinned in my thoughts. What chance did I have?

I figured I needed about fifty dollars to go to Dallas, and so far, I had only ten dollars and fifty-six cents, meaning—I did a quick calculation—it would be a year before I could make the trip. By that time, I'd be old. *Oh, woe is me*, I thought, spilling hot coffee on my fingers. The dickens!

While I filled bottomless coffee cups and served chicken-fried steak, hamburgers, and thick-cut bacon with eggs cooked in bacon fat, my extended family was having a picnic in our backyard. Now how do y'all reckon that made me feel? Y'all got that right.

We had barely finished with the lunch crowd when who should come roaring up in his silver pickup but my brother-in-law Cecil. He screeched to a halt near the side door with its flaking green paint, scattering gravel and dust across several young boys who were squatting in the shadows, smoking. Cecil climbed down from the pickup, his worn boots hitting the gravel before his sunburned face showed. As always, it was topped by a creased cowboy hat. A canvas bag swung from his freckled hands.
"Hi, Cecil," I yelled. "What brings y'all here?"

"Well, I've been running around to vending routes, y'all know, collecting money people give up for Goobers and bubble gum. So, well, can I get a cuppa?" he drawled. Cecil smiled, and his face cracked into sunflower petals all the way from his eyes to his temples and down his cheeks. Plunking the bag down next to his coffee cup, he beamed at me like the Cheshire cat.

"Want a slice of hot apple pie and ice cream, Cecil? My treat?"

133

"No, I'm kinda full."

"Yeah, I suppose y'all have been at the family picnic, drinking sweet tea, eating baked beans and potato salad, and being prayed over."

"Well, I ate a little, but needed to make my run. I'll pick up Faye and Linda in a while. They're having fun, especially Linda and Little Jimmy, pretending to be cowboys."

Never in all the time I had known him, going on seventeen years now, had I heard Cecil talk that much in one fell swoop.

"Little Jimmy told me y'all want to go to Dallas to be a model," Cecil said, twirling his coffee mug around on the green Formica counter. "Well, Patsy, Faye and I think y'all should go. We want to help." He handed me the canvas bag. It was so heavy I nearly dropped it. "The loot"—Cecil grinned— "it's for your trip. Here, I'll help count it." He opened the bag and poured out roll after roll of paper-wrapped coins right onto the restaurant counter. It was an awful lot of money, neatly bound in rough tan paper and marked in black numbers as *50¢*.

I was so astonished, I couldn't talk. Cecil beamed, put on his straw cowboy hat, being careful of his wavy hair, and was out the door before I was able to form words. I ran after him, crying happy tears and saying, "Oh, Cecil, I love y'all."

"Have a good time in the Big D," he yelled, climbing into the silver pickup. Gears were grinding and brakes squealing as he hit the pickup door with his hand three times and then peeled away.

Dallas! I was really going to Dallas! Good Old Tom would take me to the train station.

Sitting guard on the living room couch, ready to pounce, Mama sighed and fanned herself with a copy of *The Herald of Holiness*. Having told me I was not, not, NOT to go to Dallas, she was lying in wait. But a streak of stubbornness surfaced, and I said I was going anyway. The night before, we had quarreled for hours and were still at it the day I was supposed to catch the

134

Rock Island Rocket.

"Y'all never let me do anything, Mama. Don't you trust me?" I stood with my hands on my hips, trying to look calm while confronting the Holy Ghost.

"Trust you? How can I trust a girl who burned our house down, brought evil playing cards into her own home, and ev—"

"Y'all *know* I didn't burn the house down on purpose. Y'all make me sound like an arsonist."

"Don't dispute me, young lady. Go to your room this minute and put your things away. You're *not* leaving these premises. Besides, I have a pot of beans on the stove and cornbread in the oven."

"Save the beans. I'm going to Dallas, and you can't stop me!"

"Y'all think I can't call the sheriff? Just try me, young lady. You're still underage, and they can put y'all in jail."

"Ha, y'all wouldn't let them put me in jail, 'cause it would make you look bad!"

"Y'all think you're special because some old alley-cat boys look at you and go all moon-eyed."

"I don't think I'm special! I just want to make something of myself and not be so poor. Please let me go."

Mama sighed, a long, drawn-out expulsion of air. She closed her eyes and inclined her head up toward Heaven. "Oh dear Jesus," she prayed, "have mercy on my wicked daughter, who openly defies her own widowed mother. Oh Lord, you know how I have tried to do the right thing all my life. I have tried to live by the Golden Rule . . ."

I crept toward the door.

Mama opened her eyes. "Come back here, Patsy Lou. I hope someday you have a child who gives you the heartache I've had with you. Then you'll understand. But it will be too late. In fact, I don't feel well right now." She softened her voice. "Y'all better run over and get Dr. Dillard. I'm afraid I'm dying." Mama hyperventilated, her eyelids fluttering.

"Little Jimmy, y'all go," I said resentfully.

My brother had been sitting on the floor with his legs under him, taking it all in, waiting to see who won. He hopped up and ran next door to Dr. Dillard's house, happy to be part of the action.

Maybe I'd better help her, I thought, touching Mama's arm. She grabbed my arm and made a slow roll off the couch, dragging me with her. My carefully coiffed hair was caught under her feet as she fell to her knees and skewed me sideways. She began to pray. "Oh dear Lord, what am I to do?" Mama intoned. "I've done the best I know how, and now look at the sorry pass my daughter has come to."

She was still patting her chest and praying when Dr. Dillard arrived. I yanked my hair out from under her feet and got up from the floor, my face burning with shame. What if Mama really was dying?

Dr. Dillard, a nice-looking man with thick silver hair, a slight limp from an old war wound, and warm brown eyes, seemed to be halfway in love with Mama—although I couldn't begin to image it—making house calls without charge whenever she needed anything. A neighborly gesture, he said. He got a syringe from his black doctor's bag and gave Mama a shot of morphine. He took off his rimless glasses and rubbed his dark eyes, and said that Mama would be fine after she slept awhile. She was stretched out dramatically on the sofa. Dr. Dillard pulled the smoky-smelling chenille robe over her and patted her hand.

Mama was dozing when Good Old Tom arrived.

"Come on, Patsy, or you'll miss the *Rock Island Rocket*," Tom said, his voice urgent. He jiggled in place outside the front door, my suitcase in hand.

Should I go? "Mama . . . I'm . . . going now," I said.

Abruptly, as if Gabriel had blown his horn, Mama sat up, eyes blazing, fury cutting a swath through her voice. "'What ye sow, so shall ye reap,' Tom," she yelled. "I know you're out there."

Tom stuck his head inside, his nostrils quivering like a horse's.

"Tom, you're a good Christian boy. See to it that Patsy Lou don't do anything she shouldn't."

"Yes, ma'am," Good Old Tom replied, tugging at my arm.

Even after the train pulled away from the red brick station, I fretted, wondering if God would strike me dead for disobeying my mother. All the way to Dallas, I worried about her. But the farther I got from Waurika, the happier and more excited I felt.

It hadn't occurred to me to exchange the rolls of pennies Cecil gave me for dollars, and now there they were, nestling heavily in the bottom of my purse, still in the canvas bag. I counted and recounted the money: five, ten, fifteen, sixteen . . . I counted all the way to fifty-two. Fifty-two dollars. I tallied it again and again just to be sure. It was a miracle. I sang under my breath, "Gonna take a sentimental journey, gonna set my heart at ease." The sack of money gave weighty ballast to my spirit. And heavy though those rolls of pennies were, I could have carried them had they weighed ten times as much.

Dallas was as near to Heaven as I could imagine. Instead of a choir of angels, I heard the beautiful early-morning sounds of the city: the clink of milk bottles hitting together in the delivery man's basket, a streetcar humming busily along the tracks, traffic lights clicking from red to green and back to red, and the solid thud of the *Dallas Morning News* striking the front door.

At Alice's apartment, I lay between cool, crisp sheets and stretched my 110-pound, five-foot-seven-inch frame all the way to the foot of the bed, luxuriating in the smoothness of the covers. Today I was moving to the YWCA. Alice had gotten a room for me there for twenty dollars a month plus board. I didn't have a modeling job yet, but the next week I was to go to work as a salesgirl at Titche-Goettinger Department Store. Y'all don't doubt for one cotton-picking minute that I had given up on being a model, do you?

The Dallas Y was a three-story brick prison. The strict, military-like regime was enforced by Miss Colliers, a fierce-looking housemother who seemed unable to smile. Every day she wore a black suit with a white tailored blouse. The day I checked in, she read the house rules without once glancing at me. "No funny business allowed. No alcoholic beverages, no smoking. Curfew is eleven o'clock sharp." I signed a form saying she had read those rules to me. The filigreed iron entry door was always locked, so I was obliged to sign in and out in an enormous black book, recording all my comings and goings. I didn't mind. The rules gave me a sense of security, as if Mama were standing guard.

My roommate was an obese girl named Mary Ellen from a farm community in the Texas panhandle. She was in Dallas attending Baptist summer school. Well, amen, Mary Ellen! Poor Little Mary Ellen suffered from acne and dandruff and had a penchant for Prince Machiavelli perfume. "Match-a-belly," she said, pronouncing it for me. Mary Ellen let me tilt the crown-shaped bottle until a bit of the amber liquid gurgled out so I could dab it on the pulse points at my wrists. The strong fragrance lingered for days.

Down the hall, in a matching cubicle, lived Aileen Humble from an oil family near Houston. Aileen's parents had been killed in a car crash, and she had no living relatives, which was the oddest thing I ever heard tell of. I thought everyone had relatives, endowed as I was with siblings, aunts, uncles, grandparents, cousins, nieces, and nephews, more relatives than I could keep track of.

Anyway, Aileen worked as a legal assistant in the firm of her family lawyer, who was trying to get her estate sorted out. She was the smartest person I ever met. Since I had never learned proper etiquette, Aileen taught me how to set a table, turn the edge of the knife toward the plate, where to place a salad fork, and so on. I never dreamed there was more than one fork for everything. Now I learned there were salad forks, dinner forks, lunch forks, dessert forks, fish forks, serving forks, and even a thing called a spork—half fork, half spoon, like a hermaphrodite, Aileen said. Which brought up a whole new series of questions.

Never had I met anyone like Aileen. I admired her deep voice and short-cropped black hair, and while not wishing such a style for myself, I thought she looked sophisticated. That girl was the epitome of efficiency. In her room, there was a place for everything, and everything stayed exactly where it was supposed to be. Her tailored suits and blouses hung neatly in the small closet, pressed and ready to wear. I was lucky to find my clothes, stuffed as they were willy-nilly with everything jammed together, wrinkled and falling off wire hangers. My new friend even had padded hangers. Yes, truly, blue silk padded hangers! I kid you not.

One evening, three of us gathered in Aileen's room to eat Fig Newtons, talk about boys, clothes, boys, makeup, and boys. Oh, and the bad food served at the Y. Since I was the youngest one in the dorm, I was teased a lot. "Patsy, have y'all ever been kissed? I mean, *really* kissed?" pretty red-headed Ruth Anne asked.

In all my sixteen, almost seventeen years, I couldn't say I had been kissed the way I saw it done in movies—like Dan Dailey and Betty Grable or Jeanne Crain and Dick Haymes. "No," I admitted, "not really."

"Y'all better practice, then," Aileen said.
For a kiss to be meaningful, we had to have oversized mouths and wear dark red lipstick. Smear-proof Bermuda Red by Tabu was thickly applied.

"Now, watch me," Aileen said. "I'm twenty-five, so I know whereof I speak. This is how you kiss." She lifted the back of her left hand up to her lips and kissed it as if her hand was Van Johnson or Buck Jones. "Now, y'all do it."

Hands were brought up to mouths, eyes closed. I conjured up a picture of Dick Haymes, opened my mouth slightly just as Aileen had, and kissed my hand. *Smack!*

Aileen laughed. "No, that's not the way. Like this." She kissed her hand seductively like her hand was her husband.

I tried and tried, but couldn't manage to do it right. The other girls kissed far better than I did and were getting bored.

"Patsy, that was pitiful," Aileen said. "No boy would want to touch lips with you twice. You look like you're kissing a goldfish in a wet barrel. Come on, I'll show you how to knock their socks off."

We giggled. This was fun. Readjusting herself after getting a drink of water, Aileen prepared to instruct greenhorn me in the art of seduction, or at least how to kiss my hand.

Smiling, she placed one arm around my waist, cupped my head with her other hand, and curved my body into an arc. Unhurriedly, she brought her mouth to my neck and then to the swell of my breasts. Jeepers creepers, I didn't expect that. Then, bit by bit, she peppered me with tiny baby kisses until she worked her way up to my mouth. She was so close, the freckles across her nose blurred.

"Close your eyes, Patsy," Ruth Anne advised.

"Words from the peanut gallery," someone said, distracting me. Back in the kissing game, my instructor pulled me close to her body again and slowly brought her parted lips down on mine, then pulled away and did it again, teasing. Was that it, I wondered? No. Aileen's breath came in puffs as she brought her lips to mine again. Then she opened her mouth and thrust her tongue past my gaudy lips, past my teeth, and into my mouth! Golly! Was this part of the lesson? Was it ever going to end? Did I want it to end?

The memory of Jeff forcing his tongue into my mouth at the midnight preview brought me to my senses. I pulled away from Aileen, scared and confused. A tingle of alarm crept up my spine. Sex and the Devil were synonymous to me. Aileen smiled and reached for me. Cradling my head, she kissed me hard on the mouth, leaving me breathless. As she held her lips against mine, Aileen delicately circled my alert nipples with her finger. "Y'all don't need lessons," she murmured. "Just a good lover." Jesus help me, I would burn in Hell for this. Even tenderfoot me recognized this as something more than a kissing lesson.

From the dark hallway boomed the strident voice of our housemother jailer, followed by her sour face peering around the door. "What's going on in here, girls?" Aileen and I jumped apart, our scarlet faces covered with Tabu's smear-proof lipstick. "Out, everyone out!" the woman hissed. Without a word, we scurried off like clouds in a windstorm. A sense of having done something wrong haunted me, and thereafter, I painstakingly avoided further contact with my friend, although something inside me yearned for her to kiss me again.

Occasionally Aileen would knock on my door with small gifts from her office: a pen, a calendar, a box of paper clips. One day she brought me a gift wrapped in shiny flowered paper and tied up with a white bow.

"What on earth, Aileen? I haven't done anything to deserve a present."

She smiled and said for me to open it.

Feeling awkward, I slowly untied the curly white ribbon and ripped off the flowered paper, excited over a wrapped present. Nestled inside a small white box, resting on cotton, were a pair of amethyst earrings. "Gosh! Goodness gracious, Aileen, these are really, truly beautiful." I held them up to my ears to see my reflection in a wall mirror. "Golly gee whiz." Should I accept them? They must have cost a lot of money. Mama said never to accept expensive gifts from . . . boys. Well, Aileen was a girl, so that solved that!

"Patsy, I want y'all to have them. My folks gave me tons of stuff I don't wear, like these earrings. That way, y'all will have something to remember me by. Okay?"

"Okay, Aileen, thank you so much. But no matter what, I won't never ever forget *y'all*."

My friend leaned in the door, kissed me, and said goodbye.

Lesbianism was an unknown word or concept to me. Whenever I

reviewed "The Kiss," I was filled with a complex mixture of shame and longing. The longing was for tenderness, touch, and kindness, qualities I had never before experienced. No one had ever been so tender or sweet to me as Aileen. But still the image of Sally Mae being "cleansed" on that hot Sunday afternoon, so long ago, played in my head. I could almost smell the alcohol searing tender flesh, and I cried.

Even though I wasn't modeling, my job at Titche's was exciting. Assigned to the blouse department, I would unfold the pretty garments and hold them up to me to see how I would look in them. During my lunch hour and on my day off, I haunted places that used models: wholesale dress manufacturers, Sanger's department store, Neiman Marcus. Most people said they didn't need a model. Some said they would call me if they had an opening and politely took down the phone number of the Y. Every day I plunked a nickel into the black pay phone at the back of the store to check on my messages. "You're goofy," my roommate allowed when I told her about my dream of being a model.

One morning, the sad-faced manager of the blouse department, a pretend smile playing across thin lips, strode over to my counter. "Patsy, we're issuing your cash today." He acted like he was bestowing a blessing. Though I had been there only ten days instead of the customary two weeks, I was being trusted with fifteen dollars with which to make change. He gave me a drawer for the money and a key with which to lock it. I counted the bills into the designated spaces, locked the drawer, and went on my coffee break. As usual, I plunked a nickel in the phone and called the Y.

"Yes, there's a message for you, Patsy," the operator said. I held my breath. "Y'all are to go to Neiman's personnel director right away." I dropped the phone into its cradle, my new responsibilities, the cash and the key, forgotten. I grabbed my white cloth purse, the one I carried from home, and ran the few blocks to Neiman Marcus, afraid that if I didn't hurry, whatever they had called about would evaporate.

"Our junior model was in an accident and will be out all summer, so we need someone to model," the department manager at Neiman's explained. "Let's take a look at you in the clothes, and if at the end of the day, Miss Laura agrees, we'll use you as our house model."

The clothes fit. Thank you, Jesus. The only problem was that my feet were crammed into shoes half a size too small. It didn't matter; I was a model and above mortal pain. All day long, I changed from one pretty sweater and skirt set to another, showing girls and their sweet-smelling mothers the pastel garments.

"You did well today," a handsome woman in a gray dress, black patent pumps, and ten strands of pearls announced at the end of the day. "I'm Miss Laura, and we can use you all summer. Now please wash that dreadful pancake makeup off your face. Natural is usually better."

Hallelujah! The first thing I did after washing my face was to call Tom's sister and tell her the news. Then I dropped a penny postcard in the mail telling Mama my hosiery sales job was going well.

That night, lying awake in a room permeated by the smell of "Match-a-Belly," I dreamed of an ethereal future and listened to the *thump-thump-thump* of my heart. Its disturbingly loud sound and irregular beat had jarred my sleep for years. Lying on my right side diminished the sound, and I soon fell asleep.

My newfound confident self-image gave me a sense of gaiety I had never before experienced. I began attracting attention from the male sex. At a Y open house, I surprised myself by exhibiting a gravitational pull I didn't know I possessed. There was inevitably a boy named Tex. The boot-wearing, raw-boned cowboy followed me around looking love-struck. He asked me to a movie a few times and out to eat, but he never got fresh or tried to kiss me or maul my breasts the way other boys had. Tex fascinated me, not because of his charm or style—he had neither—but because of a long hair growing from his cheek. Each time we were together, I looked to see if the razor had finally

143

found it, but no, that single long hair remained. I had no real interest in Tex, so you can imagine how surprised I was when he called to tell me he had entered me in a beauty contest.

"A beauty contest! Gosh, Tex, y'all should at least have asked me first."

"Well, I thought y'all would be interested. The winner wins an all-expense-paid trip to Hollywood, California. And she gets a screen test, to boot!"

"Honest?" In spite of myself, I was intrigued. "What do I have to do?"

"Nothing, 'cept put on a swimsuit and smile y'all's sweet smile," Tex said. "I paid the fee because I know y'all will win."

Hollywood! Screen Test! Lights flashed, bells rang, cameras rolled, action . . . and . . . tra la la . . . *A star is born.*

I'll bet you would have said yes, too.

The contest was on a Saturday, so my friends at the Y were able to go along to support me. Aileen had a Plymouth painted with blue house paint, with room for five of us to ride with her. I was scrunched on the seat next to Aileen. She held my hand. It felt better than holding hands with Tex or Good Old Tom, I must say. Three other girls had piled into the rattletrap truck Tex drove on his pappy's oil well farm, he said. It was fun having friends cheer me on and help with makeup, critique my hairdo, and loan me platform high heels to wear with my bathing suit.

The bathing suit from Neiman's was a nifty white Jantzen two-piece with laces up the sides on the bottom half and a halter top. As I paraded around practicing, my cheering section beamed encouragement. I was full of confidence until the other contenders spilled into the room in skimpy bathing suits and with dinners so big they could have nursed a whole entire orphanage. The girls were done up to their teeth, long eyelashes out to here, and great big pouty lips like Joan Crawford. They looked like movie stars. I don't need to tell you that no one would ever confuse me with Ida Lupino or Betty Grable. I looked like I was ready to sun myself in my backyard instead of competing in a beauty pageant. That stupid Tex, and stupid me, believing I had a chance.

My mind flipped back to Mama and Daddy being so scandalized by the rubber suits on the Bathing Beauties whose souls they had prayed for. Mama would have fallen to her knees in supplication and bled to death right there in front of these girls. Their bathing suits were so tight I wondered how the heck they could breathe. Their dinners were pushed all the way up to their chins, where they jutted out like upside down ice cream cones. How did they do that?

Until now, I hadn't thought much about being in a contest. In my mind, it had been just me on the stage, and I would be crowned Miss Hollywood and sent off to get a screen test! If I had shown a lick of common sense, I never would have allowed my knobby knees to go out in public. The other contestants and I eyed one another with suspicion, assessing strengths and weaknesses, and then added so much powder, lipstick, rouge, and hairspray we were in danger of toppling over from the weight on our heads and faces. *Dear God*, I prayed, *what am I doing here?*

What I was doing there was marching out onto a huge, empty stage with bright lights staring me in the eyes, and standing in line with the other girls while a photographer snapped our picture. He was a full-of-himself kind of fellow wearing a shiny red vest over a black shirt and black trousers. "This way, gals," he directed us in a slangy voice amplified by a bullhorn. "Tall gals in back, short gals in front."

Was I tall or short? I went with the short gals. Y'all can't begin to believe how tall some of those girls were—Texas Tall, with a capital *T*. After we lined up, the red vest man told us to turn around with our butts turned toward him, and then turn back toward the bright lights. I couldn't see anything because of the glare, but I heard Tex yell, "Patsy, stand up straight."

My legs were shaking so hard, it was all I could do to stand up crooked. But at least I didn't have to stand very long. I was eliminated in the first go-round.

Tex was outraged. To my surprise, since Tex seemed as placid as a cow chewing its cud, he accosted the man in the red vest. "Y'all are a moron," Tex yelled, shaking his fist. "Patsy's the prettiest girl here. This is a ruse to get the twenty-five dollar fee!"

"Now, mister, hold your horses. No one's sayin' the gal's not good-lookin'. We're sayin'—"

Wham, Tex punched the guy in the stomach. The fellow crumpled to the floor like an accordion, his red vest ruched up to his chin.

"Get the po-lice!" someone yelled. The beauties still on stage stirred around like steers heading to slaughter.

"Let's go," Aileen said, pulling my arm. We took off running, me in my bathing suit, with the borrowed platform shoes in hand. My friends had gathered my stuff and were skipping along in bare feet, carrying their shoes and laughing. I looked back and saw Tex being escorted out of the place, his hands behind his back, still bellowing. I was glad to get out of there. Can you imagine Mama seeing my picture in the *Dallas Morning News* with Tex sweating and hitting and spitting like that, and me in a bathing suit? My days would have been numbered.

Bob Bates was a different matter. Nineteen, witty and handsome, he let people know right away that he was a Bates of Bates Bedspreads. He took me to the theater to hear Guy Lombardo, and as we sat in the crowded balcony listening to "the sweetest music this side of Heaven," Bob boldly put his sweaty hands on my breasts.

"Stop it," I hissed, but Bob ignored my request and continued his silent explorations. By the time we left the ornate theater, the only sound I could recall hearing was Bob's heavy breathing. His ardor cooled when we encountered the bright lights of public transportation, but flamed to a new high just before we reached the door of the Y.

"Come on, Patsy, you'll like it," he insisted, pressing me against the side of a building, kneading my breasts like they were the dough I had seen rising in Mrs. Hammer's kitchen. He scared the dickens out of me. With a violent wrench, I shoved Bob away and ran pell-mell toward the Y, glad to be quickly buzzed into the nunnery.

At least I didn't have problems at "the brightest star in the retail firmament," Neiman Marcus. The store was like a fairy tale to me: thick gray carpets, crystal chandeliers, sales ladies in elegant black dresses, the hushed ding of a paging device. Every day, I changed from one pretty outfit to another and walked through the salon to show young girls and their mothers what I was wearing.

Church sisters dropped by the Y whenever they came to Dallas. I tried to visit with them and was always polite, as Mama taught me to be, though I knew they reported directly to her as if she had a payroll of spies. Shortly after one of these visits, I was parading around the divine (as I'd learned to say) Neiman Marcus salon, when lo and behold, there stood Mama.

"Mother," I gasped. "What are you doing here?"

"You're coming with me, young lady," she sizzled, pretending to smile. "You're doing an evil thing. You told me you were selling stockings, not displaying your body around for everyone to see. Vanity will be your downfall, Patsy Lou."

"I won't go!"

"Your Grandpa Taylor drove me all the way here to get you, and I intend to do just that. We're taking you to visit your aunt Maudie in California until school starts up. I've already informed the Young Women's Christian Association to pack your things up."

"I'm not going. I—"

"Are you having a problem?" asked the department manager as she glanced at Mama, ready to call security.

"No, ma'am. It's fine."

"We don't want trouble."

With her black oxfords firmly planted in the luxurious Neiman Marcus carpet, Mama grabbed my arm. Her eyes flashed hellfire and brimstone. She would not leave without me. I was beaten.

Leaving the aesthetic paradise that was Neiman Marcus was like being cast out of Heaven. I wished time could be tied off like an umbilical cord, allowing me to stay in that aromatized bower forever.

Grandpa Taylor, Mama's father, was part Irish and part—the part mother refused to acknowledge—Comanche Indian. Six feet tall and thin, Grandpa was a model for good posture. With thick white hair and a hooked nose, he was an imposing figure. Since he was ninety and licensed to drive only during the day, our trip to California took so long, it seemed to rival the journey in *Around the World in Eighty Days*. We left Dallas on the twenty-fifth of July and arrived at my aunt's house in California on August fifteenth. Twenty-one days and one thousand four hundred forty miles! I sulked the entire time until Grandpa said he would teach me to drive.

"Now, Chicken Liver," Grandpa said a few states away from the California border, "cheer up. I'll teach you how to drive."

"Good, then I can steal a car and drive back home." It wasn't fair what Mama had done to me.

"Papa, y'all can't let that child drive this car." Mama's pupils were dilated, her face tight with fear.

"Be quiet, Myrtle," Grandpa said, flooring me. "You're getting swelled up like a toad."

Grandpa pulled over to the side of the narrow highway in the mountains of New Mexico and let me take the wheel. "If y'all can drive here," he said, ignoring mother's protests, "y'all can drive just about anywheres."

Amid Mama's frightened shrieks, Little Jimmy's cheers, and Rat-Dog's howls, I careened up and down mountain roads, sometimes weaving dangerously across the centerline, sometimes skimming the side of a hill. The thrill of independence! If we crashed, at least I would be in charge of the crash. If we survived, I would be in charge of that, too. Ah, freedom!

"You're doing real good, Chicken Liver," Grandpa said, crowing like a rooster. Each time he took the steering wheel, I chafed until he let me drive again.

"There's Californie," Grandpa declared when we eventually crossed into the Mojave Desert. Where were the fountains of orange juice, the movie stars leading us into the Promised Land—Lana Turner, Betty Grable, Gregory Peck? There was only sand, rocks, and tired-looking cactus, their prickly arms outstretched as if crucified by the burning sun.

"It's different in Oakley where your aunt lives," Grandpa insisted. "You'll like it there."

I *hated* it there. My mother's sister lived in a converted school bus with a raft of cousins, parked in a cherry orchard. They were migrant fruit pickers. Mama was so tired out that all she could do was sleep, which left me to get into trouble—which I did by reading normally forbidden magazines like *True Story* and *Real Romance*, the likes of which I had only imagined.

When Mama finally arose from her pallet bed in that cramped bus in a California cherry orchard, she was ready to go to work. Soon she found a job canning apricots, which everyone called "cots," in a nearby cannery.

"Young lady, you had better get to work picking cherries," Mama said. "You can make good money if your back doesn't break. It'll be good for your soul."

"I'm getting a better job than that, Mama. I'll save enough money to go back to Big D and be a model," I vowed.

"You go right ahead, Miss Priss," she smirked, frowning. She did not believe for one minute that I could get employment. But trudging up a busy road to a bus station coffee shop, I got my second job as a waitress.

It was unlike the Waurika Café. Customers in California were different, not gentle and mannerly like people at home.

"Hey, Okie girl," a fellow shouted. "Pour me a cuppa Joe."

"I'll bet a plugged nickel that you came to California-i-a with a mattress on top of your car. That right?"

Constantly teased, I tried to eradicate "y'all," "jist," and "git" from my vocabulary and to get rid of my drawl by copying radio announcers.

"Say 'y'all' again, honey," a customer baited me. Or, "Tell me again how many mattresses you all have on top of *your* car when you came to California." A rich Okie was someone with two mattresses on top of the car when they came to California, I was told. Occasionally a nickel would be plunked into the jukebox, and the nasal voice of a country singer filled the café. The words to one ditty went, "Hey, Arkie, if you see Okie, tell him Tex has a job for him out in Californie, picking prunes and squeezin' the erl out of olives."

I would go right on mixing thick chocolate shakes, pretending I didn't hear. But it hurt like an open sore rinsed with alcohol. I wanted to beat my tormentors until their ugly California heads fell off and rolled under the counter.

Then one day, a friendly co-waitress said, "See that nice-looking fellow at the counter? He's got the hots for you." I wasn't sure if that was good or bad, but looking surreptitiously in the direction indicated, I saw a tall man with the angular features of Gregory Peck. He had been coming in every day for over a week for a "cuppa" coffee.

The fellow gave me a big smile over the rim of his cup. "Your name's Patsy, isn't it?" he asked.

"Yes," I said, busily wiping the glass pie case.

He twirled his mug on the red Formica counter and cleared his throat. "I'd like to take you out," he stammered. "Will you go to the stock car races with me tomorrow night?"

"I'll have to ask my mother," I said, embarrassed that it was so. "I'm sure it will be okay."

He smiled again and put ten cents on the counter for his coffee. "You're pretty, Patsy."

Blushing, I looked down at the floor.

"See you at six, here," he said. "Okay?"

"Okay," I answered.

"What's his name?" I whispered anxiously to the beer-swilling cook who had sauntered out of his greasy kitchen to listen.

"Howard," he said. "He's got a construction outfit over near here."

I changed my mind about asking mother for permission. Instead I told her I had to work late at the restaurant because one of the waitresses was sick.

I had a good time that evening, although I didn't much care for stock car racing. Howard was from a ranching family in the fertile San Joaquin Valley, he said. He had recently bought a construction rig and was trying to make it on his own away from his parents. Ranching was his true love, though—I could tell because of the way his nice gray eyes looked when he talked about the rice fields and cattle.

"You are really special, Patsy," he said, kissing me goodnight. "May I meet your mother?"

"Yes," I said, wondering how it could be avoided.

We were now staying with another of Mama's sisters, my aunt Maudie, while Grandpa gallivanted around, visiting relatives until it was time to go home. Maudie lived in a quaint little house located smack dab in the middle of a peach orchard. At my urgent request, Howard let me out of the car before we got to the driveway. I was groping in the dark for bedcovers when the sun rose in the midnight sky and the Son of Man made his presence known in that small clapboard house in a California peach orchard. The overhead light swung back and forth, its black wire full of volts cascading down to a bulb that blared out more light than I thought fifty watts possessed.

"And just where do you think you've been, young lady?" Before I could utter my tip-of-the-tongue fib, Mama continued. "I checked the coffee shop and it was closed, so save your lies."

Mama was a cyclone ready to touch down. Head for the cellar, everyone!

"I'm waiting, Patsy Lou."

"I had a date." I pulled the sheet up to my chin.

"A date? What kind of date are y'all talking about, young lady, and why didn't you have the common decency to tell me about it?"

"His name is Howard Groves, and he's nice. We took a ride and got a hamburger and looked at some cars. That's all, Mama."

"Don't take that tone of voice with me, young lady. I'm still your mama, and I still have jurisdiction over y'all, and don't you forget it, you hear me? Y'all are still just a kid."

"I'm almost eighteen years old. I'm not a kid anymore! Stop treating me like I've murdered the Holy Ghost."

"Don't you dare say such things, Patsy Lou, or God will strike you dead for dishonoring your mother. Why, if your daddy were still alive, he would switch your legs for talking to me that way. Now, listen here. That alley-cat fellow Howard Groves had better come up here to see me as soon as I get home from work tomorrow, or the fat'll be in the fire. Y'all could still be sent to a detention home." Mama marched across the room with angry footsteps, reached up, and switched off the light, disappearing into the blackness and then reappearing to switch on the light again.

I cringed under the rough bed covers, fearful that she would beat me with the broom she carried.

"You should have been home to help me like a good daughter would. Today I slipped on cots at the canning place and fell down and hurt myself real bad." She made it sound like I had shoved her. "Just look here." She pulled her pink bloomers down over her ample hips to show me a purple-and-red bruise large enough to be a map of Texas. And then she knelt beside my bed in the blaring light from a fifty-watt bulb and began to pray.

"I'm sorry, Mama. Does it hurt?"

Mother looked up at me with a disparaging blue gaze that said it all. "No, Patsy Lou, it feels wonderful. Be quiet while I pray." She bowed her head. "Dear Lord," Mama prayed, "I have no friend but y'all. I pray in the name of the Holy Ghost that respect will be given to my daughter for her widowed mother before it's too late. Dear God, I know y'all did not spare angels when they sinned, but cast them into Hell and committed them to chains of gloomy darkness to be kept until the Judgment Day. Sobs arose from the kneeling figure, causing a knot of fear to lodge in my stomach. Her banshee cry produced static electricity in my bedclothes and ran up my spine. Oh Heavenly Father, I pray that y'all will save Patsy Lou so she'll not spend eternity in Hell away from her family. Amen."

Finished with her lamentations, Mama turned off the light and left my room, taking the broom with her after one final admonition. "Young lady, I expect to meet that alley-cat boy who took you on a date without asking my permission. You hear me?"

"Yes, ma'am." Okay, if Howard wanted to meet my mother, he was sure going to get the chance.

~~~

I didn't believe it. No, it couldn't be true. Mama seemed entranced with Howard, who brought her a bouquet of red roses and See's chocolates, and asked permission to take her daughter out. He was smooth. Mama was charm itself. Yes, of course I could go with him to meet his parents. Next weekend? That would be fine. Was this my birth mother speaking?
"Y'all be nice to him," Mama whispered, putting the flowers in a Mason fruit jar. "He'll be a real big brother to you."

"Salt the cow to get the calf," muttered my aunt, who stood in the background, observing the show.

On the day Howard took me to meet his parents, I was dressed in a russet-colored Lilli Ann wool suit with shoulder pads so large I could have been a linebacker for an NFL team. Large rhinestone buttons marched down the front of the jacket, which had a peplum with scalloped edges. I had discovered Lilli Ann on a brief trip to the enchanted city of San Francisco. It was love at first sight, both for the dramatic clothes and San Francisco. My determination to save money had vanished in the glamorous image of myself dressed in that outfit. I had to own it. From the moment I lifted it from its tissue-layered box, I felt transformed into a sophisticated glamour girl. The suit hung on a nail near my bed where I could see it upon waking and could be sure it hadn't vanished.

When we approached Howard's home in the San Joaquin Valley, he seemed as nervous as I felt. "Patsy," he said, clearing his throat, "do you like me?"

"Yes, I like y'all," I said, blushing.

"Do you think you could love me?"

"Love y'all? Uh, you're sure nice." Why was he asking me such odd questions, I wondered.

"Patsy," Howard said, plunging recklessly ahead, "will you marry me?"

Had I heard him correctly? Marry him? Was he kidding? A chill ran from under my breastbone all the way to my toes and curled into a toe fist. "Uh, uh, we only just met, Howard!"

"I knew the first minute I saw you that I wanted to marry you. I love you, honey." He cleared his throat. "I'll take good care of you, I promise."

Dear Jesus, what could I say? Weighing the question, I thought of the prison of life in Waurika, held my breath a moment, and said, "Uh, well, maybe, but not until I'm eighteen."

"Wonderful, sweetheart, wonderful." Howard beamed and reached across the seat to take hold of my hand.

Eighteen was ages away. I had nothing to worry about but was flattered to have someone say they loved me, not having a clue about love. There was something magical about eighteen. Mama had drilled that thought into me. "Y'all are not to get married until the age of consent, eighteen."

Howard seemed better than my prospects in Waurika or Dallas: Good Old Tom, Tex, Bob Bates, Waurika boys saying they loved me when all they wanted to do was to tear my clothes off and grope my breasts. And Howard was good-looking. Six feet two inches, with thick lashes shading nice gray eyes, straight brown hair parted on the side, and at twenty-seven an older man, better than Good Old Tom.

Most everyone I knew was already married. Some of my classmates even had babies. It was 1947. That's what we were supposed to do, get married and have babies. Once in a while, the order was reversed and the baby came first. Those girls were ostracized from the community, churches, and friends, because God sure as heck didn't want babies running around without a wedding ring having been placed on their mama's finger, and a husband to bring home the bacon every Saturday night before he went off to the beer parlor. No, sir.

In school, we dreamed and talked about walking down the aisle in a white satin gown and veil and having the whole town go *Oooh* and *Aaah*. The grooms hardly played a role in this drama; just us, the brides, were the center of attention.

Now here I was, being proposed to by a California rancher in his Studebaker on the way to meet his folks. Hmm . . . maybe, at last, I could escape the rigid confines of my upbringing. But I also had other dreams for my life. Why couldn't I be married and also be a model, or an actress, or a secretary? I hoped to do something besides be married and have babies. Growing up desperately poor and even hungry at times, I needed to figure out how to make money and how to give my spirit loft. I didn't know what that was, or what it meant, but when I had heard those words used on a radio show, they stuck in my head. That's what I wanted: spiritual loft and financial security. Married or not.

"We're almost there," Howard said, patting my hand. Checking my hair and makeup in the mirrored visor of Howard's Studebaker, I smoothed my skirt, ready to meet the people who might become my in-laws.

The Groves' five-hundred-acre ranch lay nestled in the dry, lonely foothills of the Sierras. The two-lane highway that cut through it was infrequently traveled and led on to Mark Twain's Knights Ferry, Copperopolis, and Sonora. Copperopolis—I enjoyed the way the word rolled off my tongue.

At the crest of a hill, spread across a treeless valley, were acres of green squares. "Those are rice checks," Howard explained. "The young rice plants are green. We irrigate from that dam over there." He pointed. Huge rectangles of dammed water and green rice shoots made a striking contrast to the fields of dry grass everywhere else.

How different things were in California. In Texas and Oklahoma it rained all year, and the fields and hills were green throughout the summer except when there was a drought. Howard said it didn't rain in California for the entire summer. The only way they could grow abundant crops was by irrigating. They worried about water all the time.

Mr. and Mrs. Groves came running out of their two-story beige stucco house to greet us. Mrs. Groves was short and plump, and always on a diet, she said. But she had a table full of food ready. "Mom's the best cook in the entire valley," Howard boasted. Stunning blue-and-white antique dishes and polished mahogany antique furniture took my breath away. Such affluence! Howard had one brother and one sister, both younger than he. Edith, Howard's sister, was in San Francisco training to be a nurse. Wally, his brother, trailed us around with obvious pleasure.

"You made a hit," Howard said when we left. "Mom liked you, and Dad said, 'Son, you don't need to look any further.' Let's set a date, Patsy."

"Not until I'm eighteen, Howard. I don't want anyone to know, either, not even my mother."

"After your birthday, sometime next year, though. Right?"

"Yes, after my eighteenth birthday."

Whenever I thought about actually marrying and then sleeping with Howard, I almost threw up. The specter of sex overshadowed my fantasy of wearing white satin, holding an armful of calla lilies, and being adored by my groom. Although naïve, I did know intercourse was quite different from Mr. Jack Hammer rubbing his "peckerwood" on my stomach.

Thinking about S-E-X made me so nervous that I decided to focus on school. I would be off for college three weeks after getting home. I had saved enough money to pay for part of my tuition, and I already had a job in the cafeteria to support the balance.

Grandpa gunned the car motor and honked the horn several times, announcing it was time to hit the road, to leave California orange groves and all that lushness and head home. Howard kissed me goodbye in the privacy of his automobile, and we promised to write to each other. He planned to come visit me to celebrate my eighteenth birthday, he said. Lordy.

"Goodbye, Reverend Taylor and Mrs. Montandon," he said, shaking Mama's hand. "Bye, Little Jimmy. You write me, okay?"

"Okay." Little Jimmy didn't even glance up, he was so engrossed in a Jack Armstrong All-American Boy comic book, but Rat-Dog barked at Howard.

Mama smiled, not just with her mouth but with her eyes, too. She even seemed pleased when Howard had asked if he could come visit. "We'll see y'all in December," she said, nice as pie. "You're a mighty lucky girl, Patsy Lou," she said to me after we were on our way.

Why was Mama acting like this? She hadn't even asked Howard if he was a Christian. What was she up to?

We rolled smoothly onto Route 66 in good spirits. Mama sang "Amazing Grace," Little Jimmy read comic books, and I read about Scarlett

157

O'Hara in *Movie Life* magazine and planned a flowery letter to my "intended."

Eventually, Grandpa got us back to Waurika, where all became hustle and bustle in preparation for school. But no sooner had we gotten home than there was a knock at the door. "Come on in, Tom," I yelled. "We're home." But it wasn't Good Old Tom. Of all the people in the whole wide world I never expected to see at my door in Waurika, Oklahoma, it was Tex. Mama opened the door and stood looking at the tall drink of water, a stranger in a big cowboy hat and scuffed cowboy boots that could very well be covered with oil or manure.

"Tex! What are y'all doing here?" I asked, stunned, not opening the door all the way.

"I want y'all to marry me," he said, holding out a black velvet box open to show a diamond ring shining out from it like the eye of a cyclone. Before I could get a good look at the diamond, Mama pushed me roughly aside and slammed the door. Tex stuck out a booted foot with carved alligators in full color on it and blocked the door open. With his head halfway inside, he addressed Mama.

"Ma'am," he drawled, "I'm Tex from Texas, I'm in oil, and I want to marry your daughter."

"What's going on out here?" Grandpa Taylor hobbled out from the kitchen, all bent over from having been on the road so long.

"Y'all wait just a darn minute," I said, wanting to rip that one hair off Tex's stupid face. "Tex, are you completely crazy? I don't want to marry you no matter if you own all of Dallas and Fort Worth, too. How could y'all drive all this way and buy a pretty ring for my finger without asking me how I felt? That's downright irrational."

Tex stared at me like he couldn't imagine any girl not being delighted to tie the knot with a man named Tex. As if a fellow in oil and cattle wearing cowboy boots engraved with the toothy smile of 'gators and wearing a cowboy hat banded with the hide of a reptile was some kind of big catch.

"Patsy, I've hit a gusher oil well right there in my backyard! Lookie here at the oil on the soles of my new boots." He held his foot up so I could see that a lubricant of some sort had, indeed, soaked into the soles of his boots and up the leather sides, darn near drowning the 'gators. As an added inducement to his proposal, a chunk of manure was stuck under the Cuban heel of his boot, testifying to the fact that he had at least one head of cattle.

"Well, do tell. Y'all know what, Tex? Even if you fell into a vat of oil and sold it to the flying red horse filling station folks, I would not marry y'all. Understand me? Now get in your car and go back home to your papa in Texas!"

Tex frowned, looked at me, knew I was serious, I suppose, and snapped the black velvet ring box closed. He put the pretty box and diamond ring in his red-stitched blue denim shirt pocket, tipped his hat, and sauntered laconically back to the navy-blue pickup truck parked in front of our house.

"I declare, Myrtle, if brains was dynamite, that boy couldn't blow his own hat off!" Grandpa chuckled, sounding pleased with himself.

"Patsy Lou, don't you dare go anywhere with that man," Mama warned. "He's got a crazy look in his eyes."

"Do I look like I'm going anywhere with that man? I don't hardly know that man, Mama! Seems to me the whole male species is nuts." I was trembling. "Howard asked me to marry him on our first date, and Tex is plumb weird. I've decided I'm not ever, ever going to get married. I'm going to be a career girl!"

Nevertheless, in love with love, I tied Howard's long, dry letters together with a pink ribbon the way a girl in love is supposed to do.

Thanks to my various jobs, and especially the one at Neiman Marcus, I had a nice wardrobe for college. As I packed, it gave me sensuous delight to touch the soft garments. Mama shook her head, looking grim as she surveyed my clothes. "Vanity, all is vanity," she quoted. "Remember, Patsy Lou, 'Pride goeth before a fall.'"

Mama's pronouncements were short-lived. She got a call from Indiana telling her she needed to come look after Charles. He had collapsed in his dentist's office and was now in some kind of mental hospital and needed her. Grandpa volunteered to take Little Jimmy and Rat-Dog to La Marque, Texas, to live with Poor Little Glendora while Mama was with Charles. Faye and Cecil took Mama to the Greyhound bus depot and then drove me to Chickasha, where the Oklahoma College for Women was located.

After I got set up with classes, I was sent to the campus doctor for a physical examination. I'll bet y'all will be as shocked as I was: the doctor—get ready—was a *woman!* I had never heard tell of a female doctor before. Anyway, she said I had a heart condition! She gave me a whole bunch of rules to live by or, she said, I could drop dead at any time. Well, let me tell you, that news ruined my day and the plans I had made for my life.

1. I had to live on the lower floor of my dorm.
2. I wasn't to run.
3. I was not to walk up flights of stairs.
4. I couldn't engage in sports, as if I ever wanted to.
5. I was to call my mother and tell her that my condition was very serious.

As if I was going to let Mama know about me, when she was already dealing with Charles, who might be shut up in a mental hospital somewhere. Talk about a rock falling on your head! I felt like Chicken Little, except the sky actually *had* landed on me.

I sat on a campus bench, fall leaves drifting down, laughing girls in plaid skirts walking past, and tried to console myself by wondering if a female doctor could actually know very much. Tears welled up inside me, but I refused to let them past my eyelids. Instead, I indulged in the notion of Mama grieving at my funeral. Me, dressed in a white satin wedding gown, a white veil placed delicately over my beautifully made-up face, my hair done to perfection, baby's breath and lily of the valley decorating my white casket. Poor Little Glendora sobbing . . .

"Oh, stop it!" I muttered aloud and began to pray. "Please, dear Lord, help me. I don't want to die."

The concern about my heart and my anxiety about Charles was intertwined with the joy and stress of a new school, all of it compacted by pressure into something like sedimentary rock: my childhood burns, Neiman Marcus, Tom, Tex, Aileen, the beauty contest, Howard Groves and his parents, the coffee shop Californians . . . all of it lost in memory-fog. It was as if I stood on a mountain peak where swirling mist obliterated the past, and the future was nothing more than a lifeless fantasy. I lay down on the bench, oblivious to others, and sobbed.

Reverend Charles Clay Montandon (Daddy) and Myrtle Caledonia Taylor Montandon (Mama).

Poor Little Glendora, Betty Ruth shortly before she died, and neighbor children.

Our family, 1935. Poor Little Glendora, Daddy, Mama holding Little Jimmy, Me, Patsy Lou, Charles Clay, Minnie Faye, Carlos Morrison and Jenny Lynn.

Easter Sunday in front of the parsonage in Chillicothe wearing our finery. Poor Little Glendora, Daddy, Mama, Little Jimmy and Patsy Lou.

Mama in all her severity with her sister, Aunt Loraine.

Mama was hospitalized when she got a bone stuck in her throat while tasting cornbread stuffing for a Thanksgiving family reunion. We are in her hospital room, her brood: Patsy Lou, Poor Little Glendora, Charles Clay, Carlos Morrison, Nina Aileen, Minnie Faye, Little Jimmy.

With Poor Little Glendora in Galveston, Texas. I was in route to the Azores Islands.

With my sisters at Grandma Taylor's funeral., Poor Little Glendora, Nina Aileen, me, Patsy Lou, Minnie Faye.

Poor Little Glendora sees me off on the train to Westover AFB where I will leave for the Azores Islands and Lajes AFB with my husband Howard Groves.

Howard Groves and Line Backer suited me at his parents home in Farmington, California when we first met.

Good Ole' Tom, my boyfriend in Waurika. I was fifteen.

Trying to look sexy in my Neman Marcus Janzen bathing suit. Alas, I lost the beauty contest that good ole boy Tex signed me up for.

Howard and I leave on our honeymoon in Palm Springs after our wedding on Bride and Groom a radio show in Los Angeles.

Howard and I strut our stuff at a Guys and Dolls party in the Azores.

My dear and funny friend Benny Echwald and me singing Diamond's are a Girl's best friend at the NCO Club, just as if we could carry a tune.

Wedding Bells, for eighteen-year-old Patsy Lou and twenty-five-year-old Howard Groves.

A sheer white wool wedding gown that was worn by Mom Grove's grandmother fit as if made for me. I used it and other treasures Mom had tucked away in the attic for Family Album.

I'm Only a Bird In a Gilded Cage in a play at the officer's club in the Azores.

Taking a bow after Them Oklahoma Hills, a homemade affair I wrote, produced and directed, a regular Orson Wells, on an Island AFB in the middle of the Atlantic Ocean.

An Island lost in time where I lived for over two years and where I met Malcolm whose teachings changed my life.

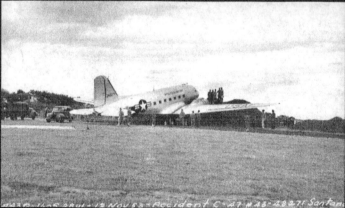

Howard crashed his plane into a pile of rocks a barrier that kept him from ending up in the ocean. This is an official Air Force picture.

My TV Show on KGO in San Francisco. It was the highest rated daytime show in the Bay Area and LIVE, which I loved.

Alex Hailey the author of Roots entertained me in his home in Rome, NY.

Modeling couture fashions for I Magnin.

I'm standing on the famous Crooked Street of Lombard about which I wrote in The Intruders, a terrifying story.

My husband, Al Wilsey and I stand on the balcony of our San Francisco penthouse. The abrupt ending of our eleven-year marriage was a shock, made even sharper when he married a woman who had pretended to be my friend.

Every summer Al and I gave a party for our friends at River Meadow Farm in the Napa Valley. Dede Traina *gas lite* me.

Three-year-old Sean Wilsey, my son, sits at my desk "writing" what I tell him must have been the beginning of his blockbuster book Oh The Glory Of It All.

My 81ˢᵗ birthday with grandchildren Owie and Mira and friend Susan Gold.

I'm addressing 6000 people in the Kremlin at an International Women's Congress with President Mikhail Gorbachev, 1987

Chapter 8

Like a Virgin

"Patsy, you have a long-distance call," someone sang out from the vicinity of the dorm. "He's phoned twice already!"

Tossing off my mantle of gloom, I ran inside and took the receiver. "Hi," I said breathlessly.

"Sweetheart, where have you been?" Howard asked in his hesitant, throat-clearing way. "I've called and called."

"Oh, Howard, I'm going to die." Tears washed the words right out of my mouth. Eventually I blurted out the story.

"I'll be there on the next train," he responded.

"No, wait until the holidays," I insisted. My drama teacher had given me the starring role in a Christmas radio show, and dying or not, I wasn't about to give up my brief moment in the spotlight. "Then we can go to my sister Nina's house in Little Rock for Christmas."

"Okay, Patsy, harrumph, I'll be out on the nineteenth of December and stay until after your birthday." That would be the day after Christmas, when I would be "of age."

~~~

My heart problem was shoved into the unthinking part of my brain, and I concentrated only on Howard.

"Howard is coming, Howard is coming," chanted the group in the overcrowded De Soto convertible. We were returning from the radio show, where I had bored everyone by bragging about my California knight. Howard was rich, handsome, sensitive, couth, and imaginative—in essence, everything I felt I was not, and far enough away for no one to know or check. It enhanced my image, or so I thought, to spread glory around Howard's head. In standing close to his imagined radiance, my own insufficient self would be absorbed

171

and replaced by perfection.

"Howard is coming, Howard is coming," my friends teased, dropping me off at a nearby hotel. As I sat waiting for his arrival in the hotel lobby, my stomach knotted ominously. It had been four months since I had seen him. Would we embrace? What would I say to him? Would I recognize him? I closed my eyes and tried to conjure up his image, but all I could see was a photograph he had given me where he stood rigidly at attention in his Air Corps uniform. I had stuck the picture in the wooden frame of a mirror that hung over my dresser.

"Patsy!" Howard came through the hotel door smiling.

I felt a rising panic. He was a stranger. Our letters and phone calls had been a romantic illusion.

He cleared his throat, *harrumph*, and carefully set down his suitcase. "Honey, I brought you a birthday gift," he said, short-circuiting my thoughts.

"You did? But I won't be eighteen until December twenty-sixth."

"I know, but I want to give it to you now," he insisted, taking a narrow black velvet box from his coat pocket. His smile grew wider when he flipped open the hinged lid. It was a wristwatch studded with four tiny diamonds.

"Golly, gee," I whispered, calling on my extensive vocabulary of superlatives.

"They're *real* diamonds," Howard said, "a quarter of a carat each." He bent down and fastened the timepiece around my wrist.

Never in all my seventeen—almost eighteen—years had I been given a birthday present, much less a real seventeen-jewel Bulova with diamonds studded into it. I gloried in the sight of the gleaming stones shining on my wrist. Okay, Mama was right; I *was* lucky to have a man like Howard interested in me.

"Don't worry about your heart, Patsy," he said. "Your heart belongs to me, anyway. I'll take care of you. You're my little girl now."

I felt protected and fragile for the first time in my life. Although deliberate in his actions and lacking wit, Howard showed generosity and consideration, qualities I had never before encountered. He was also "tall, dark, and handsome," just like fairy tales said he should be.

When we arrived at Nina and Harold's home in Little Rock, Arkansas, Mama, Little Jimmy, Poor Little Glendora, and her husband, C. L., were already there. Mama had come with Faye and Cecil after caring for Charles. The only thing she said about my big brother was that he had been bad sick and was leaving Sybil and moving to Houston. I knew better than to ask questions she wouldn't answer.

My family welcomed Howard like church members greet a sinner returning to the fold. I was afraid someone would shout, "Glory to God" or "Hallelujah! Patsy Lou is saved!"

"Why, my goodness, Howard, you need not have brought us presents," Nina said, opening a two-pound box of See's candy from the Golden State and two boxes of glazed fruit no one had ever seen the likes of before. "Just what I've always wanted," Nina said, eyeing the orange slices with suspicion. My niece Poor Little Pamela, who had inherited the title from Glendora, along with her sister Marilyn Kay and my nephew Harold Don, began stuffing chocolates in their mouths.

"Mrs. Montandon," Howard said formally three days later, "may I, harrumph, have your daughter's hand in marriage?"

We sat in the softly lit living room of Nina's antiseptic, antique-filled house. Everyone else had disappeared. Nina had just finished singing passages from every sentimental love song she knew. Sheet music for "Oh Promise Me," the classic wedding song, lay open on the piano. *They want to get rid of me*, I thought. A day earlier I had heard Nina and Poor Little Glendora tell Mama she'd better let me marry Howard. "Otherwise, there's no telling what kind of trouble Patsy might get into."

"She's sure headstrong," Mama said. "Why, she gives me more

trouble than any of y'all ever did. And now with a heart problem, there's no telling what will happen."

I burst into the bedroom where they were lounging on the bed, talking about me. "Stop it!" I wailed. "Stop talking about me behind my back. I'm sick and tired of having to find out everything by eavesdropping! So stop it. Treat me like the grown-up person I am."

"Shush," they said in unison. Mama put her hand over her mouth, Nina covered her ears, and Poor Little Glendora hid her face on the bed. They looked like those monkeys: see no evil, hear no evil, speak no evil.

"Y'all look like monkeys!" I blurted out, giggling.

"Patsy Lou, y'all are suffering nerves, that's your problem," Poor Little Glendora said. "Just nerves."

Back in the living room, Howard cleared his throat again, *harrumph*, waiting for Mama's answer. My thoughts were a jumble as I nervously wound a strand of auburn hair around my finger.

"Why, Howard, we'd be pleased to have you as a member of our family," Mama replied.

Howard jumped up and hugged me.

"Set the date, Muggins. When?"

Muggins? Where did that name come from? Golly, I was afraid I might throw up.

"April," I blurted out. Mama left the room, a satisfied smile playing over her lips. Anything could happen in four months, I thought. We could be killed by a cyclone. April was an eternity away.

New excitement electrified the house that week. "Why don't y'all get married on that radio program in Hollywood?" Nina suggested.

"What program?" I asked.

"Why, the one with John Barbour, *Bride and Groom*. I listen to it all the time," Nina said, dusting the spinet piano for the third time that morning.

I sighed. "Well, most of my friends have either gone off to school or gotten married, so it suits me. Okay, Howard?"

"Sure," he said, "if you want to."

"I'll write to John Barbour, the host of the show," said Nina, getting a pen and paper.

Howard had made appointments in Little Rock for me to see heart specialists. Mama escorted her "baby daughter," as she referred to me in front of Howard, protectively from doctor to doctor. My engagement to a landowner had given me stature in my mother's eyes. I would become Mrs. Howard Groves, a married woman, and Mama could say, "My daughter is married to a successful rancher in California." At last I had some worth.

The various doctors listened to my heart with cold stethoscopes while I hyperventilated, coughed, and did whatever they asked. "Too many Cokes and cigarettes," snapped a short, black-haired physician.

"But I don't smoke," I insisted, afraid Mama would think it was so.

"Take it easy and stop drinking anything with caffeine in it," he said, dismissing me.

The relief I felt lasted all the way to the second cardiologist. Following new tests, he announced in a doom-filled voice that I had rheumatic heart disease and should stop all physical activity. Mr. Death had his scythe ready to mow me down. My solution was to temporarily ignore them both.

Before Howard left for California, Faye took him to a jewelry store where she could "get him a deal" to buy a ring, much to my relief. How could a girl be properly engaged without a diamond ring? It would have been downright embarrassing back in Waurika. No one would have believed I was truly betrothed. Alone in my room, I held the stone to my eye, turning it slowly to catch the reflected light. I told myself I was happy, and how much I loved Howard.

Back home in Waurika, I was delighted to be the center of attention. My photograph and a two-story column appeared in the *Waurika News-*

Democrat. I clipped the article and pasted it into a scrapbook.

"Y'all sure are lucky, kid," friends said when I flashed my perfect blue-white half-carat diamond ring.

"Yes, I *am* lucky," I replied, beginning to get into the whole idea. The future shimmered before me in a Fourth of July cascade of fireworks. I imagined Howard's arms holding me as we waltzed around our immaculate kitchen. I would wear a frilly white organdy apron, and Howard would be in a smoking jacket like the one I saw Clark Gable wearing in a magazine picture. We would gaze lovingly at each other, and I would spend my entire day cooking dainty cakes and his favorite dishes. Then, in a year or two, we would welcome a blue-blanketed bundle from Heaven, just like the song "Tea for Two" says. And Mama wouldn't be there to run my life. Oh, it was becoming delicious to contemplate.

But I didn't know diddly-squat about how my body worked and how as a married girl I was supposed to "do it." Doris Faye Scott, my best friend, had recently gotten married, so I decided to ask her about sex. But when I did, she giggled and wouldn't tell me one blessed thing. Even when I slunk into the library and combed the meager stacks for something that would help me understand what sex was about, I found nothing that explained what a girl did on her wedding night. Zero. Zilch. Nil. Naught. Nothing. Like my friends, I remained abysmally ignorant of the functioning of my own body.

A church member made my wedding gown from a McCall's dress pattern of heavy white Skinner satin. The gown had a sweetheart neckline and long sleeves with points that came down over my hands. The skirt ended in a sweeping, four-foot-long train. My gossamer veil was trimmed with handmade lace topped by a spray of white silk baby's breath. When I modeled it, Little Jimmy said I looked like I was expecting "mesquites" to come bombing in any minute.

Everyone I knew dropped by our house with bridal presents and to see my wedding attire. One of our neighbors was Auntie Maud. Auntie weighed four hundred pounds and was so heavy she had to weigh herself on the scales used for bales of cotton. It was hard for Auntie to walk, much less cross the highway in front of our house without being mowed down. Her husband solved the problem, taking care of his baby, as he called her, by making a red-painted stop sign for her to hold up when she crossed the road. One day Auntie Maud held up her sign, stopping traffic in both directions, and waddled across the road toward our house as horns beeped. Pressing her forehead against our screen door, Auntie Maud tried to see inside before she knocked. Well, she didn't exactly knock.

"Sister Montie, Sister Montie," she bellowed. "It's me, Auntie Maud."

"Hi, Auntie," I said, opening the door.

"Well, Mrs. Maud, how are you," Mama said, drying her wet hands on a cup towel. No matter how long they had known each other, Mama called her friends by their last names. She would freeze up like a rooster's tail in a norther if anyone called her Myrtle. She was Sister Montandon, the widow of the reverend, and nobody had better forget it.

"To'ble well, thankee," replied Auntie, easing her bulk into the nearest chair. "I jist want to see little Patsy Lou's weddin' dress."

"Sure, Auntie," I said. "Let me wash my hands first."

"Better put those gloves on, Patsy Lou," Mama instructed.

I pulled on the white cotton gloves we kept handy and lifted the heavy white satin dress from its box of tissue paper.

"O-o-oh, ain't that purty," Auntie said reverently. She gently touched the fabric with her roughened fingers. "My, my, Patsy Lou, y'all will be so purty in that, it makes me jist want to cry." She began to weep, her tears following a well-worn path down her multi-chinned face. From the bosom of her dress, she dragged out a pink handkerchief to mop up the flow. "Y'all will look jist like Cinderella, Patsy Lou," she said, crying still. "Is that your veil popping up in that box over yonder?" She pointed to the white net frothing up in a snowy halo from a white cardboard box. "Can I see hit, Patsy Lou?"

"Sure, Auntie." I picked up the gauzy wedding veil, shook it out, and handed it to her.

With panting effort, Auntie hauled herself up and out of the easy chair and slowly wobbled to the wall mirror, the one framed with engravings of Jesus rising into Heaven. Auntie Maud's tightly permed skull was filled with romantic dreams fueled by *True Story* magazine and paperback novels with pink-heart covers that she sometimes asked me to read aloud to her. Humming softly, our neighbor stood in front of our Jesus mirror, lifted her weighty arms, and plunked the gossamer wedding curtain on top of her blue-tinted hair. Auntie Maud preened in front of the mirror, turning to the right and then the left. She smiled, laughed, raised her eyebrows, and began to cry again.

"Y'all look mighty pretty, Auntie," I said.

"I wisht y'all had a camera to take my pitcher with. I ain't never had no weddin'," Auntie said softly. "With y'all's weddin' veil a-sittin' on top my head, I'm playing like I'm a gettin' married. She whirled around, lost her balance and regained it by putting her hand on the wall. Thankee." Without another word, Auntie handed me my veil, picked up her stop sign, let the screen door slam behind her, and headed back across the road, weeping still.

"When your daddy and I got married," Mama said, watching Auntie waddle back home, "I didn't have any of these fine things, Patsy Lou. I hope you appreciate it." Now she was going to tell about how she was just sixteen and Daddy twenty-three when they started off across the Texas prairie in a covered wagon and with a few head of cattle. At night they slept on quilts underneath the wagon and sang to the cattle to settle them down. "All I had to keep house with was an iron skillet, a coffeepot, and two patchwork quilts my mama gave me," she said, looking back forty years. "It was scary, I want you to know, but I never once regretted it."

"Honest, Mama?" I said. "Not even when you and Daddy fought, and he blackened your eye once and you pretended you ran into the edge of a door?"

"We never fought!" Her temper flared; her face was red. "Never. If you ever say we did, you're lying. I didn't think I'd ever raise up a girl to be a liar."

"I'm sorry," I said, wanting to keep the peace. I replaced my wedding finery in the nest of tissue paper and ran down the street to meet the mailman. Maybe I'd have a letter from my fiancé. The word rolled satisfyingly around inside my mouth. I sprinkled the exotic noun into my conversations whenever I could.

Surprise! There was a letter from the *Bride and Groom* radio show. They had accepted us! Howard and I had filled out several application forms. Some of the blanks were easy to fill out: BRIDE'S HEIGHT: 5 feet 7 inches. BRIDE'S WEIGHT: 110. HAIR: Auburn. EYES: Blue.

Other questions required creativity: WHERE DID HE PROPOSE? "Sitting by a river looking at the full moon reflected in the water," I wrote. HOW DID YOU MEET? "I was in San Francisco modeling for the summer," I penned. "I stopped for a cup of coffee at a café in Brentwood and saw Howard at the counter. It was love the moment our eyes met."

When I completed my silly exaggerations and falsehoods, we attached a photograph of ourselves and sent it off. Lord have mercy, they bought the unlikely story.

Faye and Cecil drove Little Jimmy and Rat-Dog to La Marque, Texas, to stay with Poor Little Glendora while Mama and I made the trip to California for my impending nuptials. Howard had sent money for two train fares on the *Santa Fe Chief,* including enough for meals and a sleeping compartment. But no, Mama refused to squander "one red cent" of Howard's money on anything as frivolous as food and beds. The trip took four days, and for the entire endless time, we sat in the miserable horsehair day coach. Our meals consisted of dry rat-cheese sandwiches that we carried with us and washed down with an occasional bottle of soda pop Mama sprang for.

When we finally arrived in California, we were disheveled, hungry, and in need of baths. Howard met us at the train depot. The first thing Mama did was hand him two hundred dollars and forty-two cents, the change from the four hundred he had sent. He didn't say a word about Mama's thrift, but precisely sorted the money according to denomination, the faces of past presidents staring in the same direction, opened his wallet, and methodically placed the money inside it before we got in his Studebaker and headed to his parents' home, where we had been invited to stay until our trek to Hollywood.

That evening, Mama sat stiffly at Mrs. Groves's abundant table, afraid to tackle the strange-looking artichokes, eggplant, and asparagus, saying, "I declare, I'm just not hungry. I guess I ate too much on the train." Visions of stale cheese sandwiches danced in my head. After everyone was in bed, I snuck into the well-stocked kitchen and got Mama a safe glass of milk and a piece of cold chicken.

In Los Angeles, a billboard proclaimed, HOLLYWOOD MOVIE CAPITAL OF THE WORLD. I expected a gold velvet curtain to rise from nowhere, fairy godmother Billie Burke to wave her magic wand, and Gene Kelly to come tap dancing along the pavement.

What a disappointment! The streets were gray and dirty, without a movie star in sight. Oh, *there* was the Brown Derby restaurant, perched like Charlie Chaplin's hat with a door right under the brim. Things were looking up.

"We're almost there, honey," Howard said, referring to the Chapman Park Hotel where *Bride and Groom* originated. We were to be married in an hour. My stomach hurt. I couldn't go through with this wedding. But how could I stop it? Mama would kill me. I would have no place to go, nor could I get a good job with an incomplete education and my heart flipping around in my chest the way it did. Furthermore, I wanted to be an actress, not a housewife. So, ha, that was how I could cope. Fiddledeedee, I would pretend I was Scarlett O'Hara in *Gone with the Wind* and Howard was Rhett Butler.

Yes, I could do that! After all, I had won the title Best Actress at Waurika's state one-act play championships in Duncan, Oklahoma. Yes, I had.

I *was* Scarlett O'Hara. My imaginary chauffeur helped me out of a silver-colored Bugatti and onto a red carpet at the CBS studio. One of my fans took me to a dressing room that I envisioned as being furnished with a plushy white rug and mirrored tables and white plumy feathers instead of secondhand scuffed-up furniture, to don the wedding costume.

"Are you about ready, Patsy?" asked a woman carrying a clipboard.

"Oh, sweetie pie, is it time for my close-up?" I asked in syrupy tones.

The woman looked taken aback, but smiled and said yes, it was time for my close-up.

"Does my make up look camera-ready?" I asked in the honeyed drawl of Scarlett O'Hara.

"You look like a beautiful bride," the woman said, "and it's time to go."

"Oh, fiddledeedee," I whispered, rearranging the folds of my satin skirt. *Surely God won't let this happen*, I thought. I was not ready to get married. I wanted to be a model. Or an actress. Perhaps at the last minute a woman from Neiman Marcus wearing a sleek black dress and a neck full of pearls would step forth and say, "I object," and I would be saved. *But it's Clark Gable I'm saying "I do" to,* I thought, and smiled.

Applause leaked through the white double doors where we waited. I heard an announcer say, "And now, from Hollywood, *Bride and Groom*." Loud clapping blended with the strains of Wagner's wedding march as Rhett joined me at the door. I hardly recognized him. He looked strained and uncomfortable in a black suit and with comb marks in his hair.

We were cued. Together, Rhett Butler and Scarlett O'Hara stepped into the crowded hall as a corpulent baritone burst into song and organ music swelled, bringing me thudding back to reality.

"Here comes the bride with her groom.

They aren't married n-o-o-o-w,

but they w-i-i-l-l be soon."

We stepped into the room, and gratifying cheers burst forth from what looked like a flower garden of women. On their heads, a well-fertilized and abundant estate of pink roses, yellow mums, varicolored tulips, and violets nodded at us. I waved, but Rhett seemed frozen in place. I pulled on his arm. "Rhett," I whispered through a fixed smile, "are you coming with me, or shall I find Ashley Wilkes?"

My husband-to-be looked at me with a bewildered expression. "Rhett?" His eyes were glazed.

A man wearing earphones and a frantic expression quickly guided us to a low stage where the radio host, John Barbour, waited.

"Come on up here now, because I'm going to pry," he said.

The audience tittered, perhaps hoping that a bit of salacious gossip would fulfill their fantasies. John Barbour smiled and smiled, his mouth stretched across his round face as he beckoned us on to our doom.

"Here's our handsome couple, ladies and gentlemen," he gushed into the CBS microphone. "What a beautiful bride. Now don't be nervous. Just come right up here with me. You have no secrets from us. We're going to snoop," he said with a wink, followed by a laugh.

I could imagine all of this being carried on the airwaves across California to Arizona and New Mexico, gathering speed through Texas and Oklahoma, and finally, in a burst of static, right into Nina's house in Little Rock. I knew my fans would be gathered around the radio listening and that Carlos was having a record made so we could hear our shaky words for as long as we both should live.

On his worst day, even after Bonnie was killed by falling off her pony, Rhett Butler would never have looked the way Howard did right now.

He looked like he had been embalmed and was about to be buried standing up.

"How many in your family?" asked the master of ceremonies, thrusting the microphone in Howard's face.

"Uh—harrumph, would you mind—harrumph, repeating that, sir?" The question came back, but there was no verbal response, only four shaky fingers held up.

"Well, the groom is *supposed* to act that way," said a perspiring John Barbour before breaking for laughter and a commercial:

"Use Phillips' Cleansing Cream for beautiful skin. Look like a bride every day of your life . . ."

While the announcer read his script, a fellow wearing headphones asked us to be more loquacious during the next segment.

I can do that, I thought. *I'm Scarlett O'Hara.* And anyway, I was beginning to enjoy myself. During the next segment, I answered questions as easily as the lines I had memorized for a high school production. But my poise went skidding out the door and belly flopped on the cement sidewalk when our host sucker punched me with his next question.

"Now, Patsy, what are you going to do on your wedding night?" he inquired.

Sniggers of laughter greeted the question. I could imagine the faces of my family members when they heard it. And Mama! Had she fainted? I tried to find her in the Garden of Eden that was laid out before me, but alas, I didn't see her anywhere. I hoped she hadn't heard that embarrassing question. My face burned with shame, but I managed a honeyed drawl. "Uh, uh, well, fiddledeedee, Mr. Barbour, I'll go to sleep just like any other night. What did you expect I would do?"

Pink cabbage roses and violet violets shook as the women detonated in merriment.

It was nearing the end of the movie. Almost time for me to take a curtain call, remove my makeup, and go home to Mama. *But what a rehearsal*, I thought, then came back to reality when our radio host, with feigned sincerity, cooed into the organ music, "And now, our beautiful bride and handsome groom will walk down the tree-shaded path to the little Chapman Park Chapel, where they will be joined in Holy Matrimony by a minister of their choice. We'll talk to them later, but now . . ." His voice rose an octave or so. ". . . a word from our sponsor."

"Phillips', the finest . . ."

Mama and the Groves family trailed us down the walkway and into the chapel, where a preacher friend of Mama's waited at the altar. The only reason Mama had agreed to this charade was because we could have a clergyman friend of the family perform the ceremony.

"Hurry," hissed the clipboard woman. "You only have five minutes."

"We are gathered together in the sight of God . . . Do you, Patsy Lou Montandon, promise to love, honor, and obey . . ."

"Hurry," urged the woman.

The minister gave her a sour look and perfunctorily pronounced us man and wife. We scurried back to the broadcast, the train of my skirt ballooning out behind me, and entered the studio to thunderous applause. Many of the women wiped tears from their eyes, and those nearest reached out to touch my satin gown, giving me a memory flash of Auntie Maud.

John Barbour was describing our gifts, his ecstasy rising with each item: "A Max Factor makeup kit. A year's supply of ivory soap. A Lilly Daché hat. Luggage by Amelia Earhart. A three-day honeymoon with all expenses paid at the playground of the stars, Palm Springs. Their accommodations will be at the beautiful Desert Retreat. They will dance at the Doll House and dine in sumptuous splendor at the Desert Inn." And finally, with his lung power exerted to capacity, he said, "A beautiful Tappan gas range with the Visualite oven. When our bride cooks for her handsome husband, she will be able to see exactly the progress her baking is making."

I was led to a white-enameled stove and told to smile while a photographer recorded the scene for posterity.

"Congratulations," John Barbour said, shaking our hands. "And now," he said conspiratorially, "what is your special love song, Mrs. Groves?"

Mrs. Groves? Why was he talking to Howard's mother?

"Mrs. Groves," he repeated, "you're in a daze, aren't you?" The audience laughed—nervously this time, I thought. "What's your favorite love song?"

"Ooh," I stuttered, "uh . . ." Now I realized he was talking to me, but my mind was blank. We'd been told not to choose the obvious songs. "'Symphony . . .'"

"Isn't that lovely, folks?" Folks clapped dutifully. "Now, as our *Bride and Groom* soloist sings your own love song, you may leave for your Palm Springs honeymoon. You will be taking with you the good wishes of the entire United States."

There was a deep trill on the organ. I clasped Rhett's black-suited arm, careful to bend my fingers so my bitten-off nails wouldn't show.

> "Symphony, symphony of love,
> Music from above,
> How does it start . . ."

We ran from the studio as the assembled body of women pelted us with rice. "Hurry," my groom muttered. His car was at the curb. We got in and raced off to meet our parents at the home of a Groves family friend in Los Angeles before heading for "the playground of the stars," Palm Springs. I was still picking the rice out of my hair when we arrived.

I felt an unnatural shyness when Mama helped me change into my going-away outfit, a blue wool suit and pink flowered hat. Impulsively, I put my arms around her. She brushed me away. "Y'all be nice to Howard, young

185

lady. He's a good catch," she said sternly. "Remember, men have needs girls don't have."

"Mama," I asked hesitantly, "do you love me?"

"Why is it that you kids always expect me to go around saying that?" She busily folded my wedding veil. "I brought you into this world, didn't I?" A dark emptiness welled up inside me, leaving a void where I ached for love to be.

"I've got a bad sick headache," Mama said. "This has been real hard on me."

I left the room and went to find Howard Groves—not Rhett Butler, but Howard Groves, a farmer boy and my husband.

At least, thank the good Lord, I didn't have to worry about our wedding night. I could delay it for three days. Before we'd left for Hollywood, Howard had taken me to his doctor to be fitted for a diaphragm. The request was so disconcerting to me that my husband-to-be had to explain our mission to the doctor. His nurse strapped me to an examining table, a sheet covering my lower extremities, and pulled my legs apart. I tried not to think about what was happening.

"Ouch!" I screeched when the doctor put a gloved finger inside of me.

"That hurt?" the doctor asked.

"Yes, sir, it sure did."

"You have unusual scar tissue in your private parts," he said. "Has anyone hurt you in this area?"

"No, sir." Frozen by shame, all other thoughts were scrubbed from my head. But later I wondered if my having been burned could have anything to do with that tough tissue.

"If anyone ever tried to rape you, they would never make it," the doctor said, and even at my young age I wondered at his lack of compassion and decency. "Young lady," he went on, "I'll have to cut the hymen. Don't worry—I'll put you to sleep, and that's all there will be to it."

I wondered what the hymen was, but before I could ask, a nurse stuck a needle in my arm, and my thoughts were obliterated.

Howard was sitting beside me when I awoke. How embarrassing it was to have him there. When I stood up, it was hard to walk because of two bulky Kotex that had been placed between my legs. My vagina was on fire with pain.

"Your hymen was so tough it was like scar tissue," the doctor explained with a singular lack of sensitivity. "I've seldom seen anything like it. Anyway, it was best to cut it. You aren't to have intercourse for at least a week, and it might be painful even then."

It was painful right now. My vagina throbbed. I shifted on my chair and gazed out the window at other windows in other buildings and wondered what Little Jimmy and Poor Little Glendora were doing.

"I'll fit you for a diaphragm when you return from your honeymoon," he continued. "In the meantime, young man," he said to Howard, "use a rubber if you don't want your wife to get pregnant."

Whatever a rubber was, I sure wanted Howard to use it. *Happy is the bride the sun shines on*, I thought, watching dust motes flicker across the doctor's desk. Thank the Lord I had been granted a reprieve from sex! I had no idea what to expect, but if it hurt as much as it did right now, I was in for a lifetime of agony.

"It's time to head for Palm Springs, honey," Howard said, taking my arm.

"Goodbye," I called out, waving at Mama and the others as my husband carefully backed out of the driveway. The overpowering aroma of my gardenia corsage was sickening. I took it off and shoved it in the glove compartment, snapping the door firmly closed.

"Whee," said Howard. "I'm glad the fuss is over."

"Me, too," I said, flipping on the radio. Arthur Godfrey with his Lipton tea bags, Oxydol's *Ma Perkins*, and *Our Gal Sunday* entertained us all the way to our destination.

Funny, I thought, *I don't feel married*. The ceremony seemed like the rehearsal for a play. I hoped that at any minute the curtain would close, and I could go home.

Why is this place so special? I wondered when we reached Palm Springs. Small, flat-roofed enclaves dotted the arid landscape. Each seemed an oasis of palm trees in an ocean of rocks and sand. It was hot, and my wool suit itched. The hidden gardenia with its golden ribbon held me in the grip of its aroma. As we drove on, trying to find our own encampment, I noticed swimming pools at each enclave with people splashing and laughing.

There it was—the Desert Retreat, nestled cozily in a grove of pink oleander. We were escorted indifferently to the honeymoon bungalow, which overlooked a swimming pool.

"We're probably the only whites here," Howard said as we unpacked.

"What are you talking about?" I asked, alarmed.

"This is a place for Jews," he said, his sharp features tightening.

"What's wrong with Jews?" I had never met one, so far as I knew.

"Well, uh—they aren't like us," he answered, kissing me.

I pulled away from my husband and ventured an opinion. "Daddy used to say that Jews were persecuted because people said they killed Jesus. But Daddy said that wasn't correct, that Jesus was a Jew, too, and that we are all created equal."

"Muggins, you have a lot to learn about the world. Listen to your ol' hubby, sweetheart."

He was right about that, for sure. I vowed to start reading heavy-duty books so I could be sure of my opinions.

That night I daubed on Secrets of Venus perfume and a virginal white nylon gown and negligee set.

"You look beautiful," Howard said, while I languorously brushed my shoulder-length hair the way Scarlett O'Hara did in *Gone with the Wind*. We cupped into each other on the double bed and slept fitfully during the long night.

~~~

My heart was doing a tap dance against my ribs. It was the third day, and Howard indicated it was *time*. He had "protection" in the drawer beside our bed. When he went to the bathroom to undress, I opened the drawer, but the only thing there was a tiny, mustard-colored packet. Was that a rubber?

"I love you, Muggins," Howard said a few minutes later, pressing his hard "thing" into me.

I focused on the ceiling and tried not to think about Sally Mae and the fornicators. There were flecks of glitter in the ceiling material, a decidedly Hollywood look, I thought. Then I closed my eyes, willing myself not to scream from the pain of being ripped apart, as we consummated our marriage in silence. I clenched the pillow under my head and prayed that the cutting agony inside me would subside. Tears fell from my eyes as a fleeting memory of being burned "down there" wheedled its way into my awareness. *Fuck, fuck, fuck*, I thought. *Was that SEX?*

"Oh my God," Howard exclaimed, rolling off of me. "The rubber broke. We've got to find a doctor." He was flipping through the yellow pages of the telephone directory like some kind of Looney tunes. Is that the way men acted after SEX? "Get dressed," he commanded. "But douche first." I had never seen Howard move so fast. He was talking on the phone. "Okay, I've found a doctor who will see us," he said, pulling on his beige corduroys.

The abrupt aftermath of our lovemaking, if it could be called that, left me bleeding and more anxious and confused than ever. Where was the "moonlight and roses" feeling? In the movies, lovers were suffused in a gauzy glow as they kissed lingeringly. The camera would then pan slowly away as one's imagination continued the rhapsody of love. It was inspiring, not at all the way I had just experienced it.

The doctor sat behind a paper-littered desk and kept adjusting his rimless glasses as he played with a plaster cast of the female body and tried not to smile. "The chances of you getting pregnant from this one incident, Mrs. Groves, are virtually nil. When was your last period?"

I wasn't sure, but guessed it was seven days earlier.

"No problem, then." He thrust a plastic figure toward me, and I recoiled. "This represents the uterus."

Chagrined, I put my mind to thinking about a *Life* magazine story about Madame du Barry, a beautiful French woman. She jumped up and down with happiness and jewelry and estates when King Louis married her. But after the king died, Madame du Barry ended up having her head lopped off while screami . . .

"Mrs. Groves, are you okay?" the doctor asked. Not waiting for an answer, he tapped his pencil on a bilious-looking rosy area on the model to describe the female anatomy. A skim of fear slid through me. The memory of being burned there caused sourness to rise in my throat. I tried to deflect from the fear by focusing on the worst word I knew. *Fuck, fuck, fuck . . .* I began a repetitive mantra in my head. *Fuck, fuck, fuck . . .*

"Thank you for your time, sir," Howard was saying.

"Yes, thank you," I echoed.

"That doctor was a Jew," Howard hissed when we were outside. Seriously? He didn't look any different than anyone else to me. *I'll look closer next time*, I thought.

"Howard, what's wrong with Jews?" I asked the next day.

"Well, wifey . . ." He cleared his throat. "Jew's cheat and take our money. They're trying to take over the world. You can't trust a Jew."

"But I read that Hitler had a lot of Jews put in concentration camps and killed. That wasn't right."

"Let's not talk about things like that, Patsy. It's not good for your mind."

I wasn't so sure about that, but he was older and smarter than I was, I thought.

And Mama said I had to obey him. "Okay, h-h-husband," I stuttered and then giggled.

That day, Howard was all smiles and sweetness. "I'm real happy," he said. "Now let's go swimming, wifey." He grinned.

I put on my infamous Neiman Marcus bathing suit, wishing I could hide my long legs. Row after row of sunbathers festooned the sides of the pool, their chairs uniformly turned to catch the rays of the scorching sun. They looked like the chickens I once saw broiling in the window of a Dallas cafeteria.

"Last one in is a rotten egg," Howard said, giving me a light push toward the pool.

"I can't swim!" I shrieked.

"You can't swim?" He looked at me like I had rejected my marriage vows. "You can't swim?" he repeated, perhaps thinking he hadn't heard me correctly. "Everybody knows how to swim, Muggins."

"No, I don't know how to swim," I admitted, shamefaced.

In California, not being able to swim was tantamount to being born with two heads. Californians emerged from the womb ready to brave the Pacific Ocean. Not knowing how to swim wasn't at all unusual in Waurika. The only swimming facility we had was the Red River or Beaver Creek. Before he had gotten sick, Daddy would take his born-again converts to the river to be baptized. It was a big deal and an all-day excursion, with picnic baskets overflowing with fried chicken and jars of sweet tea. I had never heard of people, regular people, other than movie stars and queens, having swimming pools. But in the Golden State, especially in Hollywood and Palm Springs, it seemed almost everyone had a pool.

Howard and I sat together on the grass, inspecting the Desert Retreat population, aware of the heavy scent of coconut oil. Strident and unfamiliar accents sliced the warm air as drink orders were issued to white-jacketed waiters.

"Everyone's wearing dark glasses," I said, squinting in the sunlight. "Maybe they're movie stars."

"I'll buy you some tomorrow," Howard responded, laughing at my fantasy, "and you can look like a movie star, too."

A week later, I repacked my honeymoon things: the frothy nightgowns, the bathing suit, the fragile mules, and the pink rubber douche bag. It had taken me several sessions in the bathroom with the door locked to figure out the strange contraption. Poor Little Glendora had told me it was a necessary accompaniment to married life, so each time Howard and I fornicated, I would douche, letting vinegary water gush into my stinging vagina, cleansing me of the sin of sexual contamination.

We clambered into the Studebaker and headed back to the isolated Groves Ranch. Howard had given up his construction business, considering it too dirty an occupation for a married man. He would help run the ranch instead. We were to live in the pink stucco house with his parents until we could find a place of our own.

The car skimmed rapidly along the highway, taking me into my future as a wife. Checking myself out in the mirror of the visor, I couldn't help but admire the way I looked in the new white-framed, rhinestone-sprinkled sunglasses. *Okay*, I thought, *maybe this isn't such a bad situation, if he buys me sunglasses.*

Knowing that my husband enjoyed my clowning around, I began laughing and joking, pretending I was Betty Davis or Tallulah Bankhead. I acted out quotes from a book I'd picked up in Hollywood. Putting my hands on my hips and using a suggestive, husky tone, I became Mae West: "'Save a boyfriend for a rainy day—and another, in case it doesn't rain.'" Then, "'Say, boys, come up and see me sometime.'"

Howard grinned without his teeth showing and cleared his throat to speak. But I barreled on ahead before he could decide which words to use.

"'When I'm good, I'm very, very good, but when I'm bad, I'm

better.'" I hoped my come-hither voice wouldn't cause Howard to get all hot and bothered and pull into a motel. Then I would be in trouble.

"Harrumph . . . Little Okie," Howard said, "you could be an actress. Let's have some more. It helps pass the time."

A little encouragement caused me to lose perspective. "'A dame that knows the ropes isn't likely to get tied up.'"

An honest-to-goodness laugh erupted from my staid husband, encouraging me to continue.

"'I'll come and make love to you at five o'clock. If I'm late, start without me.'"

"Now, that's the way I like for you to be, Patsy," my husband responded with a grin, then cleared his throat. "My funny, sweet little girl."

Sweet? He didn't understand me at all! At that moment, I hated him for not looking below the surface of my clowning to see the fear and uncertainty there. My eighteen years and marriage had not transformed me in the magical way I had hoped for. I looked at the stranger beside me and wondered what he was feeling. Was he nervous about the future? Was he disappointed in my lack of sexual interest? It didn't occur to me to ask those questions outright. Words from the Bible that I had often heard my mother quote came floating up from the dark pool of my subconscious: *Whither thou goest, I will go; and where thou lodgest, I will lodge: thy people shall be my people, and thy God my God.*

Howard turned in quick concern. I was sobbing softly into my white lace honeymoon handkerchief, the one with the unfamiliar initials: *P. G.*

Chapter 9

Fixin' My Heart

"You've been in our family seven months now, and I think you should call me Mom," Mrs. Groves said. We had been picking flowers from her garden. Late-blooming roses, pink, red, white, and as big as pie plates, decorated the screened-in front porch and now graced the large oval dining table.

Outside, the temperature had climbed to ninety-eight degrees, but inside it was cool and comfortable. Except for the stinkbugs. They came in brown hordes, overrunning everything. They were in our beds, under the rugs, and inside cupboards. Move a sofa pillow and a whole nest of stinkbugs scurried off in a swarming scuttle of alarm. If one was crushed, the stench caused bile to rise in my throat.

"Okay, uh, uh . . . Mom." I choked on the unfamiliar word. It didn't seem right to call anyone but Mama "Mom" or "Mother."

"Get a broom and help me sweep the stinkers off the sun porch," Mom said, "but don't crush one if you can help it."

She swept from one side of the porch, and I swept from the other, gathering mounds of the squirming brown creatures before our brooms. Every spring and summer, the bugs invaded like an avenging army. Their departure was as sudden as their arrival but much more welcome. We pushed them into a dustpan, trying to ignore their vile odor as their hard little bodies wiggled, antennae waving, legs trying to gain purchase. I dumped them into a paper sack and sealed the top with a rubber band. Mom would dump it into a nearby creek on her way to work.

The stinkbug episode reminded me of the Hammers and their fly rodeo. Only that was fun, while this was no fun at all.

"I'm going now," Mom Groves announced, breaking my reverie. "Look after Gram, and be sure to get the food to the men on time." She picked

194

up the sack of stinkbugs, grabbed her big navy-blue leather purse, and left.

Mom had recently started driving the school bus and cooking in the cafeteria at the high school in Escalon, a small community about ten miles from the ranch. Gram was Grandma Huntington, who was eighty-five and lived with the Groves. Every morning, as regular as a metronome, Gram shuffled into the kitchen, looked at the cakes and pies cooling in the pantry, and said to her fifty-year-old daughter, "Ruthie, you'll be a good cook someday." Gram then put a slice of bread in the toaster, turned the dial up to dark, and proceeded to watch it burn. The smell of scorched toast was an integral part of the morning. With palsied hands, Gram ceremoniously took the cinder-like slice and scraped it over the sink, *scratch-scratch-scratch*, like a cat scratching sandpaper. The sound blended with the smoky aroma in my mind.

After I heard my mother-in-law drive away, I went to the kitchen. I leaned against the sink and gazed out the window at the brown hills in the distance. Waves of heat rippled up into a cloudless sky. Howard had left our old-fashioned walnut bed at four that morning when it was still dark outside. After eating a breakfast of ten strips of bacon, four eggs, hot rolls, pancakes, six glasses of milk, and three cups of coffee, heavy on cream, Howard and his dad, Pop, had driven off in a truck to meet the rice-harvest crew. Even after such a whopping breakfast, they would be ravenous by twelve o'clock. I had better get busy. Mom had written out a menu I was to follow:

Meat loaf

Fried chicken

Noodles

Green beans

Eggplant

Zucchini

Two loaves of homemade bread

Pat Montandon

A pound of fresh churned butter

Carrot cake (2)

Four large gallon jars of sweet iced tea

My mother had not taught me to cook. She didn't know how herself except for vegetable soup, fried chicken, sage dressing, and molasses cookies. So Mom Groves was patiently teaching me her culinary secrets.

By eleven o'clock, the high-ceilinged kitchen was a sauna. I was soaked with perspiration. I pulled my hair up into a ponytail with a rubber band from the *Stockton Record* and continued with my wifely chores.

"Need help?" Gram's thin, stooped form cast a quivering shadow on the beige linoleum.

"No, thank you, ma'am," I said, adding a stick of kindling to the ancient iron cookstove that sat in black splendor next to a modern electric one that was not to be used. "Food tastes better prepared on a wood stove," Mom had instructed.

Gram tottered over to the toaster. "They'll need bread," she said, proceeding to make her specialty.

"That's right, Grandma. Thank you." We exchanged smiles.

At last, everything was done. Each vegetable and meat had its own curved aluminum container and matching lid snapped down by double clips. Four cardboard boxes lined with newspaper held the food I had spent all morning preparing. I carried the heavy boxes one by one to the Ford truck and placed them in the bed. The effort taxed my strength. As I rested against the fender, I felt blood surge into my head.

It was five minutes until twelve; Lordy, I'd better hurry. Throwing the truck in gear, I sped along the narrow dirt road to the rice checks. The men were working in the field farthest from the house. Oh Lord, I was late again. I pressed down on the accelerator, speeding. A cloud of dust boiled straight up behind me, creating a curtain, reminding me of an Oklahoma dust storm

196

during the Depression.

The men were working on the far side of the field. Howard was driving the half-track today. He saw me and waved. The drone of the harvester engines blended monotonously with the sizzling air. Mechanical monsters spewing billows of chaff devoured everything in sight. I parked near a red oak tree and unloaded the cardboard cartons, spread newspapers on the ground, and lifted the metal containers out of the boxes. The smell of fried chicken mingled with the aroma of oak leaves.

Three harvesters and the half-track lumbered toward me, extraterrestrial warriors taking a break from the fight. The fellows climbed down from their machines and strode toward me through the stubble, kicking up puffs of rice dust on the road. Today there were only six men. Sometimes there were as many as twenty-five. The men were covered with fine rice silt, their eyes aglow with the look of fever from the ungodly heat.

"Hi, Little Okie," my husband said. I frowned. Howard seemed oblivious to my displeasure at his use of the word. He took off his sweat-stained hat and hit it against the trunk of the oak tree. Grit flew out and onto the food. A wide band of white skin showed above his hat line. My husband's face was a mask of dirt.

"You're a welcome sight." Howard sat on the ground with the others in the shade of the oak tree. "You're five minutes late, though. What held you up? We're starving."

A gap-toothed man, his skinny arms rough with sunburn, his face lean and craggy, spoke up. "We Okies are jist naturally slow as molasses in January. Ain't that right, ma'am?" His snaggle-toothed grin begged for approval.

I nodded a distant yes and poured iced tea from a large glass jar into tin cups and passed them around.

The Oklahoma fellow was one of the workers hired from the Stockton Farm Labor Bureau. I had ridden into town one day with Howard and Pop, a thin, taciturn man who enjoyed telling me he did not believe in God. They'd been looking for workers, and there was a long line of men that snaked along the side of the cement Farm Labor building and ended a full block from the office door. Some men leaned against the grim public structure, while others sat on the sidewalk, looking off into space silent, spitting, smoking, waiting.

Pop Groves's thin lips turned down at the corners as he categorized them for me. "Those bums are winos, spics, wops, dagos, and Okies," he said.

Howard had to define those definitions for me. "That's what we call the Mexicans, Italians, and derelicts. Okie is the name of someone who came here from Oklahoma during the Depression, taking jobs from real Americans. *You're* an Okie," he teased.

I pouted. "Don't call me an Okie. There are lots of good, hardworking people in Oklahoma. Educated, too."

"Don't get riled up, Muggins. We're teasing you," Howard said, trying to kiss me.

In Oklahoma, except for the black folks who lived in their own shantytown, everyone was Caucasian. They were Anglo-Saxon and Protestant, save for one Catholic family who stood out like tar on an angel's wing. "Ol' Catholics," Mama called them.

Pop continued, "They just want to work long enough to buy a bottle of Muscatel, and that'll be the end of 'em. Lazy Okies!"

I thought of my aunt and uncle living in a school bus with five kids, working to pick enough fruit to earn money to buy food and a tank of gasoline so they could get to the next job. Before the Depression, before Oklahoma became a dust bowl, my kinfolks had lived in nice white farmhouses. They brought us fresh vegetables, snap peas, carrots, and potatoes from their garden. They brought us side meat when they butchered. They had cattle and crops. They were high school educated, too, but during the Depression, there were no jobs to be had in all of the state. The land had grown tired. All that good soil that made everything grow had blown away. No rain. No crops. No jobs. No food. No carrots or potatoes, no feed for cows or pigs. No money. Just dust and then a harrowing trip on Route 66 to California, hoping the old jalopy wouldn't break down again, that there was enough money for gasoline and food to get over the border and into the promised land of California where, they were told, "All you hafta do is put a stick in the ground and it'll grow."

But in California these proud people, refugees from hunger, became slaves to rich landowners. "Okie" became the name for society's outcasts. I was told about signs that shouted OKIE GO HOME. Okies were barred from shopping in Bakersfield stores, and kids were bullied at school for being poor.

Thinking about all that history made me ashamed of my indifference to a fellow Okie. So I poured an extra glass of tea for the fellow, smiled, and told him to "take care."

The hired hands ate without conversation and so fast it seemed like this was their first meal in a coon's age. They inhaled the food like our Hoover vacuum cleaner, and paused only to replenish empty plates, wipe sweaty faces with red cotton bandanas, and then dig in again.

"You're getting to be a better cook, Patsy," my husband said as he chewed on a chicken leg, "except the meat isn't cooked through." No matter how I timed it, I never seemed to fry the chicken long enough.

"Gotta get back to work," Pop announced, standing up. The men dampened their bandanas in the leftover tea and tied them around their necks as relief from the heat.

"Bye, Little Okie." Howard gave me a peck on the cheek and patted my bottom. I prayed no one had seen. It was humiliating. Slowly, I repacked empty containers and metal plates into the grease-stained boxes and lugged them to the truck. Only twenty minutes had passed since I arrived with the feast it had taken me all morning to prepare.

Gram was asleep in her easy chair when I got home. Her soft snoring was the only sound in the house. Desultorily, I washed the dishes and then got down on my knees and scrubbed the kitchen floor. The long afternoon stretched before me like a dark tunnel.

Seven months since our wedding day, and I couldn't remember ever being so lonely. Howard had no friends, and there was no one my age in the small community of Farmington. The town had only about one hundred people in it, anyway, making Waurika seem like a metropolis. Most of the women in Farmington were older than I was, too. They kept busy raising children, cooking, and doing laundry.

"You'll have plenty to do when you have a baby," Mom had said two months after the wedding. "I'm already planning for it. Come with me." She pulled steps down from a closet ceiling and told me to follow her into the attic. "Watch where you walk," she cautioned, sidestepping a dusty rocking chair, a wooden cradle, stacks of boxes, records, baskets, an old sewing machine. Dust motes danced in the weak sunlight that filtered through a dusty window under the steep roof.

Mom Groves knelt on the floor in front of an ancient-looking brown trunk. As she opened it, the lid protested with a squeak and the odor of mothballs flew out, making my eyes water. Mom didn't seem to notice. She dug into the trunk and brought forth batiste baby dresses, booties, bibs, caps, coats, and coverlets.

"Howard was such a beautiful baby," she said. "He had the longest eyelashes I ever saw." Mom adjusted the "invisible" hairnet she wore over her short gray hair. "These are his baby things. I've kept them for my first grandchild. I hope I don't have to wait long."

Lordy, I did not want a baby—not for a while, anyway. "What else do you have in there?" I asked, changing the subject.

"Four generations of wedding dresses are in this trunk, Patsy. Four!"

"My goodness!"

Mom dove into the chest and pulled out a floor-length brown taffeta dress. She handed it to me. It felt like tissue paper.

"That was my great-great-grandmother's wedding gown. Every one of those tiny stitches was sewn by hand. Can you imagine that?"

I could not imagine that.

"They didn't have sewing machines back then. The bride of a hundred years ago had to do everything by hand; not only the sewing, but all the chores—cooking, milking, taking care of babies, if she lived through childbirth. You're lucky to have all these modern conveniences today."

"Oh my goodness, yes. Those poor women."

"Patsy, slip on that dress. The waist is small as can be, so I think it'll fit you. I'll fasten the corset top for you."

The dress fit as if it had been designed for me. The full skirt had four tiers of ruffles, and the tight bodice was made of whalebone. It looked like a picture I'd once seen in a history book of Mary Todd Lincoln. I felt like a princess as I whirled around the dusty attic, showing off the modeling turns I'd learned so long ago.

"You look beautiful," Mom said. "There are more dresses in here and old-fashioned nightgowns and all sorts of things." She reached back into the trunk and brought out the most beautiful dress I ever saw in my entire life. It was a long wedding gown made of creamy white wool. It had a high collar, a sweeping train, and fitted sleeves with tiny covered buttons marching up the arms. "That was my grandmother's wedding gown." Mom's voice was soft. "Try it on, honey."

That dress also fit. I thought about the bride of long ago, forsaking all others when she left her family, often never to see them again. She clung only to him, her husband. That passage from Ruth came often to my mind, I couldn't seem to shake it from my memory: *Whither thou goest, I will go, and where thou lodgest, I will lodge: thy people shall be my people, and thy God my God.*

I felt faint.

"Are you okay, Patsy? You look pale."

"I'm fine," I lied, "just fine."

"I have two more wedding dresses in here, along with the old-fashioned nightgowns, high button shoes, big hats, jewelry. Enough for a fashion show. I've always wished there was someone in the family who could fit into them. Edith is just too big." Edith was her only daughter. "Maybe you can use them sometime." As it turned out, I gave numerous shows at various Air Force bases with those historic garments titled "Family Album." Those shows from the prop pages of a family album traced family history by the clothing and the music of the day. They were a whopping success. But I'm getting ahead of myself.

Companionably, Mom and I refolded the historic wedding attire and fine-spun infant garments, putting them safely back in their mothball bed. But I was left with a feeling of sadness for the brides of another era—and apprehension for myself. What had I gotten myself into?

Mom Groves, a generous, capable woman, wanted desperately to become a grandmother. She made a reference to it almost every day. When I got carsick on a family outing to Yosemite, Mom beamed for a week, thinking for sure I was pregnant. Finally Howard told her he hadn't married me for breeding stock. His terminology left a lot to be desired, but at least he quieted Mom Groves.

I was lying on the living room rug daydreaming when the clatter of a truck rumbling up the road brought me to my feet. Nipper, the family's black-and-white dog, was barking his head off. The noise penetrated the thick walls of the stucco dwelling directly into my ears. Glancing at the floor-to-top-molding Grandfather clock, I saw it was almost six and getting on toward dinnertime. Nipper continued to shrilly announce the arrival of Howard and Pop, home from the rice fields. Mom was home and busy with her unending cooking chores. I had set the table hours earlier.

"Always set the table first," Mom instructed. "Even if the food isn't ready, the fellows will think it is if they see that the table is set."

Howard and Pop and Howard's younger brother, Wally, expected to eat the second they walked in the door.

Sure enough, Howard yelled out, "What's for dinner?" while letting the screen door slam-bang behind him.

"Something good, son," Mom replied.

"Hi, sweetheart." Howard was washing up at the back porch sink with a bar of abrasive gray Lava soap.

"Hope there's not a fire tonight," Pop said lifting the lids off of food simmering on the back burner of the wood stove.

"Me, too," I agreed fervently. "The one yesterday sure scared me about half to death." The grass fires of California were frightening. I had never heard of such a thing before. In the late summer the whole community was geared to fight the quick-spreading flames. Wide swaths of freshly turned soil formed firebreaks around the perimeters of dry grassland. Gunnysacks were left soaking in water troughs to be used to beat out the flames. The Groves, like most California farmers, kept a truck with a water tank always filled and ready to fight a fire. In spite of such precautions, wildfires sometimes roared out of control, destroying thousands of acres of whatever lay in its path. It seemed worse to me than the cyclones of Oklahoma and Texas. The fire the day before had been easily contained, but if the wind had been blowing, it could have been disastrous.

"Patsy, do you want to say a blessing?" Pop asked after we sat down for dinner.

I smiled and shook my head. "No, it's okay not to." It had taken a lot of getting used to, not praying before every meal.

One day in a stack of old books, I had found a copy of Emily Post's etiquette book. "Howard, listen to this," I said and began reading aloud to him. "'And yet, speak to self-made men of the need of the social graces, and nine out of ten stampede—for all the world as though it were suggested to put them in petticoats . . .'"

"Patsy, stop reading that drivel," Howard had said.

My feelings were hurt by my husband's indifference to good manners and socializing, but now at the dinner table, I practiced what Emily Post taught. My napkin was unfolded halfway on my lap. My left hand rested on my lap. The dinner knife was placed at the side of my plate with the blade toward the plate edge. Eager to be proper in all matters, I was an anomaly in the Groves family and in my birth family for sure.

"Pass the potatoes, Muggins," Howard said. The only sound was the clinking of forks against china and requests to pass the gravy or biscuits or beans. Occasionally, a loud burp escaped from someone. I stared at my plate, pretending not to have heard the rude sound.

After the supper dishes were washed and put away, we sat in the living room reading: Howard, the *Farmers' Almanac*, the only thing he ever read, and me poring over Emily Post. Bedtime was at eight, so that we could repeat the same routine the next day.

My husband was never too tired for sex. He wanted to "do it" every night, and in the morning, too. But for the life of me, I couldn't understand what the excitement was about. Howard pushing his large thing inside me and sawing away at my body made me pray for it to be over with quickly. One Sunday Howard said he wanted to talk to me about marital relations. Jesus help me! What had I done wrong? He sat me on a chair like a naughty child.

"Harrumph," he said, "Muggins, I know you aren't turned on by sex. You were a virgin when we married, so you don't know how to react. But I have a plan." He cleared his throat again, *harrumph*, looked up at the ceiling, and cleared his throat once more. Lordy, my heart pounded, and my hands were clammy. "Well, Patsy, I think I should farm you out so as to get you sexually primed."

"What? Farm me out, like a cow? What are you talking about?"

"Well, why not? I trust you, and you can learn to come. Now, wouldn't you like that?"

I expected him to laugh, but no, he was serious! "Are y'all crazy?" I said. "You think you can farm me out like livestock?"

"Calm down, Patsy, just you calm down. I'm trying to help you. I'll sacrifice myself for your pleasure. There's a fellow at the LaBaron place, a sophisticated guy. I'll bet he could turn you on."

I stared at him, wide-eyed. "Are y'all serious? How can you even think like that? I'm not a prostitute! I'm not your property, either!"

"Now, Muggins, I want you to enjoy our lovemaking . . . ."

Sobbing, I ran from the room, stumbling over the doorjamb, and headed for the creek. I slid down the muddy embankment to the cold water ahead of Howard, who was slowly following me. I took off my shoes to wade across the stream, but he caught up with me.

"Okay," he said, grabbing me. "Forget it. Just forget it. Maybe someday you'll understand that I'm thinking of you, not of me."

"Ha!" I spat in his face.

"That was disgusting, Patsy. Unforgivable."

"More than trying to make me into a prostitute?"

He looked like he hadn't given a thought as to how such a suggestion sounded. "Oh," he said. "Uh, sorry. That wasn't what I intended."

He tried to hug me, but I stalked back to the house in my muddy shoes and didn't speak to him again until I found out we were moving into our own place in Stockton. Even so, I no longer thought of Howard as my knight in shining armor. In fact, I didn't like him very much and wished I could get a divorce. But I knew I couldn't support myself, and besides, Mama would disown me for sure.

Mom and Pop Groves helped us move into our cute, minuscule one-bedroom house in Stockton. Mom stopped by once a week to bring groceries, laundry soap, and pretty dresses for me. One day she handed me a package. "Patsy, if you don't get this done, I'll never buy you anything else ever again."

What could it be? Opening the brown paper bag, I pulled out a ginormous tablecloth and twelve napkins, all neatly stamped with blue dye. "Mom, what's this blue stuff?"

"That's cross-stitch for you to embroider. And there's more," she announced, opening another bag. "When you finish that, Patsy, here's a piece of needlepoint for a chair you can work on."

"But . . . but . . . I don't know how to sew."

"It'll take you awhile, but you'll learn," she said, casually inspecting my kitchen.

~~~

My fingers and arms ached, and my eyes burned. I had been working on the needlepoint piece for a week.

"Come to bed," Howard yelled.

I pushed the thick needle in and out, in and out, pull, pull. Snip, get fresh yarn. And so it went. I did needlepoint from the first glow of dawn until I could no longer stay awake, barely stopping to eat or go to the bathroom. It had taken ten days, but now it was finished. I could hardly wait to show it to Mom.

She looked surprised. "You sure are determined. I expected that needlepoint to keep you busy for a year."

Every time I looked at the needlepoint, now on a bedside chair, I felt a twinge of pride. But I never, ever wanted to do another needlepoint anything. The tablecloth didn't interest me. I worked at it spasmodically and eventually finished it three years later.

~~~

The days stretched emptily ahead. Married life was not the end in itself I had expected. Life did not begin with that walk down the aisle. "Down the aisle and into a pan of dirty dishes," I was fond of saying. Every day I poured a tablespoonful of Dr. Miles' Nervine into a glass of water and drank it to try to calm what Howard called "nerves." Whenever the sound of a train click-clacked into my eardrums, that mournful hooting like an owl's cry called out to me. I longed to hop a boxcar and take off like a drifter, off to somewhere else, anywhere away from this godforsaken place and my boring life.

"You let your nerves rule you, Patsy. Try to be more like other girls," my husband said.

There *was* something abnormal about me. I hated ironing, mending, cooking, and sex. All day while cooking and cleaning, I listened to the radio: *Stella Dallas, Our Gal Sunday* ("Can a girl from a little mining town in Colorado find happiness as the wife of England's richest, most handsome lord?"), and the inevitable Arthur Godfrey with his Lipton tea bags.

I prayed, yes, actually prayed the way Mama prayed, down on my knees, begging God for something to relieve the deadly boredom. Our social life consisted of an occasional movie and dinner at a third-rate Chinese restaurant on Sunday night. Howard always ordered pork chow mein and sweet-and-sour spareribs that we ate without talking to each other. When we finished our meal, he would fortify himself with a handful of toothpicks from the roller dispenser near the cash register. "Gonna build?" I asked. Emily Post would not have approved of my husband.

Mama wrote brief, illegible letters reminding me of the pitfalls of the Devil, who was lying in wait behind every tree. She wrote on the backs of envelopes, wrapping paper, and the edges of newspapers. Trying to read one of her missives was tantamount to working out a crossword puzzle without the clues. Except I knew exactly what she said without even reading it. Mama always included enlightening mottoes or an article from *The Herald of Holiness*. She never signed her letters with anything other than her title, *Mama*. Forlorn, I telephoned her.

"Mama, this is Patsy."

"I know who it is. What's wrong? Why are you calling long distance?" Our conversation never lasted beyond my asking about Little

Jimmy: "He's fine." And Poor Little Glendora: "She's fine." And Mama: *Sigh.* "As well as can be expected." She never said goodbye, but always dropped the receiver back on its hook in the same abrupt way she ended her letters. Mama had long since been replaced as pastor of the Waurika Church of the Nazarene, and now survived on a small church pension and donations from her children. I hated asking Howard for the five dollars I sent to her every month, but I felt an obligation to Mama.

"I'm getting a job," I said to Howard one morning at the breakfast table.

"You think I can't support you?" His tone was a rebuke. He had a tight look around his eyes.

"It isn't that, honey. I'm bored." It would be nice to have money of my own, too. Whenever I wanted to buy something, I had to make a request and have a good reason for needing it. It made me feel as if I were back in Oklahoma on welfare. With all due credit to my husband, with his lack of understanding about my lack of a monetary education, he had opened a checking account for me when we were first married, but I'd made such a mess of it that he had closed it and forbidden me to write checks.

"What do you think *you* can do?" he asked, spearing a sausage. "Wait tables?"

"No, I'll get something good."

"Okay, if you think you can get a good job, I'll allow you to work until you get pregnant."

After we kissed goodbye and he left for the ranch, I rushed to get the dishes done. I already had a job. I had gotten it two days earlier and was due to start work that very morning. A doctor had hired me to be his receptionist and secretary, a job I was not in the least qualified for.

An actress at heart, I was ready for a starring role in this slice of my life's saga. Cast as a nurse of sorts, I knew that I needed to look the part to succeed. Since I had no money—and as a married woman I couldn't open a charge account without Howard's written permission—I forged his consent the way I had faked Mama's signature on school report cards and opened an account at a specialty store.

On my first day of work, I changed into my costume: crisp white uniform, white stockings, white shoes, and a perky starched cap. *I look like a real nurse*, I thought as I greeted patients, found their charts, and placed them in the proper sequence on the doctor's desk, with no less zeal than Florence Nightingale during the Crimean War.

One week later, the glow of my job faded in floundering ignorance. Having lied about my nonexistent secretarial abilities, I found myself face-to-face with a steno pad and Dr. Collis, my employer. He looked exasperated. "O-B-E-S-E," he spelled for the second time. "Patsy, don't you know what that means?"

"No, sir."

"Fat, it means fat! Where did you go to school?"

"Uh, Waurika, Oklahoma, sir."

"War, where? In Oklahoma? Didn't they teach spelling there?"

"No, sir, not very much, I guess."

"Let me see your notes," he said, and held his hand out for my steno pad.

It was time for me to show how good an actress I really was. Following Mama's example, I clutched my chest. "My heart," I gasped. Having told him about my potential heart condition, the ruse worked. He called his nurse, and they half-carried me into the examining room as I swooned.

"Please undress from the waist up," the doctor commanded. "My nurse will give you a gown."

I complied, hiding the shorthand notebook under my clothes. I hardly dared breathe, even though I had to cough and breathe deeply as the doctor listened to my heart. I was terrified that he would find out I was a liar and send me home or have me arrested. I could feel my heart tumbling around in my chest from the nerves Howard accused me of having.

Dr. Collis finally completed his examination and told me to get dressed and come to his office. He looked serious. "Patsy, you *do* have a heart condition," he said, as if he were surprised. "I hear a murmur, and your pulse is much faster than normal. We'll have to do some tests, but I think you have patent ductus arteriosus." He looked up at me. "They've been doing experimental surgery for such problems for almost a year now. You could be a very lucky girl."

"Surgery? I've never heard of a heart being operated on."

"It's new, and there are only a few doctors that know how to do it. Lots of patients died, but they would have, anyway." He was busily writing a prescription. "I'm giving you a prescription for digitalis. You're to take one twice a day and come back in two weeks for tests."

"Am I fired?" I asked, trying to suppress my fear.

"You need complete bed rest, so you really can't work." He stood up and dismissed me.

Numb, I collected the Hershey candy bars from my desk and got my white purse, trying to control the old familiar shakes that were beginning to take over my body. *I'm going to die. I'm going to die, and I'm only eighteen. I haven't done anything with my life yet.* My only solace was that I hadn't been arrested. Then my mind conjured up an image of my mother bent in sorrow over my untimely demise. Mentally occupied with that image, I climbed aboard a city bus to go home.

~~~

Mom Groves plumped the big white pillows at my back. She placed two at an angle and one straight across, creating a cozy nest in the old-fashioned walnut bed. For three weeks, I had been at the ranch in her efficient care.

"Now I'll get your breakfast," she said, dusting her way out of the

210

room. The digitalis prescription had worked against my body's needs, and the smallest action, even turning over in bed, caused my heart to beat in a tango of protest.

The smell of food created a nauseous reaction when Mom placed a steaming tray in front of me. "You've got to eat, honey." She spooned a dollop of butter onto a stack of pancakes that were topped by a runny egg. "Ninety-eight pounds just isn't enough for you to weigh!" she said.

Dutifully, I pushed the food around the plate, pretending to be interested.

Rain played tic-tac-toe on the metal roof of a nearby barn. A curtain of water covered the bedroom windows the way I imagined my insides looked, flooded by my inner tears. It was California's rainy season, and it had been pouring for three days. There was no accompanying roll of thunder or jagged flashes of lightning like we experienced in Oklahoma—just water, as if God and his angels were cleaning Heaven with all the faucets turned on.

Back home, we expected sandstorms and the black fury of cyclones and tornadoes to uproot houses and trees, sending us scurrying to a cellar carved from the earth in a neighbor's backyard. We would sit crowded together on wooden benches, our feet held up, watching water gush down the sides of the wooden entry. Dirt shelves around the perimeter were filled with fruit jars of peaches, corn, and tomatoes. The strongest person stood watch by the door, holding an ax to be used if an object were blown against the exit and we had to chop our way out. The damp smell of earth and waste and fear permeated the shelter. A lantern, held high to illuminate the dark recesses in case a rattlesnake lurked there, created ominous shadows that danced across the walls. I shivered.

California weather was different; the only things Californians worried about were earthquakes and out-of-control grass fires.

"Hi, sweetheart," Howard said as he came into the bedroom. He shook the rain off his coat and onto the bed. "How's my girl?"

"Fine." I forced a smile.

"We'll be taking you to the University of California hospital tomorrow." He bent his lanky frame over the bed and kissed me, showering the covers with dampness.

"I'll be glad to get it over with," I replied.

We were finally going to the UC Medical Center in San Francisco. After two weeks on digitalis, I couldn't walk without my heart flitting around in my chest like a flock of humming birds. Howard had to carry me in his arms to the doctor's office. Dr. Collis admitted me to the local hospital. I never knew there were so many medical tests: basal metabolic rate, X-ray, and so much blood was drawn that my veins collapsed or jumped away from the needle whenever a nurse approached to draw blood. It was decided that a hole between the aorta and pulmonary arteries of my heart had not closed at birth, as nature intended. My heart had to beat much faster than normal to supply enough blood to my lungs, which were shortchanged because of the defect. The digitalis slowed my heart down, making the cure seem worse than the disease. As the doctor had said, the condition was medically known as patent ductus arteriosus.

Dr. Collis stood at the foot of my hospital bed, filled with pride at his diagnosis. "You will die by the time you're twenty-five without corrective surgery," he said bluntly. "Your heart will simply wear out. Only three people in the United States are qualified to perform this particular surgery. But there are two places in the West where you can go to have it done: the University of California Medical Center in San Francisco, and Stanford."

I began to tremble. *I'm going to die*, I thought.

"The operation takes eight or nine hours. They give you curare, an Indian poison, to stop your breathing after they open you up so the beat of your heart won't interfere with the cutting. You'll need several blood transfusions, too." Dr. Collis continued with the bloody details, oblivious to the fact that he was scaring me silly.

"Which hospital do you think you would like to go to?" he asked as a nurse plunged a needle into my right buttock.

"Howard's sister is a nurse at UC, so I guess I'll go there." I tried to act casual.

While waiting for the okay to go to UC, we lived at the ranch, and I tried to forget the bloody details my former employer had supplied. But every night I awakened from a nightmare of death and got up to pace back and forth across the bedroom floor. Stopping in front of a Victorian dresser with small marble shelves jutting out on either side of a mirror, I stared at my emaciated self. Deep shadows hollowed my cheeks and eyes. *I'm already dead*, I thought.

When Mom Groves asked if I wanted someone from her Presbyterian church to come pray for me, I said no. Although my parents and church parishioners often sent solicitations swirling urgently up toward Heaven for the sick and afflicted, my thoughts were on the fate of little Tommy Sweetie.

We were living in some piddling Podunk town in Southwest Texas, a town full of tumbleweeds, barbed wire, and a picture show that I passed on my way to school, when I found out what could happen if you depend only on prayer to make you well. It was a Saturday, and I was playing cars in the dirt of my neighbor's front yard when my playmate, six-year-old Tommy Sweetie, his arm swollen to twice its usual size and radiating heat from fever, commenced vomiting up green stuff. I jumped up and scampered to the Sweeties' screen door to yell for help.

"Mrs. Sweetie," I screamed, banging on the screen, "come quick! Tommy is throwing up his insides!"

Mrs. Sweetie's skinny limbs hardly stirred the dirt as she moved faster than a lizard on a wall to reach her son, with her long red hair flying around her like a kite in the wind. "He was bit by a black widder yesterday," she shouted to Mama, who had come out to see what the problem might be. "We thought God had healed him already." She swooped up her son and

213

wiped his flushed face with her apron, then headed home, loudly beseeching the Almighty to heal her son. "Make him whole, dear Lord, make him whole, if it be thy will."

"I'll go get the doctor for you, Mrs. Sweetie," Mama yelled, her voice a combination of iron and fear.

Mrs. Sweetie came to an abrupt stop, with Tommy still clutched in her arms like a bag of flour. "Mrs. Montandon, we are holiness people. We don't believe in medicine or doctors. God will hear our prayers if it's his will that our little Tommy should live." And with that, she carried her sick offspring into their dark house, letting the screen door slam shut behind her.

Shortly afterward, members of their sect came hurrying to the Sweetie door, and immediately the air was rent by prayers entreating God to heal Tommy Sweetie.

"Those folks are speaking in tongues," Mama said, condemnation in her voice. "No telling what they're saying. Oh, poor little Tommy Sweetie." She turned to my father with something close to panic in her eyes. "Daddy, y'all better march over there with your Bible and show those folks that it's okay to get a doctor for that boy. I could tell by looking at Tommie Sweetie that he is bad sick."

Daddy tried to reason with the Sweeties, but they told him to leave. "They don't seem to realize that just because you may die if you do nothing, that doesn't mean God wants you to do nothing," he told Mama.

Two days later, my playmate, little Tommy Sweetie, died and was carried out of his house in a small white casket. His sobbing mother and father walked along behind it with his four bewildered-looking siblings.

I never forgot what I learned that day: Don't rely on prayer to heal a medical problem, unless you're a saint or an angel.

"No, thank you," I said to Mom Groves. "I believe in prayer, but I believe in good doctors, too." I smiled at her, and then said a silent prayer that God would not let me die.

Mom Groves loaned us her new Chrysler, roomier than Howard's Studebaker, for the drive to San Francisco and the UC hospital. A comfortable nest of blankets and pillows was made for me in the backseat. I curled up in the blankets for the 150-mile drive to the City by the Bay. *At least I'm not bored*, I thought as we rode along.

San Francisco captured my imagination. It was alive and romantic with bridges, fog, rain-slicked hills, cable cars, and corner flower stands. It was a magical city of dreams.

When we approached the University of California Medical Center at the top of a steep hill, I wondered what lay ahead. There had been long discussions on the phone between Howard and the administrator at UC. The operation would cost over eight thousand dollars, they said, but because it was such a rare procedure and UC was a teaching facility, I could go through the clinic as a semi-charity patient. We would only have to pay for medication and blood transfusions.

The antiseptic smell of the hospital met us halfway and then was lost in the odor of bodies cluttering the uncomfortable waiting room. Crutches leaned against walls, and wheelchairs held shrunken shells of humanity. My numbed buttocks seemed to meld into the hard wooden bench on which I sat hour after hour. Howard leaned against a pale green wall until space finally opened up for him on one of the benches.

In the unnatural silence of the wounded, I remembered a photograph in *Life* magazine of the Lourdes grotto in France where miracles occurred from drinking the water. In the picture, there were snaking lines of sick and crippled folks waiting for a sip of the health-giving water. Inhaling the fetid air of the afflicted, I began to pray. I prayed for myself, but also for a young boy whose head was heavily bandaged and who seemed very sick. Maybe we would get a miracle, like some of the people at Lourdes experienced. They had left their crutches and wheelchairs in the grotto, as proof of their healing.

Each time a name was called, everyone surged forward, only to sink back, discouraged. We had arrived at nine o'clock in the morning; a doctor finally saw me at three o'clock that afternoon. I was tired and hungry, but a shot of adrenalin coursed through me when my name was finally called.

"We'll have to hospitalize you for tests," the doctor said after checking my heart. "You'll be put through the mill, but that's the only way for us to find out what we can do for you."

"Are you going to operate?" I hoped he would say no.

"You'll be under observation for months before we make that decision," he said, handing my chart to a nurse. "We've only operated on a few patients—about five, I think—with your condition. It's a very new procedure."

Howard carried my turquoise Samsonite suitcase up to the third-floor ward and then said goodbye. He had to get back to the ranch.

"Your bed is over here," a student nurse said, indicating a curtained area. Thirty-six hand-cranked metal beds lined the open ward. Each had a rod with a short shower-like white curtain, hanging from it for privacy. Every bed except one had an occupant. Seventy eyes followed my nervous progress to the fourth place on the north side.

An overwhelming stench assailed my nostrils. "You'll get used to the smell," the nurse said. "It's Alice, in the last bed. She has ulcerative colitis." I looked in the direction indicated and saw a frail-looking young woman with long black hair. Her space was filled with plants, photographs, and assorted objects.

"How long has Alice been here?"

"About a year, I think," the nurse said. She pulled the curtains closed and gave me a faded blue hospital gown to put on. It barely covered me.

The ward was alive with action and politics, I soon learned. The old-timers knew how to get strawberry ice cream and the best blankets, which were issued from a rolling gurney every night.

"You want three?" the orderly asked. "You must have ice water in your veins."

During the long hours between tests, I became acquainted with my roommates. There was Mrs. Hernandez, an obese woman (I now knew the meaning of the word) in the eighth bed with a bright laugh and a smile. Her smile never seemed to fail despite her severe diabetes. Her children showed up at every visiting hour and at unscheduled intervals in between, bringing her forbidden cookies, flowers from the garden, and the youngest baby, sneaked in under cover of a coat casually draped over one arm. The crisp Spanish consonants and trilled *r*'s rolled back and forth around Mrs. Hernandez's bed, blanketing out other conversations.

To my left was a thin, taciturn woman with a mysterious illness. She never left her bed, never had a visitor, and never smiled. She was dubbed "The Sphinx." And of course there was Alice, who had made her home there. Her hanging pictures and domestic touches gave her cubicle an air of permanence.

We were all dissimilar, yet together made a curious family, united in the quick friendship of distress.

The hospital routine was preferable to my life in Stockton, for sure. Here, there were people to talk to, and as a patient preparing to undergo a rare surgical procedure, I rated special attention. My bed was the focal point for visiting medical celebrities, such as Dr. Blalock from Chicago, who had just perfected the "blue baby" operation, I was told. He casually pinched my toes to see how quickly they became pink again.

Groups of eight to ten interns surrounded my cubicle several times a day, listening intently as the doctor-in-residence described my symptoms: shortness of breath, palpitations, and a murmur. I closed my eyes in embarrassment at having to disrobe from the waist up with young interns looking on. Although they tried not to stare, I was aware that my bared breasts were a magnet for the fellows, especially since they were unusually plentiful

217

and plump and rosy. A cold stethoscope was pressed against my chest, and I was told to breathe deeply. In my imagination, I left the room, making a mental escape into movie star fantasyland, as I had on *Bride and Groom*. Would I be June Allyson? June was perky and cute, with an infectious smile. She usually wore gingham dresses with puffy sleeves. People said she was wholesome. No, that wasn't who I wanted to be. I liked drama and glamour. Joan Crawford was more my style. Yes, I would be Joan Crawford starring in *Mildred Pierce,* confined to my bed when I won an Oscar, Clark Gable at my side.

The naiveté and fear that kept me suspended between fantasy and reality helped me cope with what I thought would be my death. The type of heart surgery I underwent as a guinea pig of sorts is now—today in 2013— easily done by a variety of means, but in 1948, it was a yearlong and iffy ordeal.

The examinations were without end: X-ray, electrocardiogram, blood draws, fluoroscope, basal metabolism rate, and a test where I had to run up the hospital stairs as fast as I could and then quickly have my vital signs checked. It was the crude forerunner of the treadmill stress test. One day I was driven to the Laguna Honda home for the elderly to be checked on a machine called a phonocardiogram.

Finally a decision was made. "We'll operate in two months," Dr. Stevens said one day. "You can go home for now, but we'll need to check you every week."

"Goodbye," I said to my ward mates. "See you in two months, if you haven't gone home." There had been a big turnover since my arrival. Only Alice and two others remained of the original cast.

"Your mother is coming," Howard informed me on the way home. "She'll be here for your operation."

"Oh, I'm glad," I said, forgetting how Mama affected my emotions.

After being taken off of digitalis I felt stronger, but the waiting period for surgery was unnerving. "Howard, I think I'll join that little theater group I read about. Okay?"

"Well, okay, Patsy, if it makes you feel better."

I tried out for the role of Ann in *Outward Bound* and got it. Rehearsals were fun, especially since I was mentored in the role of Mrs. Clivenden-Banks by Jeanne Cooper. (Jeanne became a star in the soap opera world with a long-running role on *The Young and the Restless*.)

True to form, Mama arrived in a cloud of distrust. We unfolded the living room sofa to make a bed for her.

"Are you sure you need that operation, Patsy Lou?" she asked, as if I were sinning against the Holy Ghost.

"Yes, Mama, I'm sure."

Mother's mouth tightened, and she crossed her arms over her bosom. "Seems wrong to me," she said, "but of course I don't know anything. I'm just an old woman whose children try to tell her what to do."

"I'm going to rehearsal," I said, slamming out of the house.

"Wait, I'm coming with you," Mama declared, following me out the door.

From the center row of the empty auditorium, I could actually feel Mama's angst. I could hardly say my lines.

I looked up at the pimply-faced boy playing my love interest. "You see, I love you. I love you so much. I love the way you walk . . . " I whispered to the actor.

"More feeling!" the director shouted. "Patsy, you are *supposed* to be in *love!*"

"I love you. I love your mouth," I purred, as we stiffly embraced to kiss. The sound of wooden seats clattering against chair backs shattered the scene. I peered beyond the footlights and saw Mama thundering up the aisle, muttering as she went.

I jumped off the stage and ran after her. "What's the matter?" I asked.

Mama stumbled across an imaginary platform. "I've hurt myself," she said accusingly, as if I had pushed her. "The very idea of kissing a boy that way. You're going to Hell in a handbasket and wrecking your marriage on the way."

"Mama, Howard knows I'm doing this play."

"Your daddy would turn over in his grave to see such goings-on. 'Rear a child up in the way they should go, and when they are old, they will not depart therefrom,'" she quoted. "I'll be glad when you get old."

We reached the car, and Mama got inside, slamming the door behind her. Reluctantly, I got in beside her, waved an embarrassed goodbye to the startled cast, and left.

"I'll probably not live to be old," I grumbled.

"Well, it's your own fault if you die. Your daddy said I would have to bear the burden alone."

My mother's attitude toward me was demoralizing. I was more disabled by her constant low opinion of me than by my heart problem.

"Howard, will you please ask Mama to leave," I begged. I didn't have the courage to do it myself.

"Okay, honey," he said. He was trying to make up to me for wanting to farm me out, but I had trouble forgetting it. Now I needed him in ways I never expected to.

Two days later, Mama went to stay with her sister in Brentwood.

My feelings toward Mama were ambivalent. I desperately wanted to please her and to gain her love and admiration. Conversely, I disliked her intensely and grieved because I missed having a warm family relationship. From my childhood on, Mama had inculcated in me a deep sense of guilt for any action that was contrary to her wishes.

"'Honor thy father and mother, that thy days may be long on the earth,'" she often recited. Would God abandon me in my time of need because I asked Mama to leave my home, I wondered?

My favorite sister, Faye, arrived on the Greyhound bus from Oklahoma with my nine-year-old niece, Linda, and Little Jimmy. I was touched that she cared enough about me to bring two rambunctious kids on a hard three-day trip across America. *They're gathering for my final hours*, I thought.

Mom Groves was gently reassuring when she hugged me goodbye. "You're going to be fine, Patsy."

Would God punish me for dishonoring my parent? And would God let me survive the operation I had decided to risk? I was so afraid I would die that I closed my eyes when we drove past cemeteries, and I battled "the shakes" almost every night.

My operation was to be in seven days. Dr. Brodie Stephens, my surgeon, kept a chart of heart surgery patients prominently displayed on a wall in his office. It had a horrifying attraction for me. I noted the names that had been scored through, the ones who had died, and I always looked for my own, as if to reassure myself that I was still alive.

"I don't care if I die," I blurted out to him two days before "O" day. It was an attempt to be consoled and reassured.

"Why not?" He seemed alarmed.

"There's nothing to live for."

"We'll delay your surgery for a while," Dr. Stephens said. He patted me on the shoulder. "We'll have you talk to a psychiatrist at Langley Porter." He was referring, I learned later, to the Neuropsychiatric Institute that was part of the UC Complex.

~~~

The psychiatrist sat comfortably behind his scarred brown desk while I sat rigidly opposite him. His paunch stretched his white doctor's jacket snugly across his overgrown midsection. I expected a button to pop off and zing across the room any second.

"So you are one of eight children," he murmured, breaking a long silence. "Do you think you were planned?" Was he trying to make a joke? Was he serious? What did that have to do with anything?

"Sure," I answered sarcastically. "My parents needed another mouth to feed."

"How do you feel about your mother?" He had asked that several times during the past three appointments. The question always made me perspire.

"My goodness," I said, trying to appear unconcerned. "Everyone loves their mother." I couldn't possibly tell him I hated Mama. If I admitted such a thing, a bolt of lightning would suddenly come out of the clear California sky to find me and, without so much as a warning, strike me deader than a doornail.

"Did you bring me a dream?"

"Yes, sir. I've been writing them down the way you told me to."

"Let's hear it," he said, lighting a Camel cigarette.

"Well, I dreamed I was with a group of friends in Waurika, the town where I lived in Oklahoma. We were having fun, you know, laughing and eating French fries and all. Mother suddenly appears, and she's really mad at me. The next thing I know, I'm standing in the center of a round table, and Mama's shouting and pointing her finger up at me and telling everyone what a bad person I am, a sinner . . ." My throat tightened. I fought back tears.

"It's okay to cry," the doctor said, handing me a box of tissues.

Permission was all I needed. Tears burst forth from a reservoir inside of me as if Hoover Dam had broken wide open and formed a vast new lake. I swam toward a far-off shore, crying so prodigiously that the body of water grew ever larger and the shore farther away with each stroke of my flailing arms. My tears turned to hiccups, and I lay down on the floor of the doctor's ugly office, hiccupping and sobbing for over an hour.

"You must keep Patsy's mother away from her," the psychiatrist told Howard. The man was a genius—what insight!

The days became a countdown: five . . . four . . . three . . .

A new patient came to the ward. She was a frail-looking brunette, about my age, I thought. She was given the bed next to mine, and like prisoners meeting in jail, we began to talk.

"What are you in for?" I asked.

"Tests," she replied. "And you?"

"Heart surgery." I felt infinitely superior to "tests."

Her name was Debbie. We quickly became friends in that encapsulated space of time. Debbie's home was near Fremont, California. She was engaged to marry her high school sweetheart in the spring. He came to visit her, bringing boxes of chocolate-covered orange sticks.

The long days shortened. I was to "face the knife" the next morning. I lay awake, staring holes in the ceiling. "Oh God," I prayed in a reversal of my previous attitude, "please don't let me die. I promise I'll never do a bad thing again—just let me live."

Debbie leaned over the side rail of her bed. "I'll be praying for you," she said. There was caring in her voice, and a sympathy that reached through my loneliness and braved me for the morning ahead. But the fear still lingered deep inside me. I was scared—scared—scared.

Daylight arrived in a haze of shots and pills: "To make you drowsy, Patsy." White balloon-like leggings were slipped on me. "Please remove your ring, and take all the bobby pins out of your hair." A white cap covered my head, and in a state of grogginess, I signed a form of permission for surgery.

I was wheeled out of the room on a gurney, past a distorted mirage of shapes and soft goodbyes from beds far, far away. I tried to reply, but only slurred sounds came forth. A cluster of people bunched around the gurney at the end of the hallway. Dimly, I recognized Howard, his mother, and my sister Faye. The question I tried to form was but a drunken slur. "Tooo early . . . :early tooo morning." Kisses, the dampness of tears—mine or theirs? I didn't know.

There was an enormous white light overhead, and then a shot of sodium pentothal . . .

There stood Daddy and Dead Bette Ruth, both shining like silver in the light that shone down on me. I tried to reach out, "Daddy, how did you and Dead Bettie Ruth get here?" They embraced me tightly across my chest . . .

Someone pressed on my stomach. "What are you doing?" I whispered. "Where's Daddy?"

A disembodied voice said, "You're pregnant."

"I'd better not be," I muttered, my rusty throat throbbing.

Ten hours after they took me to the operating theatre, I was wheeled to a private room. I was under an oxygen tent. Shots of morphine, intravenous feedings, blood transfusions, and mumbled prayers passed in a blur of delirium. My left arm was paralyzed. The nerves connecting my vocal cords were pulled during surgery, and I could only speak in a whisper.

"The Lord is my Shepherd, I shall not want."

Through the cellophane of the oxygen tent, I saw Debbie. She had come to my newly assigned private room, which was still in the line of sight of my old friends.

"I'm to switch the lights on and off if you're okay," Debbie said as she flicked the lights. "They're all waiting to see. I'll go now." She squeezed my hand.

Dr. Stevens checked on me several times a day. He was warm and sympathetic. He regaled me with football stories, having played for Cal during his college days. He had caught the longest pass in football history. His real interest in me, and his unflappable attitude, helped stem the shivers of panic I would feel as the nerves in my chest and arm began to heal.

When the mummy-like dressings were changed, I was surprised to find out the incision had been made across my back, not on my chest. The seventeen-inch scar curved from the nape of my neck to the bottom of my ribs—one of which had been cut and rejoined with a permanent silver wire. Periodically, a hollow needle would be inserted through my back to draw fluid from my lungs. "We don't want you to drown," the doctor said as liquid from my lungs gurgled into a container.

Debbie visited me every day. Her tests had determined that she, too, had a heart condition and needed immediate surgery.

"It's my turn to pray for you," I whispered.

"I'm not afraid," she said. "If you can make it, so can I."

"Just the same, I'll say a prayer."

Fourteen hours passed, and Debbie hadn't returned from surgery. I kept pushing the nurse call button to inquire about her. They weren't even answering.

Although I was walking some every day, I was still weak. I climbed slowly out of bed, pulled a robe over my useless left arm, and shuffled down the corridor. I opened the door to Debbie's room and peered inside. A weeping man and woman leaned over a still form lying in a tangle of tubes.

A nurse standing in the shadows told me to go back to bed. Debbie had not survived the surgery, she said.

I ran back down the hall to my room as fast as my condition allowed. I fell into bed, covered my head with a pillow, and cried until I had no tears left.

Chapter 10

Suffocation

My friend's death made me question God and the biblical teachings I had been subjected to throughout my childhood. *What's life about?* I asked myself. Why was I put on earth? Surely not to cook, wash dishes, do laundry, and cater to a man. *If there even is a God*, I wondered deep in the hidden part of my brain, down where curse words went and all my true feelings were stored—my wishes and dreams and desires. *God, if you exist*, I asked, *why do you allow cruel defects such as the ones I've seen in hospitalized children? Why the grinding poverty so many of us experience?* By questioning the Almighty, I imagined Christians in Daddy's church rising up to condemn me. "Oh ye of little faith," they intoned, "you are doomed to the pit of Hades forever."

Was I doomed? I quickly recanted my conversation with God, hoping to avoid Hades.

And what about my dreams of making something of myself? Were those dreams to be thrown on the ash heap of my life and amount to nothing at all? And did they matter?

~~~

Two weeks later, it was time to leave the comfort of the UC hospital—and also the comfort of being cared for and appreciated by friends. I packed my nightgowns and various bits of debris. I was going home, back to Stockton, boredom, and SEX. My arm was still partially paralyzed, but my voice had mostly returned.

But it was my mind I worried about. I couldn't control my thoughts—thoughts of burning in Hell and thoughts of SEX. *Fuck, fuck, fuck . . .*

When my husband came to get me, I was still shaky and weak, so he helped me navigate the steep hill overlooking San Francisco where the Chrysler was parked. We headed out of the beautiful city that was air-conditioned by God and into the devilish heat of the San Joaquin Valley. Before we even crossed the Bay Bridge, I missed the hospital and the kindness I had experienced there.

I made trips to the UC hospital every three weeks for checkups, even though the nerve had reconnected in my arm and I was fully recovered. The journey to the city was the highlight of my existence. Boarding a Greyhound bus to San Francisco, I immediately transformed into a white-gloved city dweller. In my mind, I became one of the sophisticated society people I read about in the *San Francisco Examiner*. On the ranch with Howard, my life felt like a dead end. These trips to San Francisco breathed new life into me.

After one of these outings, I got an idea of how I could go to the city more often. Nervously, I approached my stern husband with a daring pitch. Howard liked it when I was funny, so I went all out to get him to laugh at my zany antics. After he was in a jolly mood, I seduced him with a steak dinner and then aroused him sexually—which was not difficult—by prancing around in a filmy black nightie while singing "Put the blame on Mame, boys . . ." He quickly threw me onto the bed, just as quickly did his business, and rolled over, ready to snooze.

No way. I had a plan. "Sweetheart," I implored, "don't go to sleep yet." I nudged him awake. "I've figured out how I can repay you and your parents for what y'all spent for my operation."

"Yeah, how's that, Muggins?" He yawned. Having gotten what he wanted, he now wanted sleep. I had to act fast. "Muggins," he said, yawing widely, "tonight you acted the way I want you to be all the time, funny and sexy."

"Okay, but will y'all please listen to me?" I blurted out my idea before he could nod off again. "Market Week begins in San Francisco tomorrow. They need models. I could make twenty-five dollars a day for two weeks!"

"Yeah? Market Week? That sounds like a made-up story. Since when does a week turn into fourteen days?"

I was pushing for extra days, but had hoped Howard wouldn't notice. "Wholesalers show their clothing line to store buyers during Market Week. I need to be there to get settled and get bookings before the local models swoop up all the good deals. Since I have to go to UC anyway, a few more days shouldn't matter. Please, honey." A prisoner pleading for her life could not have been more passionate.

"Go to sleep," he said. "Turn out the light."

Could I appeal to my husband's substantial ego? He often said he wanted to leave the ranch and get a white-collar job. He had once tried to sell life insurance but wasn't able to memorize the spiel and was fired before he got started.

I prodded him again. "Are you awake?"

He opened his eyes and tried to focus on my face.

"Darling, think. If I'm a good model. You can become my manager!"

He was suddenly awake and grinning. "Harrumph. Where would you stay?"

"At the YWCA. It's right downtown and doesn't cost much. I've got to do something with myself, Howard. I feel so useless. I might as well be a pet cat."

"Pop says you're like his aunt Millie. She ran away from her husband, and he lost his mind. Ended up in the Napa Mental Hospital. Pop and I visited him once. All he did was wring his hands and talk about Millie. Said he would put a gun to her head and kill her if he ever got out of the asylum."

I shivered. Was that a threat? "Well, I hope he never gets out!"

"He died there."

I leaned across the rumpled sheets and kissed my husband. "I would never, ever run off from y'all."

"You had better not. When you say y'all, I kinda believe you. But I know you haven't adjusted to married life yet, so I worry."

I looked down at the faded blue carpet, noting the worn spots, not knowing what to say. I hoped he wasn't going to suggest farming me out again. If he did, I would get up off the bed, pack my clothes, and walk out the door so fast I would be a blur.

"Mr. Howard Chandler Groves, I want to be more than a cook and cleaner. I'll end up in Napa myself if I don't have something interesting to do. Let me go to San Francisco to model!"

He sighed. "Okay! But only for two weeks. Got it, sister?" My spouse cleared his throat, turned away from me, and was soon snoring.

I got out of bed and crept around the room, packing a suitcase so I could get out of there the next day on the first Greyhound bus to San Francisco.

~~~

The small room I shared at the Y with a girl visiting the city from Indiana was a haven to me. My first morning there, I dressed carefully in a Macy's copy of Christian Dior's New Look, a black crinkle nylon dress and black suede opera pumps, and topped it off with a huge straw cartwheel hat I wore flat on my head like an oversized pancake. Standing on a chair in order to see the lower part of my body in the splotched dresser mirror, I did a slow turn. *I look snazzy,* I thought, pulling on elbow-length black gloves to complete my ensemble. Sashaying down windy Post Street to the House of Charm modeling agency with one hand on the crown of my hat to keep it from blowing away, I felt the thrill of belonging to the exciting city.

"Have you ever modeled professionally?" asked a chic blonde behind an enormous black desk. "I'm not talking about small-town events at your bridge club, but professionally." The woman hardly looked at me, discounting me before I got a chance to say anything.

Suddenly feeling gawky and uncomfortable, I perched on a small love seat upholstered in leopard print, my body positioned at an angle and my legs crossed at the ankles in approved model pose. "Yes, ma'am," I mumbled, intimidated. "I modeled for Neiman Marcus in Dallas, Texas." I tilted my head back in order to see her face from under the brim of my overwhelming chapeau.

The woman arched finely penciled eyebrows over her awning of false eyelashes into an expression of skepticism. "Neiman Marcus? Really? Well, then, you'll have no trouble walking for me, will you? Do a pivot, too," she added, turning to the more pressing chore of filing her long scarlet fingernails. *Rasp, rasp.* The sound challenged my frayed nerves. She glanced up at me.

Nervously, I walked to the end of a cream-colored carpet, accompanied by the sound of her nail file. Would I fall and twist my ankle the way I had when I was learning to do a pivot? My knees shook.

"Got a problem?" the woman asked.

"No, ma'am." I took a deep breath. "I just need to recollect myself. It's been awhile." My mental gears turned with a noise that seemed louder than the blonde's nail file as I shook the rust off my memory. After a fast mental rehearsal, I began to walk toward the blonde. As I glided across the carpet, my toe caught in a loop, but I regained my balance before Miss Blondie noticed. I subtly indicated the pocket on my dress and executed a smooth pivot. Success! But if I expected applause, well let me tell y'all, I was sure let down.

"Okay, sweetie. Is that it?"

"Yes, ma'am."

"That's better than I thought you would do. You need practice. Where's your portfolio?"

"Portfolio? Oh, you mean pictures. Well, ma'am, I'm getting pictures shot next week," I fibbed.

"Please don't call me ma'am. I'm not one hundred." She smiled, revealing tiny Rat-Dog teeth. "Here's the name of a photographer." She handed me a card. "We don't want amateurish stuff. We want pictures like the ones hanging on our walls."

How could I not have seen the large black-and-white pictures? They were huge. The models looked like movie stars. *Lordy*, I thought, my heart sinking to my throbbing feet, *I could never look like that.*

She must have read my mind. "Don't for one minute think the girls in those photos look that way in person. Hell no, far from it. It's lighting and makeup that makes the difference, that and knowing how to pose. On the street, you wouldn't look at those girls twice, but the camera loves them." She dropped her nail file into a drawer and blew the fine nail dust off her desk. She rummaged around in a file cabinet, found some forms, and handed them to me. "Fill these out, and you will officially be a House of Charm model."

My resolve to appear detached and sophisticated collapsed. "Hooray," I half-shouted, catching myself just in time. I was now a House of Charm model! The blonde gave me a nice Rat-Dog grin. I hope y'all agree that that was applause enough!

"We get ten percent of what you earn," Blondie said after I signed the papers. "I have a go-see for you right now. A Lilli Ann rep needs a size six. He's showing in Room 12B at the Fairmont Hotel." She handed me two introduction forms. "If you're hired, you'll be paid twenty-five dollars a day, but the money comes through the agency. Okay? Tomorrow you'll go on audition for a new wine gig, Joanne wine. Can you imagine a wine named Joanne?"

"No, ma—uh, no."

"Wear flats so you can negotiate the steep hills and carry your high heels in a model's hatbox with your makeup. Never drink with a client. Always be on time. Time is money, and that's the name of the game. Welcome to our agency. Good luck."

An hour later, I was happily modeling the elaborate wool suits and coats in the Lilli Ann showroom.

"That was fine, baby," the salesman said at the end of the day. He eased himself into a chair and slipped off his shoes. "I'll send your check to the agency." He poured himself a shot of whiskey from a bottle on the dresser. "Wanna little nip before you go?"

"No, thanks. Don't you need me anymore?"

"Not this week, but I heard the other girls talking about trying out for a job at Elizabeth Arden's. You might try there."

"Well, thanks again," I said, pinning my hat in place.

The next morning, I auditioned for an advertising company that was touting Joanne wine. I was thrilled to be chosen to be red wine, and a blonde was to represent white wine. We were taken to the Mark Hopkins Hotel. When we walked into the lobby—well, let me tell you, I very nearly fell over. The ritzy establishment was like something out of a movie. My mouth actually fell open, and my neck hurt from looking up at everything. Marilyn, the blond model, and I were whisked up in an elevator that made my eardrums pop, and we were taken straight into a conference room with floor-to-ceiling windows swathed in white drapes. When the "draperies" abruptly parted and the sun shone in, I realized that what I had mistaken for window coverings was instead thick fog.

A quartet sang about Joanne wine:

"Put Joanne to your lips
It's love at first sip
I'm that way, that way about Joanne."

Meanwhile, Marilyn and I poured glasses of wine, me the red, Blondie the white, and passed them around to dark-suited men at a long table.

Mama would have had a pure *D* fit if she thought I went anywhere near the Devil's brew of any color, much less that I poured men wine. It wasn't the kind of modeling I thought I was going for, but Lordy, I got paid big money for one hour of pouring, smiling, grinning, and evading pinches from a guy with painted-on black hair.

On my way out, I stood in the lobby of the Mark Hopkins, gawking at the red velvet upholstered furniture and marble floors and gilt-edged doors and enormous paintings of what looked like a queen, before I headed down the hill to Elizabeth Arden's. Outside, I stepped into swirling cold fog. Shivering, I half slid and half walked down Mason Street, the steepest street imaginable. It was vertical! I kid you not. Finally, I took my shoes off so my Oklahoma toes could get a grip, or I feared I would end up in the bay.

After putting my shoes back on over dirty hose, I pushed open the red-lacquered door of Elizabeth Arden's elegant new Sutter Street salon. The heady fragrances of jasmine, lavender, and orange rushed out to greet me. It was the aroma of their signature Blue Grass perfume, I soon learned.

The black-haired manager was dressed in an elegant black crepe dress that skimmed lightly over her slender body. Her voice was like Katherine Hepburn's in the movie *Adam's Rib*. She was fashion royalty, and I was mesmerized, eager to do her bidding.

"Please take off that ridiculous chapeau, dear," she ordered in a genteel tone. I quickly removed the offending article and tried to hide it behind my back. "There now, isn't that better? A smaller hat is more appropriate for day, except at the races, of course. The style rule at Arden's is less is more, dear."

I nodded, grasping the need to keep my Oklahoma mouth shut.

"You're very pretty," she said, holding my face in her hands and examining me as if with a microscope. "We are just opening the salon"—she pronounced it *say-lon*—"and we need a model with a fresh, open look. If your hair is styled and your makeup changed, you might do. Come—let's find out. Miss Arden arrives tomorrow, and we need to be ready."

She led me into a sweet-smelling, pink-walled cubicle where a pink-uniformed attendant waited behind a rosy chair. The luxury of face cream and gentle fingers lulled me into an unfamiliar feeling of extravagance. After that, silky makeup base was applied to my face, and my eyes were outlined with

233

black liner and mascara, making them look enormous. Soft tones of rouge and lipstick were finishing touches.

"Yes, you'll do," the woman said, inspecting my new face, "as soon as we change your hair color. Mr. Craig, please take charge of our model," she said to a thin young man brandishing scissors.

"You'll look good as a blonde," said Mr. Craig, combing a thick white paste through my hair. The sting and stench of peroxide battered my nostrils.

"I sure do hope so," I breathed, panic-stricken. *Howard will kill me*, I thought.

Hours later, I stared at my unfamiliar reflection, trying to absorb the shock. Short golden ringlets replaced my long auburn locks. Understated makeup enhanced my complexion. I was dressed in a magnificent lavender silk taffeta ball gown made by Castillo—a name I was at a loss to pronounce. Crystal earrings sparkled from my earlobes but were quickly replaced when Miss Arden arrived. She said I needed the real thing, not crystal, and took her own diamond and gold earrings off and clipped them on my ears.

"You're in the rarefied world of haute couture," she said, smiling at me. "Wear the real thing or nothing."

All week I modeled throughout the "say-lon" in a cloud of incredulity, while being photographed for *Harper's Bazaar* magazine and the local press. Society women shopped for opera gowns and got massages and facials and their hair curled and cut and piled on top of their head in the pink-and-white salon. Maids in black with frilly white aprons brought trays of sandwiches cut into tiny triangles with the crusts removed, and tall, frosty glasses of iced tea with wedges of lime for women under the hot hair dryers. I was not only learning about haute couture, but also a different way of being in the world. As the days floated by in the luxurious atmosphere, I was lulled into a false sense of security and promise.

"Why, I feel just like Scarlett O'Hara or Cinderella," I told Mr. Craig.

The second week of my big San Francisco fashion adventure, I was on Arden's main floor modeling a ball gown when I heard the familiar "harrumph." Oh my God in Heaven, it was Howard Groves. My husband stood on the edge of the room looking ungainly and out of place among delicate Louis XIII furniture and soft pink walls.

Spotting me, he glared at my golden curls. "What have you done to yourself? You look terrible."

"I'll change my dress, and we can go talk at the coffee shop up the street," I said, trying to buy time. "I'll meet you there." The scene with Mama at Neiman Marcus flashed through my mind. Nervously, I changed into my own clothes.

"I'm taking you home," he said when I met him at the coffee shop diner. "You look ugly. You're my wife, and you need to get your feet back under yourself."

"I won't go with you, Howard," I said as I slumped over my Coke. "I have three days before the Arden job is over."

"Patsy," he pleaded, "you made a vow to obey me." He cleared his throat, the annoying sound that accompanied his speech. "My family spent a lot of money to make you well, and I won't have people thinking we're separated. You're coming home." He plunked down a dime to pay for our drinks and pulled me to my feet. "Let's go."

He *had* been thoughtful and sweet to me when I had heart surgery and when we were first married, too. So he did have that in him. I wondered what I had done or not done to turn him into the bully he was now. It must be about sex, although I never refused him and tried to be loving and receptive to him even when I was in pain.

The long, hot drive to the San Joaquin Valley and away from the cool, romantic city of hills broke my heart. I sobbed quietly all the way.

"Soon now, it will be time for a baby," Howard said, reaching across the seat to pat my leg. Lord have mercy, I didn't want to have a baby. I was only twenty-two; I had plenty of time to make a family.

Inside of me was a searing desire to make something of myself. I checked books out of the library and studied constantly—reading, learning, observing, working hard to educate myself. I listened to radio announcers to emulate the way they pronounced words. I stopped saying "y'all" and "cain't" and "jist."

My dreams of being more than a housewife seemed a betrayal to womanhood, to God, and to my husband. Many times, I had listened to preachers stand behind the pulpit and bellow about a wife's place in marriage: "Wives, submit to your husbands as to the Lord. For the husband is the head of the wife as Christ is the head of the church, his body, of which he is the Savior. Now as the church submits to Christ, so also wives should submit to their husbands in everything." How unfair! Thinking about that Bible verse gave me a roaring sick headache.

The scorching heat inside the Studebaker did little to refresh my dejected spirit. Stretching before me were endless days of cooking, mending, and eating chow mein every Sunday.

Melancholy merged with a sense of doom, becoming my constant companion. Depression overwhelmed me. A routine trip to the grocery store caused sweaty palms and shaky knees and a feeling of suffocation. Fear became the dominating feature of my landscape. Was I losing my mind?

Inside my head, like a movie on an endless loop, the piercing screams of Brother Webber shouting out the forbidden word "fuck" in Daddy's church played over and over. The crazy old man had ended up in an insane asylum. Lost his mind, people said.

What would happen if I yelled, "*Fuck!*" as loud as I could with Howard and Mom standing beside me at the Farmington General Store? That would get attention. Why, I'd be whisked off to the loony bin so fast you would never know I had existed. *Fuck, fuck, fuck.* The forbidden word repeated itself in my mind like a blinking neon sign. Could people read my thoughts? Had I said *fuck* out loud without hearing myself? Would I go to Hell for thinking the word *fuck*? *Fuck, fuck, fuck*!

Sister Ruth, my Sunday school teacher when I was six, popped into my consciousness. Sister Ruth usually had a faraway look in her eyes, and people said her husband had up and left her when she was pregnant. Just like that. Afterward, she sat in a field weaving wildflowers between her toes and singing to herself until her folks hauled her off to the state insane asylum at Norman, Oklahoma. She came home after her baby was born, but she would disappear again, and we knew she was back at Norman.

Was I like Sister Ruth? Was I going mad? Would I be sent to an insane asylum? *Fuck, fuck, fuck, fuck*! Suddenly a trembling sensation stirred inside of me, and the shakes moved in, just as they did when Daddy died. I could hardly walk, my legs felt like rubber bands, and my vision blurred.

Finally, with my heart beating in overtime, I summoned the courage to confide in Howard. We were in our cramped bedroom getting ready for sleep. "Howard," I said, not daring to look at him, "I'm . . . I'm . . . having a hard time. I'm shaking, and I can't see well, and . . . uh, I'm afraid . . . afraid I'm going crazy." It was as if sharp-edged boulders had erupted from my mouth, and now my lips and tongue hung in ribbons of flesh.

"What did you say?" Howard questioned. His intense look frightened me. "What did you say?"

"I'm afraid I'm losing my mind."

"Speak up if you want to be heard! That's not usually hard for you."

"Oh, Howard, I'm scared that I may be losing my mind."

"Well, I'm not surprised." He turned away from me. "You and your high-flown ideas. They are bound to disturb your mind."

That was it. No catastrophic appearance of angels with raised swords had swooped in when I revealed my innermost secret. *Fuck, fuck, fuck*. How I hated that man. He offered me nothing—not kindness or understanding or compassion or love, just confirmation that I was on the brink of insanity. Was this the reality of married life? A husband was the head, forever in charge of his wife, and there was nothing she could do about it? When Poor Little Glendora married Edgar Woods, Daddy said she had made her bed and now she had to lie in it. But Poor Little Glendora had gotten an annulment. When I asked how that had happened, she said they hadn't consummated the marriage. Okay, so much for that.

Howard's response to my need created within me a fracture, a black hole I crawled inside of and from which I wanted never to emerge. I tried to help myself by swallowing spoonfuls of Dr. Miles' Nervine, but still I shook. My life force was drawn into that dark hole, leaving me without the desire to do anything: chow mein on Sundays, shopping, or indulging my husband in his idea of lovemaking. Unspooling from my brain, an endless stream of profanity gushed silently forth in words I didn't recognize. *Fuck, fuck, fuck.*

Six months went by. I lost weight. My usual luxuriant, shiny hair became stringy. I didn't care about anyone or anything. My life was over. *Fuck, fuck, fuck . . .*

Chapter 11

Selma, Alabama

Suddenly, just like that, things changed. The letter. It was *the letter* that changed tracks and shunted us off in a new direction: an official letter recalling Howard to the Air Force, for what he always described as the "Korean Conflict" and an automatic promotion from first lieutenant to captain. For me it brought relief from self-destruction and distracted me from my thoughts and overwhelming fears—fears that were leading me inexorably toward ending my life.

Adrenalin began pumping through my veins once again. All was hasty preparation—deciding what to take and what to leave behind, sorting out Howard's kit and uniforms, packing, settling up our home, saying our farewells, sending letters to distant family.

Of course, Mama had to be told. "You're going into a den of iniquity," she said when I called her with the news. But Mama couldn't sustain interest in my affairs for long, because Granddad Taylor had gotten married. He was ninety-four, and although ailing, was by no means senile. His new wife was seventy. Mama's self-righteous wrath was directed toward Grandpa. "The very idea of a sick old man like that getting married! She just wants his money." As usual, Mama's tone had the bite and finality of a hanging judge.

"What money?" I asked sarcastically. "It seems to me she's taken on the care of a frail old man."

In the face of my contradiction, Mama froze up like a rooster tail in an ice storm. She was also fretting over the remote possibility of school integration. "That awful Brown versus the Board of Education bill is contrary to the laws of God," Mama said. "It's against his law for races to mingle! I will never let Little Jimmy go to school with a nigger. And I don't think anyone else in the United States of America will allow it, either, certainly not your brothers and sisters. We're a God-fearing country."

I was so outraged I could hardly speak. "And you profess to be a Christian? Daddy preached equality, and you know it. Narrow-minded people calling themselves Christians give me a royal bellyache. And furthermore, Mama, why should God be feared? Is he a dictator? How can y'all—" The receiver banged down in my ear.

Lordy, I sure let Mama get under my skin. I was shaking. It took me awhile to cool down, but I felt better for having had my say. I was sick and tired of Mama and sanctimonious churchgoers acting all sweet and mealy-mouthed and then practicing hate. Where did they get off doing that?

When I told Howard I believed in the rightness of integration, he laughed, saying it would never happen and suggesting that I save my energy for important issues such as packing up our stuff.

The next day, I felt better. Speculating on my future as the wife of an Air Force officer sent my mind soaring into the wild blue yonder.

Howard was ordered first to Palm Beach, Florida, for two months and then to Selma, Alabama's Craig Field for training. In Palm Beach, I sweated in the high humidity and strolled Worth Avenue gawking at the fashion-filled windows. On a whim I applied for a modeling job at Saks Fifth Avenue and became their house model for the summer.

When folks named Kennedy came into the store, the manager flustered around like a setting hen when her eggs are threatened. "These people are Big Time in Washington. John is in Congress," he whispered, his smile tight. "Help them in any way you can. The older woman is Rose, the mother. She's a buyer, not a shopper."

Engaging the sons in small talk was easy, but I soon realized they were comfortable lounging in the gown salon's overstuffed chairs, contrary to most men whose women folks shopped there, and preferred teasing each other instead of talking to me. Let me tell y'all right now, those fellows were good-looking as all get out, with thick, wavy hair, twinkling eyes, and an air of confidence and good humor. Little did I know that in 1960, one of those boys would become president of the United States of America.

When Oleg Cassini, the famous designer for Jacqueline Bouvier, waltzed into the store, took me in his arms, and swirled me across the floor to piped-in music, I knew I was no longer in Waurika.

Howard was happy to have me occupied, since he was focused on learning to fly Military Air Transport planes. He didn't mind a bit when Mr. Lewisohn, an elderly gentleman for whom New York's Lewisohn Stadium was named, invited me to have dinner with him and a friend at the tony Palm Beach Patio Club. There was such a change in my husband that it crossed my mind he might be having an affair, but I quickly dismissed the idea. Not Howard. The manager of Saks said that Adolph Lewisohn was a lovely man, a financier and philanthropist who wanted to show me off as his arm piece for the evening, which proved to be the case. Mercy, I was learning a lot about how some parts of the world worked. Mr. Lewisohn sent a limousine to collect me at our apartment in West Palm Beach and to swish me home after dinner.

Alas, the hubbub and glamour of Palm Beach ended too soon. It was time to move to Selma, Alabama. We found an old coach house to rent, and I finally attempted to use the Singer sewing machine Howard had given me for my birthday. I sewed crooked seams on long red cotton panels for window curtains, proud of my effort. I loved the old coach house until one night after we had gone to bed. I turned on a lamp, and let me tell you, I found myself in cockroach hell. It was like being in the middle of a military assault—the scurrying, flying, marching, scrunching, and the *odor*! Pew-ee! I screamed and stood straight up on the bed, not knowing what else to do. I refused to get down until Howard Hoovered up the mess of bugs and ran a wet mop over the floor. There was satisfaction in seeing him do a little housework, even though he did it to keep me quiet, afraid neighbors might think he was beating me. The next day, we complained to the landlord, and hightailed it out of there until the place was fumigated.

Well, so much for living in the Deep South, although I loved their singsongy way of talking and being called sugar, sweetie pie, honey, and darlin' and hearing women say, after putting someone down, "Bless her little heart." Their accents were close enough to my drawl that I was soon talkin' like a native sweetie pie.

As a military wife, I had a lot to learn and plenty of documents and "old-timers" to guide me. When I was presented with a copy of *The Air Force Wife Handbook*, the bible of military protocol, I plunged into the intricacies of Air Force etiquette with the enthusiasm of an actress studying for a challenging new role.

TIPS AND TABOOS FOR ALL SERVICE WIVES

1. It is considered unmilitary for an officer to carry an umbrella.
2. It is considered unmilitary for officers in uniform to be the motor power for baby carriages.
3. Most officers in uniform avoid carrying anything unless absolutely necessary; the reason being it is difficult to salute.
4. Promptness is a military must. Never keep anyone waiting unnecessarily . . . or even necessarily.
5. Don't go downtown to tell some merchant, "I can get it at half price at the commissary." Loose talk of this sort has cost the Service many of its fringe benefits.
6. Don't be esoteric. For instance, it is wonderful to understand man talk, but don't try to outdo the men in hangar flying.

The rules seemed absurd, but the older wives condoned them and encouraged the rest of us to do likewise. "We are made from a man's rib, you know," cautioned the president of the Officers' Wives' Club at one of the frequent meetings. I was the only one who laughed.

An important list of rules concerned the selection of calling cards. They had to be absolutely correct. Over and over I read:

1. Cards are left at formal calls.
2. A lady leaves cards at a formal tea for hostess and guest of honor.
3. Cards are used to accompany gifts.
4. Cards are left when friends aren't home.
5. Cards are convenient for brief messages or an introduction.
6. Cards are left for PPC calls. PPC written in pencil in the lower left hand corner means Pour Prendre Conger (to take leave).
7. Cards are left at hospitals, particularly if one is unable to visit the patient.
8. A lady leaves a card for each adult member of a family, a maximum of three.

So much new information made me dizzy. Could I remember which corner of the card to turn down when the colonel's wife was out? Should I wear white gloves at card parties and teas? Who was supposed to sit where? Who pours? Did coffee outrank tea?

This strange new world came with the realization that I was—that I could be—popular. I made friends easily with other wives, some as young as myself, and joined them for card parties, although, when I said I didn't know what a trick was, their reaction sent me home in tears. It gave me a guilty feeling of pleasure when I finally learned to play cards. Mama was still looking over my shoulder, but it was another source of guilt that I no longer felt quite so guilty. The pleasures of friendship were driving fears of hellfire into the background, if not dispersing them all together. Even Howard relaxed a little. He allowed me to buy a few pretty dresses so I could compete on an equal level with the other wives.

Relax is perhaps not quite the right word. Howard enjoyed being told what to do and when to do it. It was a congenial role. He had become very militaristic. He enjoyed endlessly polishing his captain's silver bars and sprucing up his accouterments. When he put on his uniform, he put on a new personality with it. Just as he obeyed orders himself, he became a rigid disciplinarian toward his subordinates, enforcing the strictest obedience. He had found his niche.

One day my domineering husband brought home sixteen boxes of canned goods, having stocked up at the PX so if the End of the World came, or some other disaster, we would be prepared. There were dozens of containers of canned corn, canned beans, canned deviled ham, canned beats, canned tomatoes, canned peas, canned carrots, canned milk, canned spinach, canned pickles, canned soups, canned okra, canned mixed vegetables, canned fruit, and finally, four dozen cans of Spam.

"Howard Groves, have you lost your mind? Y'all know I don't like Spam. What were you thinking?"

"Patsy, my commander said in case of a food shortage, Spam is a source of protein that you can make all sorts of things from. Harrumph." He listed them, counting on his fingers: "Spam burgers, Spam sandwiches, fried Spam, baked Spam, barbecued Spam, Spam cubed in vegetables, Spam with pineapple rings, Spam and beans, Spam . . ."

"Howard!" I punched his shoulder. "For heaven's sake, stop it! Lordy!"

"Spam hash, Spam patties, Spam . . ."

"Howard, so help me God, if y'all don't shut up, I'll plain kill you with a can of Spam to your head!"

"This is information you need to know, Patsy! Your mother should have taught you this stuff."

"Yeah, like we had the money to stock up on Spam or anything else."

"Pay attention, Patsy. I'm going to show you how to organize things."

He took the heavy boxes to a storage closet, where he had built rows of sturdy shelves. Captain Groves, otherwise known as my husband, taught me the correct method for stacking cans. While he guided me, I stacked the cans, careful not to mix peas with green beans or corn with carrots. After I finally got that done, Howard took a wooden ruler and measured the rows to make sure they were even, like dancers in a chorus line.

After that, I had to make Spam burgers for supper! Can y'all imagine how many Spam burgers I made over the next year?

Oddly enough, except for my husband's demanding rigidity, I didn't look on these days as being as limiting, unbending, or disciplined as they were. For me there were parties and friends. I was *chosen*—elected and *chosen*—to be Program Chair of the Officers' Wives' Club, and that meant an outlet for my craving to create. I inaugurated musical fashion shows to benefit the Heart Association and came up with new ideas for dances and entertainments. Howard even unbent enough to stumble around the dance floor with me. I found I was distinctly popular with Air Force bachelors. And I enjoyed sinful experiments with cocktails such as a Cuba Libra. What might have been purgatory for other young girls who had come from a more normal, permissive background was an unusual freedom for me; and the sharply defined framework within which we lived was more a stage to play on than a confining cage.

Even the indoctrination classes for wives did not faze me.

"An Air Force wife is loyal, unquestioning, ready to move to any base anywhere in the world at a moment's notice, however many children are involved."

I swallowed it all, reveling in the prestige of the Gate Pass and the social whirl. Altogether, Howard and I, a captain and his wife, were almost at the bottom of the exactly regulated ladder of precedence, as unalterable as the laws of the Medes and Persians. I absorbed the experiences and struck out into new fields as never before. I had never had such a good time in my life.

One of the benefits of living in the South was the financial ability to hire a maid. I never, ever thought I would have a maid! There had been a deceiving moment in my youth when Mama had announced she was getting a "chore girl." Chores meant only one thing to me—housework—and for one brief, shining instance, I imagined we were going up in the world, to a dizzy level where servants were the order of the day and I would no longer be expected to scrub floors and wash dishes. Alas, a Chore Girl turned out to be nothing more than the brand name for a scouring pad—a metal mesh pad that I had to use, resentfully, to clean our crusty skillet.

When Howard said I could hire a girl to do the ironing, I was giddy with joy. Of all my domestic chores, I hated ironing shirts the most. Howard said he wanted his shirts ironed without a single crease in them, and the way I ironed was pitiful.

Idessa Lee was the same shade as my morning coffee after I poured a big dollop of cream in it. She said she was seventeen, but with her hair in short braids all over her head, she looked like a kid. When I asked why she wasn't in school, she said no one in her family had ever gone to school. She couldn't read, but she could write her name, she said. And boy could she iron a shirt. With his shirts crisp and starched exactly right and without a single wrinkle, my officer husband was a happy man. Idessa worked for a pitiful seventy-five cents an hour, and when I paid her, she treated me with embarrassing deference.

One day, Idessa arrived during pitchfork lightning and a downpour of biblical proportions. She stood on the back porch dripping and shivering in the slashing rain. "Idessa Lee," I said, "get yourself inside this house right now, hear?" I pulled her into the kitchen and grabbed several raggedy towels with which to mop up the rivulets of rainwater that poured from the soggy newspaper covering her head and whispered down her skinny body. Mushy newsprint plopped on the floor in clumps. Water spilled into her falling-apart shoes and streamed over the uneven floors. My housekeeper-ironer stank like

Rat-Dog did after a good drenching. "Idessa Lee, take off those wet clothes right this minute and get into a warm shower, or y'all will catch your death of cold." I pushed her toward the bathroom.

"Oh, no'm, I cain't do that. It's not right." She stood there trembling, not wanting to use the white folks' bathroom.

I twisted the corroded bathroom faucets until the pipes began knocking and hissing, a good sign. Yelling so Idessa could hear me, I issued an order. "If y'all don't get yourself in here as soon I finish adjusting the water, why, I'll come out there and undress you myself."

"Yessum," she muttered and edged into the bathroom with me.

Adjusting the temperature, I closed the shower curtain, relieved to see steam rise from the antiquated system. "Now, get in there and take a good long shower. Relax, Idessa Lee. Y'all have all day to do the ironing. And here's a bar of good-smelling soap to use." I held a bar of green soap under my nose and inhaled the freshness of pine before handing it to her.

"Yessum," she said, slowly beginning to peel off her blouse.

Turning my back to give her privacy, I continued to talk. "I'll get one of my old dresses for you to put on, and underwear, too. Maybe you can fit into a pair of my flats, so I'll get those, too. I'll leave everything just outside the door."

"Yessum," she said.

From the kitchen I could hear the change in water sounds and knew she was in the shower. The young girl was out of the shower and dressed in my clothes a few minutes later. After she set up the ironing board, I got her a cup of canned hot tomato soup and a plate of saltines and left her in peace.

When it was time for my maid to go home that day, it was still raining, so I said I would drive her, only to be puzzled by her awkward resistance. Protesting that she had only a short way to go, the girl reluctantly got into the backseat of the Studebaker. Obviously, it would not be right for her to sit in front beside me. The muddy road she directed me to was a hazard.

I drove carefully, slipping and sliding over red mud, wipers on full.

"It's jist a little bit on up here a ways," Idessa said several miles later. "I'll get out. It's right close now."

"No, it's a mess out there. I'll take you all the way if I don't get stuck."

Good heavens, she must have walked at least five miles to get to my house. And still she didn't want me to drive her all the way up to the dilapidated shack, our destination. The house wasn't a house at all but a chicken shack on stilts. It sat in a muddy yard with a big black wash pot in front, reminding me of Poor Little Glendora on the Woods farm.

"Idessa," I said, "next week I have the car, so I'll come get y'all. Okay?"

"Yessum, ma'am." She smiled.

Before collecting Idessa the next week, I went to a bookstore and bought *Curious George, The Little Engine that Could, The Tale of Peter Rabbit,* all children's books, so I could try to teach her to read. At first my student was reluctant to sit down in my "classroom" and acted dimwitted. She wouldn't even try to pronounce the words, but she did like looking at the pictures. Eventually, she learned a word and then another and another, and then she put an entire sentence together. We celebrated with dishes of vanilla ice cream. She began to trust me and rushed through the ironing so she could find out what happened next to Peter Rabbit or Curious George, and she appreciated the lesson of persistence in *The Little Engine that Could.* The stories in the colorful books were as new to her as to a five-year-old. Little by little and with sweat-drenched effort, she learned to read those simple books. It was cause for a major celebration. Together we baked a chocolate cake, and I put birthday candles on it. She said it was her first birthday cake, though it wasn't exactly her birthday, she didn't think. Helping an illiterate girl learn to read was more satisfying to me than a game of bridge could ever be.

Everywhere in Selma was talk of "niggers," often pronounced

"nigras." The "nigras" were getting above themselves; they had to be taught a "lesson." The soft, drawling voices belied the bigotry behind hate-filled words. The "lesson" was both brutal and violent. A black male selected at random late at night was wound up with bailing wire and thrown off the Edmund Pettus Bridge to deter any uppity niggers from getting above themselves, so people said. The image of a helpless man trapped in the swirling, muddy water of the Selma River haunted me. I kept asking myself what I could do about it. There was no answer.

Other savage customs prevailed. Neighborhood dogs barked endlessly and attacked black folks. When one nipped Idessa Lee, I asked her why she didn't teach it a lesson with a well-placed kick.

"Oh, no'm!" She was clearly scandalized; her eyes rolled. "If'n I was to kick white folks' dogs, they would plumb send me off to jail!"

I was so incensed that I marched "where angels fear to tread" to the police station to lodge a complaint, unaware that in two years, blood would be shed in that small, sleepy town of cypress- and oak-lined streets as blacks marched for the right to vote. Selma would become central to the civil rights movement. But in the police station on that day in 1952, when I complained about folks letting their dogs attack colored people, they laughed.

"Y'all need to have the folks at the dog pound come pick up those dogs," I said to an officer.

"Y'all aren't from here, is that right, ma'am?"

"No, sir," I said. "We're from California. My husband is stationed at Craig Field."

"Well, guess that explains it." The man rolled a toothpick around in his mouth, grinning all the while. He called to a buddy. "Hey, Jim, this little lady here thinks we should stop our dogs from barking at the fine Negro citizens of our little community. She and her husband are Californians. He's out there at Craig Air Base. Talk to this nice little lady, Jim."

Jim guffawed and then smiled at me. "Y'all wanna know why we can't stop dogs from nippin' at colored folks' heels?"

My discomfort must have been obvious. They were making fun of me. "Yes, sir, it's not right for dogs to go around barking and biting black folks."

"Well, coming from California and all, I understand that y'all can't know how it is here in the South. Oh, sorry, I forgot my manners. Please have a seat, ma'am." He pulled out a slat-backed chair. "Standing there in those high heels must be tirin'."

"Thank you," I said, taken in by his Southern charm and good looks.

"Okay, sugar, let me explain the barking dogs to y'all. See, ma'am, no one wishes harm to come to black folks—we love our Negroes—but y'all need to understand that they have a different smell than us white folks do. Our dogs go plumb crazy when they get a whiff of that smell. We cain't do a thing about it."

With my lips compressed to steady my trembling chin, I departed the police station, red high heels clicking on the wooden floor. I felt shame and helplessness. When I told Howard what I had done and what the officers said, he was furious with me. "We're in the South, Patsy. When in Rome, do as the Romans do. You will get me in trouble yet!" I thought about the coffee shop Californians and felt kinship with the Negroes of Selma.

Increasingly unattractive as I found the relation of white to black in the South, I could not ignore or fail to respond to the nostalgic charm of the beautiful old plantations, relics of another era. *Gone with the Wind* whispered to me in every oak tree, in every old mansion, in the soft drawl of native Alabamans. One in particular was still inhabited by the direct descendant of the original owner. She was usually referred to as "The Colonel's Granddaughter" or "Miz Nancy Jane." With the passing of time and the family fortune lost in the Civil War in her grandfather's day, she was now relegated to one corner of the mansion, otherwise occupied by a boutique and antique shop.

There hung about her an air of breeding and distinction. I can still "see" her as she clasped the graceful banister of the staircase with one arthritic hand, while pointing out with the other the decaying grandeurs of the past. The house had a musty aroma befitting its crumbling age. The floors shone with wax and the banisters were polished, but cockroaches scuttled in the shadows, and the damp air foretold the mildew of dissolution.

When my wisdom teeth needed to be extracted, I was sent to the Maxwell Air Force Base military hospital in Montgomery, Alabama, fifty miles from Selma. Because of my history of heart surgery, the doctors there thought it best to hospitalize me. I loved the drive to Montgomery on a traffic-free highway lined and overhung with a forest of green trees, and I enjoyed receiving attention from the medical staff. It was like old times at the UC hospital in San Francisco. For an instant, it crossed my mind that something was wrong with my life when I got more pleasure from being hospitalized than from being with my husband.

A few weeks after my wisdom teeth were removed, I kept an appointment with an internist at the Montgomery hospital. The doctor was a looming presence, tall with the beginnings of a belly, his moon face topped by a head of silvery hair. The man exuded authority. After a number of questions, the doctor sent shock waves through me by asking a question I wasn't expecting.

"How's your sex life, Mrs. Groves?" His brown eyes were those of a seer.

"Uh, fine," I lied.

"Really?" he asked. "Are you orgasmic? Do you have orgasms?"

"Orgasms? Oh, you mean do I enjoy sex?" I said, my words muffled by mortification.

"Yes, that's what orgasmic means."

"Uh, not exactly."

"What do you mean by 'not exactly'?"

"Uh, well, I haven't had one yet."

"And how long have you been married?"

"Four years."

"Four years?" His round face reminded me of a setting sun, now growing dark with concern. "That's a long time. It's unhealthy not to enjoy sex. Does your husband caress you and make love to you? Or is he the slam-bam-thank-you-ma'am type?"

I giggled nervously. "Slam-bam, I guess."

"You know, it doesn't have to be that way. Get undressed and put on this gown." He handed me a faded blue robe. "I'll examine you and see if I can help." He indicated a gurney-like table with a green pad on it and told me to hop aboard. "I'll step outside while you undress."

I lay on the hard table, feeling exposed and uneasy, until the doctor reappeared. The feelings only worsened when, after he examined my breasts and thumped on my stomach, the doctor put one of his big hands on my pubic area. It was all I could do to stay on the table when he began to massage me. "How does that feel?" he asked.

"Uh, kinda uncomfortable." I tried to pull the skimpy robe over me, to no avail.

"You're just nervous. Remember, I'm a doctor, schooled in matters of frigidity. Do you trust me?"

"Well, as you said, you *are* the doctor." My reply was a strangled laugh.

"Please close your eyes and relax. Imagine you are lying in the hot sun on a beautiful beach, green trees moving softly overhead."

His fingers made circular motions on my skin. I tried to imagine the sun shining down on me, but Lord have mercy, I couldn't focus. My muscles were so rigid that quarters could have been bounced off my stomach. I tensed my sphincter muscles and tightened my vagina, fearful that I might pee all over the doctor's hand and soak his white coat in urine, or worse. The physician continued his languorous massage, but his fingers were going deeper into my body. I began to sweat. "Uh, doctor, uh, stop . . ."

Suddenly, in one swift movement, he lifted the green table pad off the gurney and onto the floor with me on it. I was startled, but before I could utter a sound, the doctor covered my mouth with one hand and unzipped his pants with the other hand. His engorged member jumped out. The doctor's heavy body flopped down on top of me. Panting, he worked to push his penis into me.

Flooded with adrenaline, I opened my mouth and bit down so energetically on the heel of his fleshy hand that I tasted the man's blood. He yelped and rolled partway off of me, his rumpled white coat catching dribbles of sperm. Immediately, I raised my feet and kicked him in the groin with as much force as I could muster. He rolled away from me, moaning and cursing. I scrambled to my feet.

"I'll scream bloody murder if you dare touch me!" I hissed. Moving quickly, I threw on my dress, grabbed my shoes and purse, and ran out of the room, unbuttoned and barefoot, leaving the doctor on the floor of his examining room, groaning.

It wasn't until I was on the highway, driving under the green, arching branches of the forest, that I began to cry. My tears fell in an unbridled waterfall, pooling at my feet, flowing across the highway, creating a flood of such profound intensity that I turned on the windshield wipers. I glanced in the mirrored visor and saw that a blood vessel in my right eye had burst and I had a nosebleed. I pulled off the road and tumbled out of the automobile, holding a handkerchief to my bloody nose, and allowed the dense forest to swallow me whole. Through a tangle of kudzu, I headed for a flowering pink dogwood tree. Sitting on dirt and fallen leaves, I leaned back against the slender trunk of the beautiful tree and wailed. I must have sat there for an hour until the forest grew dark and silent, and finally I wandered back to my car and drove home.

At home I cried continually. Not out loud, but silently, morosely, fearfully. I didn't tell Howard what had happened to me. I knew he would accuse me of leading the doctor on, of being a loose woman. No, I couldn't bear the thought of confiding in the man I had married. So I didn't. The shame I experienced for allowing that doctor to touch me made me feel as if polluted water sloshed around in my bloodstream, poisoning me.

My confidant became my maid, Idessa Lee, who noticed there was something bothering me. She asked if she had done anything wrong. That was all I needed, a sympathetic voice, and I let it all out. After I told her about being raped, Idessa opened up about being "taken advantage of" by an uncle and an older brother when she was ten. We sat on the living room floor together, my maid and I, comforting each other with pats on the back and cups of black tea as we sobbed.

~~~

One Sunday when Howard was away, I decided to go to church, thinking it might make me feel better. Maybe I would even request a prayer. I chose a Baptist church because there were more Baptist churches than any other kind in Selma. There was one on every street corner, it seemed. The first question a native Alabaman asked me was "What church y'all belong to, honey?" I always said I was a Baptist, as it saved explanation.

The church I chose to attend that Sunday in Selma had Southern charm to spare, having once been a plantation-style house. "Welcome. Where y'all from?" I was asked in sugared tones and soft voices by ladies wearing flowered hats and with sweet expressions. Settling my dressed-up self onto a folding chair and adjusting my own flowered chapeau of pink cabbage roses, I joined the congregation in singing the familiar old hymns.

Overwhelmed by memories of childhood, I felt tears start to run from my eyes, and I pushed them back under pale lids with a white linen handkerchief. But all that softness and tearfulness ended when the preacher, in a flowing black preacher's garment and with graying hair, got up from his high-backed, red velvet king's throne and announced the text of his sermon. "Leviticus 20:13," he intoned with a twang that was neither soft nor educated.

Oh no, I thought, knowing what was coming.

"'If there is a man who lies with a male as those who lie with a woman, both of them have committed a detestable act; they shall surely be put to death. Their blood-guiltiness is upon them.' Are y'all a-listen'? Are y'all a-listen'? This here is the Bible, and we are given the right to slay those who disobey his Word."

"Amen," someone shouted.

"Yest'day," the preacher continued, his eyes squinted up tight and his arms waving in the air, "an effeminate-like fellow wanted to talk to me 'bout his soul. That fellow said he was attracted to men! Can y'all imagine that? Made me want to puke! We have a name for aberrations like that, and it ain't Brother. It's Queer, it's Homo, it's Fairy, it's Fag, it's the D-E-V-I-L! I tole that fella that he would have to repent of his sins and ask the devil be cast out from him. *'You shall not lie with a male as one lies with a female; it is an abomination,'*" the man screeched, as parishioners shouted encouragement.

"Glory to God," a woman shouted. "Amen."

That preacher's hateful words and his obvious relish in saying them sure made me want to puke. I covered my mouth with a hankie and edged quietly out while hearing the lascivious and disgusting words of the Christian cleric.

~~~

Staying in bed as much as I could, I felt removed from my body, from reality. When Howard told me he was being transferred overseas to the Azores Islands, I hardly understood what he was saying.

"The Azores Islands? Where is that?" I queried.

"Two thousand three hundred miles due east of Philadelphia in the Atlantic Ocean," Howard answered, as if reading, "and nine hundred miles off the coast of Portugal."

My deep-seated insecurities exploded into view, my weeping became visible. Howard told me to get hold of myself, that moving wasn't the end of the world. Was I having my period? Was that why I was crying? Yes, I said. I was having my period.

I longed for a home, for roots. I had always been leaving, all my life. Just when I made a friend, our family would move—two years in one parish, then off to another. And here I was, getting ready to go to a place I had never heard of, having to say goodbye to my only friend, Idessa Lee.

On the day of the move, Idessa and I made a strange pair, the two of us, with matching tears of the same color, the same sadness, the same longing for something solid in our lives. My maid stood near our car, crying. Through blurred vision, she read aloud from all three of the books I had given her: *The Little Engine that Could*, *The Tales of Peter Rabbit*, and at last, *Curious George*. It took her about an hour to laboriously read those books, and Howard was none too pleased. But for once, he showed a little gumption and kept quiet. Idessa and I were both blubbering when Howard pulled away from the curb.

We sped down the highway, our heaving Studebaker packed tightly with cardboard boxes. I could have been riding in Daddy's Model A Ford, my long-gone cat Bluie purring on my lap, quarreling with Poor Little Glendora, Rat-Dog at Charles's feet, Daddy falling asleep at the wheel, Mama saying, "Lord help us," and singing "Amazing Grace." But it was my stern husband in the driver's seat, and we were en route to Farmington, where I was to stay with his family until the Air Force issued permission for me to join him in the Azores.

Howard drove like he owned the highway, scaring me so much I forgot to cry. Somewhere on the outskirts of Albuquerque, New Mexico, a siren wailed and red lights flashed. Sure enough, it was the Highway Patrol. Howard slowly got out of the car, shook out his lanky frame, and walked up to the officer, who kept telling him to get back in the car.

"There was no traffic," Howard said, pointing his finger at the man. "Prima facie law says it's okay to drive whatever speed is safe when the traffic is light." Lord help us, Howard was going to get himself arrested.

I opened the car door, thinking to corral him, when my husband was advised in sharp tones to get back in the car. "You too, lady," the officer admonished, "back in the car."

The highway patrolman, his face red, the veins in his neck throbbing, leaned in the open window and addressed my fuming husband. "Mister, when I tell you to get in the car, I mean it. You were exceeding the speed limit by twenty miles per hour. Now if you want to fight and contest this ticket I'm writing out for you, well, take it up with the judge." With that, he handed Howard a speeding ticket that carried a fine of fifty dollars. "The courthouse is just inside the city limits on the right-hand side. I'll be there to tell the judge how you threatened me, mister."

After he thought it safe to do so, Howard cursed the stupidity of the Highway Patrol, New Mexico in general, Indians specifically, Mexicans especially, and cacti. "Dumb-ox Highway Patrol, they don't know their ass from a hole in the ground. I'll get that ticket voided and that officer fired. His face will be even redder, the jackass." He cussed all the way to the courthouse, which was closed. We spent the night in a dusty motel room so Howard could get the ticket fixed the next morning.

Albuquerque was familiar to me. The hot sun was still shining down hard on the rough landscape when Howard fell asleep on the thin motel room mattress and began to snore. I decided to go for a walk along the rocky highway, hoping to spot the place where Daddy once held a revival meeting, or the store where I worked stuffing kapok into cloth Navajo dolls when I was ten and dressing them in soft ruby and green velvet dresses with turquoise jewelry.

Daddy's revival meeting was held in Albuquerque over two weeks one summer. He worked in a defense plant during the daylight hours, earning a whopping ten dollars a day. Mama's sister, Aunt Fanny, and her husband, Robert, along with grown grandchildren Jerry and Gwendolyn, lived in Albuquerque, so we stayed with them. Jerry and Gwen were cutups, unafraid of anything. They made us laugh with their crazy antics, and Jerry let Little Jimmy read his large stash of comic books. On a vacant lot, Uncle Robert helped Daddy pitch a faded red-and-white striped tent loaned him by a defunct circus. The local Nazarene church lent him their black upright piano, a patched-together pulpit, wooden folding chairs, mimeographed songs, and a straggly volunteer choir. When I wasn't stuffing Navajo dolls with kapok, I helped Jerry, Gwen, and Little Jimmy hand out flyers printed on a mimeograph device announcing healing services.

People flocked to the tent the first night, some of them thinking that a circus was in town. They sat fanning themselves and fending off an extravaganza of moths buzzing, beetles mating, assassin bugs pouncing, praying mantises praying, web spinners and thousands of other bugs swarming around the bare light bulbs hanging on wires from the two peaks of the Big Top.

"Where are the animals?" a man yelled when Daddy took the pulpit.

"Son, open your eyes. Y'all are looking at him," my father said, laughing. "And if I'm not animal enough, take a gander at all those acrobats up there swinging around the light bulbs."

Laughter rippled. Daddy was just getting warmed up.

"If y'all were expecting a circus tonight, y'all will not be disappointed. Open your eyes and see the animals sitting there on either side of you. And look over there at that wild lion." He pointed to a scruffy-looking fellow in the fourth row. The man's tangled hair looked like it hadn't experienced the teeth of a comb in years, and his beard was bushy and unkempt, his eyes bleary. "Brother," Daddy said to the man, "y'all look like a lion that lost a few tussles with bottles of booze somewhere along the line. You've lost your way. But I'm here to help you find your way back to the

Lord."

The lion grinned and saluted the pulpit. "And over there, another animal, a raggedy black sheep that was once a lamb white as the driven snow, but is now tarnished, having been gored by too many bulls."

The sheep lady frowned, her frizzy red hair standing on end.

"And there, hiding out on the back row, a sleek panther, ready to slip in and steal your wallet, an animal once an angel, now burdened by sin. Oh, my dear brethren," Daddy bellowed, "fellow members of this circus of life, I am here to tell you, there is a Savior, and he can change you from a drunken lion, a black sheep, a fallen angel . . . He can heal your illnesses, your spirit, your wayward ways . . ."

By the time the choir burst into "Softly and Tenderly," people were shouting, the lion was stumbling toward the altar, the fallen angel was weeping, and the woman gored by bulls was storming out of the tent. Those on crutches made space at the improvised altar for bandage-wrapped heads, while the able knelt on the straw-covered dirt. The praying was powerful, but I think even Daddy was surprised when a fellow threw his crutches away and danced around the center ring, shouting that he had been healed. Daddy didn't recognize our cousin Jerry disguised with a mustache, sunglasses, and a cowboy hat. Jerry was making sure that Daddy's revival was a success. We laughed about Jerry and his crutches for years afterward. Daddy laughed too, and praised the Lord for unseen blessings. After Jerry's "healing," the revival meeting was packed with sick and afflicted sinners for the entire two weeks of services.

Lost in memories of another time, I stumbled along the shoulder of the road, kicking white rocks with the toes of my sandals. The highway was littered with car lots, blinking neon signs, curio stands, and fast food restaurants. The air sparked with heat, the same way it must have centuries earlier. But look over yonder—look beyond the debris-strewn lots—look past the fast food stands—gaze upon the mountaintop clothed in a russet-gilded cape designed in the premeditated glory of the setting sun. Observe the ancient cliff dwellers as they light cooking fires in clay ovens and prepare flatbread in the cool comfort of their cave. And for a moment, just one moment, remember the Cherokee tribe forced into exile on a heartbreaking walk along the Trail of Tears.

My own tears, always near the surface, began to seep from my eyes as I thought of the cruelty imposed on the powerless. A chill skittered down my spine. Nothing stirred except a star that blinked in the milky sky above the Sandia Mountains, but I was spooked and frozen even in the unrelenting heat of Albuquerque. I ran back to the motel where my obtuse husband slept, oblivious to the history of this desolate place, oblivious to my inner turmoil . . . oblivious.

In court the next day, I got perverse pleasure from hearing the judge shoot down Howard's prima facie argument and increase his fine to one hundred dollars. Well, let me tell you, that sure pissed Howard off, to use his phraseology. He fumed all the way to Farmington as I sang and wrote jingles. One such masterpiece was the result of buying a piece of Indian pottery from a roadside stand. When I looked at the bottom, it said *Made in Japan*. I laughed. All manner of curios were being imported from Japan, so I hoped to get my jingle published in the *Saturday Evening Post*, since they were paying three hundred dollars per.

The sign said authentic curios
Direct from the Indian Nation
I never knew that Made in Japan
Was an Indian Reservation.

~~~

"You had better have fun," Mom Groves said in her brisk, practical way. "You'll never be able to shop like this again in your whole life." Howard was in the Azores, and I was stocking up to go there. I needed clothes and supplies for the entire two-and-a-half year tour of duty.

Mom would be shocked if she knew what an effort all this was for me—how anxious I felt. Whenever I left the safe, familiar environment of the ranch, I almost threw up; my hands became drenched in sweat, and my stomach clenched in a fist of pain. I began imagining that people stared at me and whispered about me. I was paranoid to the point of refusing to join in any outside activity. How could I possibly get on an airplane and fly over an ocean of water all the way to the Azores? And if I did, would Howard send me back to an insane asylum? My mind was a churning maelstrom of such thoughts, my imagination feeding off my fears and my fears feeding off my imagination. It was a desperate time for me.

Now it was time to go. Mom and Pop and Wally said goodbye to me on the tarmac, and I forced myself to board a DC-9 at San Francisco's International Airport. My first stop was to be New York, and from there I would board a train for Westover Air Force Base in Massachusetts, and then endure the additional horror of flying fourteen hours on a Military Air Transport plane over the Atlantic Ocean to the Azores Islands.

The contours of the DC-9 seemed to change shape, expanding and contracting. I fastened the seat belt and willed my crippled mind to think of pleasant things. Was it the prospect of flying that was causing my mental problems? I had never flown before, and I could only conjure up fatal crashes and scary Bible verses my father had often recited. Whenever an airplane flew over the house, my father quoted from Revelation. He equated airplanes with war, death, and destruction.

"'In the last days there will be wars and rumors of war,'" he would intone, or, "'I saw a star fall from heaven unto the earth: and to him was given the key of the bottomless pit.' Revelation 9:1."

When I heard these doom-filled pronouncements, I hid under the bed and stuffed my fingers in my ears to try to close off the words. Images of fiery stars falling, angels with ferocious red eyes and drawn swords, and bombs raining down on earth filled my impressionable mind with recurring horror. Daddy had been dead ten years. I was now twenty-three, and still the phantasmagoria planted in my childhood blossomed into full-blown reality in my broken-down mind.

Chapter 12

Fly the Ocean in a Silver Plane . . .

It never occurred to me to seek professional help for my penetrating confusion. I was afraid if I dared breathe a word of my craziness or of being raped to anyone, the earth would open up and swallow me whole. All I had to do was remember Howard's reaction when I had tried to confide in him. I replaced the image of that moon-faced doctor in Montgomery with the word *fuck* and repeated it in my mind continually like a mantra.

During the six-hour flight to Westover Air Force Base, I had plenty of time to think. The TWA propellers lulled me into a state approaching calm. My nervous mind settled down, and I was soon able to go deep inside myself to try to ferret out my honest feelings. Fastening my seat belt ever tighter, I prayed for help to cope with my unreasoning anxieties. Were my panic attacks due to the fear I harbored of an avenging God, or because of my stifling marriage, or because I was raped, or perhaps all of those things? By facing my immobilizing terrors straight on, I realized that my marriage was built on quicksand and the increased weight of rape caused my "Tea for Two" illusion to collapse in the light of truth. Howard wasn't my companion; he was my boss. Our life together was a wasteland, an intellectual desert. We never discussed books or poetry, or did anything of consequence.

Should I continue to accept my husband's autocratic attitude as his helpmate? "Helpmate" seemed only to apply to a wife. When I'd said, "I do," what exactly had I agreed to do? Was I expected to endure painful sex, painful to contemplate and painful to endure? Line up canned goods correctly? Cook and scrub and let my creativity rot? Put up with offensive behavior? No! That wasn't right! I was twenty-three and had been married four years. I would live in the Azores for two and a half years. Then what?

As I continued to dig for the essential truth of my anxiety attacks, a truth that played hide-and-seek somewhere inside me—my heart, or my liver, or my brain—I had a revelation. My skin tingled with the electric current of recognition. We were flying over the jutting pinnacles of the Rocky Mountains when it hit me: my crippling anxieties stemmed from an aching need to be loved. My mind hungered for intellectual stimulation; my body cried out for comforting arms; my soul sobbed for sweetness, gentleness, and kindness; my inner self longed for respect. And, to my surprise, I found that I throbbed for a tender and passionate sexual partner.

As for a baby, or rather the lack of a baby—Howard said there was something physically wrong with me because I hadn't become pregnant.

"There's something wrong with you, Patsy," he said. But when a doctor determined that Howard had a low sperm count, he railed against the medical profession. "Bunch of stupid jackasses," he summed up. "There's nothing wrong with me. It's because of your operation." How my heart surgery could affect my reproductive organs, I had no idea.

His attitude made me so frustrated that I threw an entire set of dinner plates on the floor, breaking them into sharp-edged fragments. *Crash—wham—crash!* I stood amid the shards of white china, crying. Howard stood in the kitchen doorway, a toothpick in his mouth, his hands on his hips, hostility distorting his angular features. After he had cleared his throat, he told me to clean up the mess, and then he walked away and left me to it. Why didn't I throw a plate at him? Although I argued with him and occasionally won, I allowed my husband to rule me. That idea originated in the Bible. Why? Jesus wasn't married. Just before my wedding, Mama had read a Bible passage about marriage.

"'After Adam and Eve had sinned,'" Mama read, her rimless glasses perched over grooved frown lines, "'God appointed the husband as leader: To the woman he said: I will greatly multiply your sorrow and your conception; in pain you shall bring forth children; your desire shall *be* for your husband, and he shall rule over you.'"

"Mama!" I yelled. "Why would you read such a thing to me? Lordy!"

"You kids don't appreciate how I suffered to bring you into this world." Her face, powdered with Rachel #2, was the very picture of a pale-faced martyr.

"Well, I didn't ask to be brought into this world, Mama, so please stop preaching at me!"

"You are stubborn as a mule, Patsy Lou, but you better let your husband rule, or you'll rue the day, I'm telling you!"

Outside the airplane window, apocalyptic-looking clouds towered. They seemed an accurate reflection of my thinking. What if I weren't married? Not married. Single. Alone. Could I survive? I had no marketable skills, no money, and modeling was not a sure thing. Besides, wasn't I a *dependent*? Right there in my big brown traveling bag were papers issued by the United States government, saying, *Patsy Lou Groves, Dependent wife of Captain Howard Chandler Groves.*

The plane shuddered, and a distorted voice said we were experiencing turbulence, to fasten our seat belts. I pulled my belt tighter and thought about turbulence. That was the perfect word for the geographic map of my brain. What if I got a divorce? Divorced. Single. Solitary! *Mother!* Why, Mama would kill me! It was a sin against the Holy Poltergeist to divorce. Bible verses that laid out God's law with no room for deviation, preached at full volume by a variety of male Bible thumpers, resonated in my head. "'Wives, submit to your own husbands, as to the Lord. For the husband is the head of the wife even as Christ is the head of the church, his body, and is himself its Savior. Now as the church submits to Christ, so also wives should submit in everything to their husbands.'"

Wither thou goest, I will go . . . all the way to the insane asylum.

Stop it—stop it, I said to myself. Thinking such traitorous thoughts made me fear that God's wrath would cause the plane to crash in flames. Downing another swig of Dr. Miles' Nervine, I reassured myself that as soon as I saw my husband, everything would be okay. He supplied the money, but maybe I hadn't done my part. Okay, I would be funny and sweet just the way he liked me to be, and Howard would respond with loving tenderness and all would be well.

After spending a night at Westover Air Force Base, I boarded a Military Air Transport Service (MATS) plane for the Azores at five o'clock in the morning, rickety with apprehension. Our one stop during the fourteen-hour flight was Newfoundland, where we landed in a glacial whiteout. Three people deplaned, leaving the crew and an Air Force major and me as the only passengers. As we waited to take off again, the major got up from his seat, stretched and yawned, and sauntered over to me.

"We might as well keep each other company," he said. "Looks like we're the only travelers to the Azores. Mind if I sit here awhile?" Without waiting for an answer, the dark-haired major sat down beside me. "I'm Malcolm Kerkorian, an Armenian." He smiled.

"Patsy, Patsy Groves," I replied. "You know what a patsy is? Describes me to a tee."

"Good one." He laughed, a real, resonating laugh, nothing phony or forced. "Your husband stationed at Lages Field?"

"Yes," I said, staring out the small window into nothingness.

"It's a hell of a place to live," Malcolm said. "I've been stationed there a year with one more to go. Be glad to get my tour over with and back to civilian life."

"We'll be there for two and a half years."

"Why so long? A tour of duty is two years."

"My husband extended it so we can go to Europe. As a dependent, I can go on a space-available basis for an additional six months." I looked at the man beside me, seeing him for the first time. He had pleasant brown eyes, olive skin, and black hair parted on the side. His tie was off, and his open collar revealed the metallic glint of dog tags. He needed a shave.

"You'll enjoy Europe, though parts are still in bad shape from the war." He pulled a thin silver flask from a leather bag. "Care to join me in a drink? A little vodka might help you relax."

"Do you think I need to relax?" I demanded, chagrined that he read me so accurately.

"I'm a doctor, a psychologist, trained to recognize signs of stress. This is a long flight to a small dot in the middle of a vast ocean, and there's a fierce snowstorm outside this plane. Anyone with good sense would be a bit apprehensive."

My defenses weakened, and I laughed. "Glad to know I have good sense. Okay, I'll try a sip of vodka, but I'm not much of a drinker."

"Don't worry, it's a fourteen-hour flight, and you can't get lost." Malcolm poured us both shots of vodka. "Well, down the hatch," he said, and drained his cup.

"Down the hatch," I said, feeling reckless. The liquid burned my throat. I gasped. I grabbed the glass of water provided by our flight steward and quickly downed it. My seat companion laughed.

"No, I guess you aren't much of a drinker," he said after I recovered enough to talk. "Do I detect a drawl?" he asked, pouring another jigger of vodka. He stretched his long legs under the seat in front of him. "No, wait, I'll tell you about you. You're from the South, you're beautiful but don't know it. Intelligent but don't realize it. You're married and know it. You hate flying, and you'll never be a barfly. Right so far?" His off-kilter grin caused lines to explode from the corners of his eyes, reminding me of my brother-in-law Cecil.

I smiled, my first genuine smile in a long time. "Right," I said, sipping my drink. "I couldn't possibly disagree with such flattering words." A pleasant sensation stole over me, beginning in my fingers, progressing to my limbs, and quickly moving to my head. I felt light and carefree. The major was right; I *had* needed a drink. "How about you?" I asked. "Married?"

"No, divorced."

"Oh, I'm sorry."

"Don't be. We're happier now. Thank God for divorce. How terrible to be stuck with someone who just tolerates you or whom you've outgrown. There's nothing wrong with divorce," he said, looking straight into my brain, "unless children are involved, and then I'm not sure."

"Maybe you're right," I replied, and then startled myself with the feathery words that flew out of my mouth like swallows returning to Capistrano. "I'm thinking of a divorce."

"Tell me about it," Malcolm said.

Our plane was well on its way to our destination when I unfurled the fearsome thoughts skittering around inside my skull. Slowly, haltingly, between long sips of vodka, I confided my innermost secrets to the pleasant stranger sitting beside me. I told him about Mama, my marriage, my mental breakdown, and eventually, with the help of a few more jiggers of vodka, I told him a little about being raped. Periodically, he asked me questions. Revealing my fears and panic attacks to him was an enormous relief. I felt the way I imagine sinners feel when praying through to Victory. Hallelujah!

"Patsy," he said when I finally ran out of words, "you need a friend, and I would like to be it." He scribbled a number on a card. "Here's my phone number. I live just outside the base gate. Call me if you need to talk." He chuckled. "We've already had the equivalent of ten therapy sessions, and we've only scratched the surface. You have a bright future if you make good choices." He leaned over and kissed me lightly on the cheek. He looked abashed. "I'm sorry. I shouldn't have done that."

"It's okay. We're drinking."

"Alcohol offers an excuse to do what we lack the courage for when we're sober. Can't blame the vodka." Malcolm stood and moved up the aisle. "We'd better catch a little shuteye," he said. In an overhead rack he found a blanket and handed it to me. It was military-issue khaki and stamped with

USA in large black letters. "There must be pillows," he said, looking overhead until he found two. He put one pillow over the seat armrest to pad it and one under my head, then helped me swing my legs across the armrest. After I settled down, my new friend spread the blanket over me.

"Sweet dreams, Mrs. Groves," he said and moved off to his own seat.

How thoughtful, I mused as I drifted off, aided by the lullaby of propellers and vodka.

~~~

Someone was shaking me awake. "Patsy, wake up. We're almost there. We only have time for breakfast."

I rubbed my eyes and sat up. Malcolm stood in the aisle of the bouncing plane, attempting to keep a cup of coffee balanced.

"Your coffee, madam," he said. He was freshly shaved, his hair combed and his shirt buttoned. He even wore a tie.

"You look ready for the day," I said, smoothing my tangled hair.

"Gotta hit the tarmac running," he said. "But first . . . breakfast! I conned our lazy flight steward into orange juice, croissants, and hot java."

"Umm, sounds good," I said, "but I'd better get myself together first." In the miniscule restroom, I freshened up the best I could. When I returned, the *USA* blanket and the pillows were stowed away and the seat trays were down. There was one red rose by my plate.

"Where on earth did that come from?" I asked.

"It came from a pilot who now has eleven roses he's taking to his wife, although he thinks he has twelve."

Laughing, I pinned the flower in my hair.

"Lovely, Mrs. Groves," Malcolm said as he buttered his croissant. "Let's eat. I'm famished, and I want to take this opportunity to talk to you. Okay?"

"Sure, it's your turn, after all."

"Patsy, what I'm going to say might sound strange since you don't know me, but your use of the word 'dependent' concerns me. Even though the military uses that designation, please don't think of yourself as a dependent. A female doesn't need a male to complete her. It's good to have a companion with whom to share one's life, but it should be a mutual experience in every way. You are intelligent, gifted, and smart. Remember that, all right?"

"Thank you. You've helped by listening to me."

"Anytime, Patsy. Anytime." He paused as he sipped his coffee. "One more thing. The rape you told me about was not your fault. Understand? No way was it your fault."

Suddenly emotional, I nodded, unable to speak.

Time skittered quickly by until the flight steward announced our imminent arrival in the Azores.

"There's Terceira, your island home, Patsy," Malcolm said, pointing to a small patch of land amid white-capped waves. "One island of the nine that make up the Azores."

The plane made a slow descent through layers of clouds, and little by little, the outline of a patchwork quilt of fields in varying shades of green emerged. The outer fringes of Terceira were rimmed with dark sand on which frothy waves crashed and receded, and crashed again. One gigantic boulder reached out of the frothing sea like a monster from the deep as silvery ocean knights sent vast amounts of salt water slamming into it, attempting to slay the stone dragon, failing but never giving up the battle.

The long runway on which our plane was trying to land was pinched into a narrow valley between a steep cliff and a towering mountain. Malcolm said that Lages Field was the only refueling stop on the way to Europe and the Near East, and the runway was long enough to accommodate all manner of aircraft. I hoped he was right, since it was taking forever for the wheels to touch down.

When we were finally on solid ground, Malcolm said goodbye, reminding me to call him if I needed help, and quickly exited the aircraft. I combed my hair, put on lipstick, and straightened my wrinkled dress before deplaning, as I wanted to be as pretty as possible for my husband.

There he was, waiting for me at the foot of the steps. I felt a sense of relief as I rushed into his arms. I was glad to be with Howard. He was my lifeline in a world of strangeness. Never had I been so cut off from familiar sights and sounds. The long journey had made me conscious of the remote speck in the Atlantic Ocean I was to call home for two and a half years.

At sunset, the American flag was lowered to the evocative resonance of "Taps." The reverberation echoed against the cliffs and mountains and traced the fifty miles of shoreline of that distant base. "Taps," that poignant reminder of loss, filled me with haunted isolation.

There were seven beds in the bare, impersonal Quonset hut where we were billeted, but we were the only ones sleeping there that night. We chose a bed near one of two windows and settled in. Howard kissed me and said he had missed me, and then, without another word, he made silent love to me. I wished he would caress me and talk to me, but he simply plunged in. The act was over in two or three minutes, give or take a few seconds.

"Did you feel anything?" he asked when he finished.

"I felt loved," I lied.

"Harrumph! No, damn it, did you get a thrill out of our lovemaking? Did you come? Or did you fake it?"

I had taken to pretending I enjoyed sex so Howard wouldn't interrogate me afterward. He made me feel guilty. "Howard, please don't act this way. I like feeling desirable to you. I *want* you to make love to me."

My husband sat up and fumbled for a pack of cigarettes in the weak light that leaked into the room from a window. He pulled out a cigarette and lit it.

"When did you start smoking?" I asked, surprised.

"When I first got over here," he answered. "Listen, Patsy . . ." He paused to inhale smoke, and with a soft whooshing sound, blew it out.

271

"There's something I've got to tell you."

"Okay."

"Well . . ." He hesitated.

"Well, what?" I said, sitting up in bed beside him, alarmed.

"Harrumph. Never mind, it's not important." He cleared his throat and stubbed out his cigarette. "I'm tired. Let's call it a night."

"No, tell me what you started to say."

"It's not important." He paused. "It's just . . . well, it's just that . . ." His voice was so low I had to strain to hear him. "I slept with someone else on a trip to Germany."

I couldn't have heard right. My husband had sex with another woman?

"She didn't mean anything to me. I wanted to prove I could make a woman come."

"And did she?" I hardly recognized my cold voice.

"Yes, damn it, she did. I am a man, you see, by God! She said it was the best she ever had!"

"Well, hooray for you!" I flew out of bed and stumbled along the blank wall until I found a light switch and flicked it on. The space was suddenly flooded in what seemed like a thousand watts of harsh light. We could have been in an interrogation room. Howard leaned against the metal headboard, squinting, and lit up another Winston. Curls of smoke rose to the ceiling.

"Turn off the damn light," he demanded.

"Screw you, Howard Groves. Don't tell me what to do!"

He leaped up and pulled me back to the khaki-clad bed. I kicked him, but his strength prevailed even with a cigarette clenched in his teeth. He pinned me against his shoulder and exhaled smoke out the side of his mouth. "I love you," he said.

"Take your hands off me." I pulled away from him and moved to the edge of the bed.

"I'm ashamed of myself."

"You betrayed me. You and your moralizing, ha!"

"It's different for you. You're a woman."

"How do you know it's different for me, you bastard?"

"Bastard? When did you start cussing?"

"About the time you started fucking another girl!" Judging by the look on his face, he was scandalized. Good, that was worth the fight. He *was* a bastard!

He scrunched down into the bedding, as if hiding. A twinge of compassion for the sad man I had once thought of as my Prince Charming surprised me. His sharp features were gaunt; he appeared helpless—a feeling I understood, but one I had never seen in Howard.

"Please," he said, "it won't happen again. Forgive me."

"We're stuck on this island for now," I said, "but I'll only stay if you promise not to touch me. And I expect you to show me respect from now on."

The dictatorial Air Force captain, the man who used white gloves on his big hands to check for dust, was gone. In his place, a person I had never seen before wept like a lost child. My better nature did me in. I took him in my arms and cried along with him.

Eventually, we agreed to work on our marriage. But my eyes were now open. I had made a giant leap forward in the way I viewed myself and the way I viewed my marriage.

~~~

Howard had bought a trailer house from a previous owner, set on a permanent foundation on a corner lot, which gave me room to plant flowers and make everything look pretty. We owned the trailer but not the land. The interior was knotty pine and consisted of a living room, a miniscule kitchen with an illegal Dutch oven that we had shipped over, two bedrooms, a walk-in closet, a bathroom, and, as was true throughout the base, a storm entrance.

When the stiff winter wind caused hammering rains to rage sideways across the island and nail into the sides of our domicile, I could barely make it across the yard, step into the storm entrance, catch my breath, and use all my strength to pull the cumbersome outer door closed before—*pant-pant*—yanking the living room door open to safety.

The month I arrived in the Azores, the weather was pleasant, so I took off in the little green Austin-Healy Howard had purchased and drove across the island. A narrow cobblestone road wound over the Brasilia Mountain, where boisterous blue hydrangeas embraced pink roses and sprawled wantonly across the bordering stone walls. The scenery was incomparable, as if filmed in CinemaScope. Halfway across the mountain, a barefoot man sat on a three-legged wooden stool in the center of the road, replacing stones in the roadway by pounding them in place with a mallet. I waved, but he didn't acknowledge me and kept hitting his mallet against a cobblestone. On the mountaintop, I encountered a magical swirl of mist that reminded me of San Francisco. It felt adventurous to emerge from the mystical shroud of fog into gentle sunshine, and in the distance to see the spirited sapphire sea. Nestled in a cove were numerous red-tiled roofs covering the joyful pinks, yellows, and blues of the houses in Angra, capitol city of Terceira.

The Portuguese people were a patient tribe. The pace was slow, their lives hard, primitive, and simple. As if caught in a time warp, women in black dresses washed their clothes at a community well, and farmers tilled fields with oxen hooked up to tree limbs roughly fashioned into plows.

Every week the people celebrated a religious "fiesta" of some sort. A procession would wend its way over the cobbled streets and around the town square of Praia da Vitória. White-clad children carried an assortment of plaster saints, garishly colored and gilded, waving unsteadily overhead. Artificial flowers decorated everything in sight, and the devout leaned out their wide windows, crossing themselves as the procession wound its way along their street.

Apparently no one in authority had given much thought to the tediousness of life on an island. The only newspapers to keep us in contact with the world were a few well-read copies of the *Air Force Times*. Visitors to the commissary were not cheered by the meager choice of foods, almost all of it canned, which pleased my can-crazed husband, along with unappetizing frozen eggs.

The most apparent evidence of boredom, however, was heavy drinking at the officers' club. Even the base chaplain had to be assisted as he made unsteady progress from bar to dining room each evening. My rigid upbringing made it difficult for me to believe he was truly a "man of God." Mama would have knelt in the bar and prayed for the priest's soul even though he was an "ol' Catholic." She would have put Carrie Nation to shame by smashing all the booze in the bar and causing a riot.

Slowly, I made friends and learned that if I kept busy, the unreasoning fears that troubled me could be shoved into the recesses of my mind . . . and controlled. Now that I had spoken my mind to Howard, though, I felt better than I had for years. The bastard!

I inherited two beautiful Siamese kittens from a couple who were going stateside and couldn't figure out how to take the cats along. Those animals became my family. I drew on my usual creative talent for naming pets, and they became Brother and Sister, joining a long line of similarly named pets: Dog, Spot, Bluie, MeowMeow, Rat-Dog, Kitty, Whiskers, Cat, Cat-Cat, and Kat.

It was a thrill when I was elected president of the Officers' Wives' Club, but it was torture to speak in front of the group. It felt different than in Selma. But I forced myself to speak, though my heart beat faster, my hands trembled, and my mouth went dry. I forced myself to look confident. Afterward, my stomach knotted in spasms, and I spent hours on the toilet.

More and more, I recognized that the Azores also created problems for Howard. His natural slowness seemed aggravated. It took him hours to get dressed in the morning. He flew into a rage at the slightest provocation, although now he knew better than to lash out at me. He also had trouble maintaining his record of flying hours. And as month succeeded month, he was repeatedly passed over for promotion.

One dreary day, in an effort to get in more flying time, Howard flew a C-47, or "Gooney Bird"—a plane that could accommodate a crew of three and 6,000 pounds of cargo, or twenty-eight troops, or fourteen stretcher patients and three attendants—to Santana, a runway on the neighboring island of Santa Maria. But he didn't make it home on the same plane. Somehow, although his copilot tried to warn him, Howard crashed the C-47 into a heap of gravel at the end of the runway. He was lucky—lucky that he plowed into the gravel and his plane came to a halt. Otherwise he, his crew, and the 31,000-pound aircraft would have tumbled down a steep cliff and ended up in the frothing sea. Or perhaps he would have sunk onto the lost continent of Atlantis, rumored to lie under the ocean at the base of the island.

Poor Howard.

Just when the time arrived for our highly anticipated trip to Europe, word came down from on high that dependent travel was suspended indefinitely. But I was not without resources. Having become popular at the Portuguese base connected to Lages, I was acquainted with the commanding officer and his wife. The commanding general's aide said a Portuguese military plane was leaving for Lisbon the day after Howard flew off to Germany without me. The general gave orders that I could fly to Lisbon on their aircraft. From there, I flew commercially to Rhein-Main Air Base in Germany, where I met up with Howard.

Europe was a mind-altering experience. As if the European continent hadn't existed for eons before I set eyes on it, I was startled to encounter a world beyond the United States of America. We rented an English Austin and drove first to France, where in youthful naiveté I called on Elizabeth Arden's sister Gladys, who managed the Arden salon in Paris. When I hailed a taxi to take me to Place Pigalle, the driver didn't understand what I was saying. I showed him the address on a map, and he shrugged and gave me a sharp lesson in Gallic superiority. *"Plas Pigal!"* he sniffed.

I'm happy to say that Elizabeth Arden's sister was hospitable and kind and even took me to lunch. *Ask, and it shall be given you; seek, and ye shall find; knock, and it shall be opened unto you.* I was my father's daughter, for sure.

My husband purchased a Leica camera and a light meter at the Rhein-Main Post Exchange and thought he was the next Ansel Adams. Hour after hour passed, along with the light, as Howard held his light meter up to the view, me, passing motorists, mountains, and the Eiffel Tower, while the meter hands jiggled, the light changed, and the resultant photo was often dark. My impatience bordered on revolt.

When we arrived in England via an overnight ferry, I was struck by the White Cliffs of Dover, and in London I lapped up the pageantry of the changing of the guard at Buckingham Palace. The majesty of Switzerland was awe-inspiring, too, but it was in Mannheim, Germany, that a startling snapshot became embedded in my memory and would influence the trajectory of my life.

On a sightseeing tour, the guide pointed out the shell of a bombed-out seven-story building. Jagged bricks had sheered off the front of the structure, leaving twisted metal, molten glass, crumbling mortar, and blackened bricks, exposing the lives of former residents in the manner of a macabre dollhouse. We gazed upon rooms with shredded curtains that hung limply from shattered and warped window frames, rooms with metal beds twisted into knots where couples had once made love, rooms with overturned rusted stoves where potato soup once boiled, rooms with the innards swollen out of chairs and now awaiting ghosts, rooms where people undoubtedly cried, laughed, fought, made up, and tried to be happy. These were the rooms in which actual flesh-and-blood persons once lived. There hovered over the place now, eight years later, the putrefying stench of war.

Those who had called these broken rooms home were Germans, our enemy. But they, like millions of others, had been ensnared by the vitriol and cold-blooded ambition inflicted by a megalomaniac leader—Hitler. The evil of that despotic leader seemed to permeate the very air we breathed, the walls we leaned against, the nervous tension on the faces around us, the fear. My consciousness about the effects of war was being raised. In my mind I heard the whistling of falling bombs. Panic I could barely control rippled through my body.

> Through clever and constant application of propaganda, people can be made to see paradise as hell, and also the other way around, to consider the most wretched sort of life as paradise.
>
> —Adolph
> Hitler

That evening, in Mannheim, Germany, there was no ambient light, no streetlights or bright signs. We were in the dark, except for one candle on our table and one dim light bulb hanging over the bar as we sat in a pub having supper. It was a fitting atmosphere for the accompanying sounds of battle, as in the distance, Allied troops practiced wartime maneuvers. The ominous *boom-boom-boom* of guns firing in the motionless fever of a summer night was unnerving. Sorrow conquered me. I pushed away a bowl of chicken broth, put my head down on the rough table, and wept.

Leaving Howard in Germany, I flew to Lisbon, where I was to connect with the Portuguese military plane for the flight back to Lages. I had one day in Lisbon before catching the once-every-ten-days flight back to my island home. With my last few dollars, I bought a souvenir: a black, red, and yellow painted clay rooster, tucked it under my arm, and headed for the airport. Marching confidently up to the desk, rooster in hand, I gave my papers to the woman who appeared to be in charge. She looked at them and then said in a tired, cheerless voice, "Señora, your plane, she has left!"

"Left? No, that can't be right. She can't have left." I fumbled in my voluminous purse and brought forth another paper that I shoved across the counter at her. "See, it says right here that she departs this afternoon."

"Señora, your plane, she has left!"

"No, that can't be right. She can't have left," I insisted. Sweat ran down my sides. It was hard to breathe.

"Si, señora, she has left. She flew away."

"She has left? No! Look at my papers, just look," I was losing control. My bowels churned.

"Senora, the plane she has left!" the woman said with a modicum of asperity. "She has left." She waved her arms like a bird in flight in an effort to make me understand. "She flew away, byes, byes."

The crowd of black-clad women grew larger. They wrung their hands and muttered, "Oh, poor lady, poor lady." I had an audience and was putting on a show for them. They probably expected me to break out in a dance number like Betty Hutton in *Annie Get Your Gun* or as Stepin Fetchit doing a comedy routine.

"What am I to do?" I asked the hapless woman behind the counter. "There won't be another flight for ten days. Help me. What'll I do?"

She didn't know. With a presence of mind I didn't feel, I called the American Embassy and the American air attaché, but it was a weekend and both agencies said to call back on Monday.

"Am I to sleep in the airport for ten days?" I cried. "I have no money." The person on the phone did not offer assistance.

Well, I came undone right there in the hollow-sounding blue-tiled airport. My audience would get a show, all right. I followed the example set by Mama at the Greyhound bus depot when she learned I had burned down our house. Right there in the Lisbon Airport, without regard for my last pair of nylons or my black leather opera pumps or the constraints of my slender beige traveling skirt, I carefully placed the painted rooster on the stone floor, hiked up the narrow skirt, and knelt down. An embarrassment of runners popped into my last pair of stockings, making ladders on my legs from my thighs to my toes. Mama and Daddy's lessons were deep-seated, and I was in a jam, so I began to pray.

"God," I said out loud, "please help me out of this fix, and I'll never do another bad thing in my life." As if I ever had done anything that could be classified as a sin except wear lipstick. My prayer continued, a litany of promises, until I heard an English-speaking man ask what the problem was.

I opened my eyes and clambered ungracefully to my feet, knocking over the rooster in the process, but thankfully not breaking it. In the audience I had attracted was an American man who said he was en route to New York via TWA, and his plane would be stopping to refuel in Santa Maria, a neighboring island to Terceira. He would pay my way there, and I could pay him back when I got home.

"Oh, I can't let you do that!" I said.

The dozens of Portuguese women surrounding me were invested in my welfare, and said in unison, as if choreographed, "Señora, yes, you can." And so I did.

My rescuer was Jay Smith—a name that was to cause hilarity back at Lages, where the commanding general called on me to tell the story of being rescued by a Mr. Smith to visiting admirals, generals, and senators. Jay Smith was a vice president with a Dun and Bradstreet Fortune 500 company based in New York City. During the long trip to Santa Maria, Mr. Smith told me about his poor childhood, of sleeping on pallets, and being hungry during the Depression. His story was not unlike my own.

In Santa Maria, I was put up in a bunkhouse full of construction workers, many of whom knew me from trips to the Post Exchange at Lages. Did I tell you that I had a job at the PX? Well, yes, it was the only job available for a civilian *dependent* like me, and though there was lots of competition for it, I was the one hired. I sold diamonds. Yes, real diamonds, not knock-your-eyes-out stones, but satisfactory nevertheless. I was hired by Reinhold Brothers in New York City to run their diamond counter. Lages Air Force Base was the first foray of the Reinhold brothers into Post Exchanges. Thus I had friends—or at least friendly faces—on the island of Santa Maria.

Anyway, there I was on Santa Maria with no way of getting to my island and no way of letting friends there know what had happened to me. At night, in the bunkhouse, I pushed a heavy chest across my door after making sure it was locked. I was the only female among a bunch of horny construction workers, all of whom wanted to escort me to breakfast, lunch, or dinner and do anything else I would permit, which wasn't much. Every day, I traipsed down to the runway, the one with the gravel pile still at the end of it, and tried to find out if any planes were coming from Lages.

During one of my scouting safaris, I heard the drone of an airplane engine and recognized it as one of ours. I ran to the runway and literally threw myself onto it, causing the plane to veer and then stop or run over me. When the angry pilot climbed out of the cockpit, ready to call me crazy, he called my name instead.

"Patsy? Patsy Groves? Where have you been? The whole Air Force is looking for you!" And it was true. Well, not the whole Air Force, but two MATS planes from Lages had been sent by the commanding general to Lisbon and Rhein-Main Air Base in Germany to try to find out what had happened to me. Howard didn't know, and even though I had left all my information with the US Embassy in Lisbon and the air attaché's office, they didn't know, either. It was as if I had disappeared from the face of the earth, so far as they were concerned. So much for what one can expect from our embassy.

Captain John Eubanks was not supposed to give me a lift in his plane, but he did it anyway. He had me lie on the floor in the back of the plane, where he covered me with a canvas tarp and showed me a strap to hang onto when he landed on Pico Island after he cleared cows away so he could deliver something or other. After that, we took off for Lages. John tried to spirit me off the plane so no one would be the wiser, but word had traveled much faster than we did. There was so much fanfare over my arrival that I expected to be hoisted on shoulders and paraded up the hill to the Officers' Club.

After that, I was a celebrity on an island where nothing much happened and a celebrity was whoever got your attention that day. With the commanding general on my side, I took advantage of the moment to write and direct a musical, *Them Oklahoma Hills* that involved the whole base. The men assigned to build the stage had forgotten to measure the gym doors and had to tear out one whole side of the gym and rebuild it. The beauty of doing things in the military, I discovered, was that anything could be done. The general gave an order, and that was it.

I had bonded with a woman named Bennie Echwald, a fellow Oklahoma girl and a stellar talent. She was a hoot of a comedienne, and at her instigation, I also became a hoot. We wore long, slinky, black satin dresses, decked ourselves out in all the rhinestones we could find, and gave performances at the NCO Club and the Officers' Club singing "*Diamonds Are a Girl's Best Friend.*" Since there was no competition and everyone was starved for diversion, we were hugely popular. I was feeling my oats—or, as Poor Little Glendora liked to say, I was "something on a stick."

On New Year's Eve at the Officers' Club, I ended up seated next to Howard's commanding officer, a bird colonel. He was a bird in other ways, too, a bantam of a person, short and cocky. He had a clipped reddish-brown mustache that he regularly smoothed with his right index finger. He was annoying. "Do you want your husband to get promoted?" the colonel asked while drinking his Jack Daniels dessert.

"Why, sure," I replied.

"Let's talk," the colonel said, and waltzed me onto the dance floor. His grip was strong, and as we danced, he pushed his lean body hard against me. "You're cute," he said. "A good dancer, too."

I felt clumsy and thought I was sinning when I danced. Mama would have had a wall-eyed fit. "Ole' honky-tonk stuff," she would have said.

"Thank you," I replied, endeavoring to create a sliver of light between our bodies.

"Listen, honey," he said, dancing me into the shadows, "I'll pick you up tomorrow after your husband leaves for work."

"Why, I can't do that," I sputtered.

"Of course you can. You have free will. And you want to get your husband promoted, don't you?"

"Yes, but . . ."

"Meet me tomorrow," he whispered and blew into my ear. My face burned. I pulled away. What had I done to invite such an advance?

"Well?" he questioned.

"No!" I replied.

The previous softness left his face. "Young lady," he said, "there's such a thing as R.H.I.P., or haven't you heard? Rank Has Its Privileges." His grip on my wrist was steel. "Your husband is a captain. I'm a colonel. I'll see you tomorrow."

He released me, and I headed back to the table where Howard sat. Oh, dear Jesus, what had I ever done to make that man think I was that kind of girl? Did I dare tell Howard?

Back in our small house, my husband demanded I tell him what his boss had said to me. "Tell me what the colonel said," he insisted. "Tell me!"

"I told you, he wants me to meet him tomorrow."

"You're lying, Patsy. Now tell me."

"I'm not lying. I'm not."

"You led him on, didn't you?"

"No!" I screamed. "And you're a fine one to talk—after all, you slept with someone else."

His stinging slap sent me reeling into the sofa. "You agreed not to mention that!" he said.

Humiliated, I stared at the man who had promised to love and honor me. My tears dried like a drought-starved stream. A certain resolve hardened into a plan. I deserved better than this. There was no question about it. As soon as we got back to the States, I would divorce this dumb, cruel man. "Howard, if you dare touch me again, I'll report you to an MP. And don't think I won't. I will not tolerate your abuse. I am through with you!"

The next day I called the colonel and told him he was not to show up at my home. He seemed so taken aback that he mumbled a quick apology and hung up. I was surprised at my strength and willpower. Well, I said to myself, I must have inherited Mama's determination.

I was no longer troubled by unreasoning fears, although I still had nightmares about a vengeful God. The fact that I had reached a decision about my marriage made me feel better.

"Howard," I said the next day, "I want a divorce." I was calm and controlled, concentrating more on the heavy rain lashing at the windows than on the effect of my statement.

"So do I," he said, throwing a slicker on over his uniform. "I want a woman who will give me a family." He turned and opened the door. "My tour of duty is nearly over. We can file for divorce when we get back to the States." With that, he disappeared into the rain. From then on, I slept on the sofa, listening throughout the night to the crackling Voice of America broadcasts on a shortwave radio and ignoring my husband. It didn't occur to me that Howard was the one who should have moved to the sofa or to a barracks. I had a lot to learn.

Chapter 13

S-E-X

At last I saw Malcolm again. We had run into each other at various events, and I saw him sitting in the fourth row on the left-hand side of the gym at my Oklahoma Hills offering, but we hadn't talked to each other. Howard was on a flight to the States, and I was eating dinner alone at the Officers' Club. I was supposed to be with my friend Bennie, but she couldn't come at the last minute.

"May I join you?" Malcolm asked, already sitting down. "I've been hoping to see you."

"Me, too," I said quietly. "I need to talk to you, okay?"

"Okay, that's fine with me, but we should get away from prying eyes." He glanced around at the all-too-familiar faces in the dining room.

"Where?" I asked. "Howard's away."

"I know. I've kept track. Would you be comfortable going to my place?" I nodded yes. "It's the third house past the main gate. You can't miss it." He grinned. "Brilliant pink with neon-blue shutters to announce my address. I'll be waiting." He said a casual goodbye and left.

I forced myself to finish eating, slowly and calmly, but I was filled with excitement. I was attracted to Malcolm, even though he was old enough to be my father. But more than attraction, I wanted someone trustworthy to listen to me. I needed to talk honestly about being raped and how unclean I felt.

As soon as I was out the club door, I ran to my little green Austin and drove directly to Malcolm's house. The restive ocean beating against my eardrums, along with the tang of salty air carried on wisps of fog, created a de-energizing chill that caused me to shiver and pull my red sweater more tightly around my body.

"Park here," Malcolm said, directing me to a place behind a rock wall. "We should be careful. Everyone knows everyone else on this island, and I don't want you gossiped about."

"Maybe we shouldn't meet like this," I said, feeling unsure of myself.

"It's okay. There's nothing to be concerned about."

Rows of candles splashed light against the white stucco interior of his small abode and painted shadows along the walls. On the record player, Jo Stafford's clear voice belted out, "Fly the ocean in a silver plane, see the jungle when it's wet with rain . . ."

"Quite a romantic bachelor pad, Malcolm," I said with a chuckle.

He grinned. "Yeah. As usual, the electricity went off, so I made the most of it, even though it sputtered back on a few minutes ago." He came across as relaxed, in a beige cable-knit sweater and fatigues rather than a uniform, more accessible somehow. "I keep candles at the ready," he said, pointing me toward a bulky old orange-red sofa fronting a fireplace of blue tiles. Stacks of wood piled on the stone floor and in outsized wicker baskets furthered the air of rustic ease.

My shivers abated when I felt the warmth of a fire blazing in the grate.

"I'll get a bottle of Mateus rosé to sooth inner demons, and then we can throw our glasses in the fireplace in a toast to the land of *não faz mal*," Malcolm said.

We laughed. That was a common saying on the island and meant, I was told, the land where nothing matters. I slipped off my leather loafers and, feeling suddenly shy, snuggled into a fluffy red pillow tucked into a corner of the comfy old sofa. The warmth of the fire and an earthen pot of yellow and blue wildflowers revealed Malcolm's appreciation of beauty. After pouring us each a glass of the rosy liquid from the oval-shaped bottle of wine, he sat down in a cozy-looking chair across from me. "Okay, my friend, tell me what's bothering you. How are you faring?"

A sigh, a sip of wine, and I began to unburden myself. "I'm miserable with Howard, and I'm definitely getting a divorce. He's mean, he slept with another woman, he . . ."

"Whoa, wait a minute, slow down," Malcolm said. "Take a deep breath. You have plenty of time to talk."

"Oh, Malcolm, I'm ashamed of myself. My marriage hasn't all been bad. Howard allows me to put on plays and work at the Post Exchange selling diamonds, and he goes to the costume parties that I enjoy, but he orders me around like a slave, and . . ."

Malcolm interrupted my stream-of-consciousness soliloquy by asking a question. "Patsy, one question. Are you in love with your husband?"

Lordy, I didn't know the answer. Some part of me did love him, at least the part that had caused me to marry him. But did I love the dictator he had become? No. "No, I don't love the person he is now."

"Love is a misunderstood word, Patsy. It's not the flush of romantic feelings we associate with it, but should personify positive actions. Your husband isn't your boss. He doesn't have the right to 'allow' you to do things. Otherwise, you have a child-parent relationship instead of a marriage of equals."

My mind whirled with new thoughts. Ah, that was it: I had let myself be Howard's little girl—a child—and Howard the parent. "By any definition, I can't attach the word *love* to Howard."

"Okay, it's good to be clear. You don't have to explain anything to anyone. Please don't be influenced by what you think others may say. They should be working on their own lives, not yours. Remember that, sweet girl. Often we think we need to explain our reasons for doing things out of fear of what others may say, instead of embracing the unique music our own life offers."

"That's beautiful, Malcolm. For sure, I refuse to be Howard's little girl any longer. If I have to live with that boring, mean man one minute longer, I'll scream and jump into the ocean!" I stood up and covered my mouth with both hands in an effort to stop a weeping cry that fought to make its presence known.

"Go ahead, Patsy, let it out. No one can hear through these thick walls, and it will probably be good for you."

The scream that bubbled up from four hundred feet below my surface felt like an artesian eruption. If I allowed it to explode, it might shatter the windows. "Hang on!" I shouted. Then a wail shot from my throat, spread to the rafters, and awakened every dog in the neighborhood, I felt sure. "Aieeeeeeeeeeeeeeeeee!"

Candles blinked, fireplace logs flared, bugs crawled under furniture, and Malcolm laughed.

At last I said, "Okay, I got carried away. I'm through." I felt better for having vented my frustration in a childish manner. For a long moment, I stared out the window at the black eyes of the Atlantic Ocean, and then flopped down on the sofa again.

"Thanks for making me feel comfortable enough to do that," I said. "Thanks, too, for what you said about divorce during that long plane trip. I've mulled it over ever since."

Malcolm smiled. "When my hearing returns, I'll answer your question. Lady, you can yell! Next time try screaming into pillows so there won't be an MP alert."

"Funny. Ha-ha." I threw the red pillow at him.

"Patsy, I recall saying that one should never feel sorry for people getting a divorce, but that was too flip. Divorce is a traumatic experience regardless of how anxious one may be to make a change."

"If my experiences are what one can expect in marriage, any marriage, I don't want any part of it," I said. "I want to accomplish things and have fun and not be a servant under the high and mighty rule of a man. I want connection and empathy—a friend, not a taskmaster."

"All relationships aren't like that, Patsy." Malcolm patted my hand, comforting me. "You're very young still. I wonder if you're prepared for the real world. Military life isn't like civilian life, you know."

"I know I'm lonely. I'm hungry for romance and love, for a trustworthy connection with someone I care about, for gentleness." Longing made my voice husky.

Malcolm urged me to keep talking. His tenderness penetrated my trembling spirit and lent me the courage to talk about the details of being raped. I avoided his gaze as, with the usual stops and starts, I told him the particulars, things I hadn't revealed before. "Uh, the man who, uh, raped me was a doctor . . ."

"A physician? A military doctor?"

"Yes, a bona fide military doctor. Uh . . . ahem . . . that doctor asked if I had orgasms, and . . . uh . . . when I said no, he told me to undress so he could examine me . . ." My voice quavered.

"I'm here for you, Patsy," Malcolm said, taking my hand in his larger one, calming me.

"Well . . ." Geysers of words shot from my mouth like Old Faithful in Yellowstone Park, as if ridding myself of them. "That man said I suffered from frigidity and he could help me, and then . . . then . . . he raped me." Tears coursed down my cheeks. Wood shifted in the fireplace, spitting sparks onto the hearth.

Soft curses exploded from Malcolm. "That fucking doctor! Forgive my language, but I'm outraged. How unconscionable! How outrageous!" He stood up and began to pace the floor. "What's that doctor's name? I can report him. He should not be allowed to practice medicine."

"No, please!" The thought of a public report made my stomach roil. "If I had to testify, I would die. No one would believe me, not then and not now. I wanted to report him at the time, but to whom? No one would believe me, no one. And I would be branded a slut!"

Malcolm hit his fist into his other hand as he paced, not his usual calm self. His eyes flashed. "Sadly, you're right. A woman in a rape case usually gets blamed. Oh, Patsy, I'm sorry you had such a horrific experience. But you do realize that it wasn't your fault. Nothing about it was your fault. Do you know that?"

"I'm beginning to know that. Thanks for believing me," I said, meaning every word. "Howard would have blamed me, so I didn't tell him. I told my maid. She was the only person I could trust."

"I'll ask you again. Do you know, *really* know that nothing about that rape was your fault?" He sat down next to me, took my arm, and turned me toward him. "Answer me. Look in my eyes and answer me."

"Yes, I do know that," I said, crying.

"Promise me you'll not let that experience define you. As traumatic as it was, it was only a blip in your life. Okay?"

I nodded agreement. Malcolm encircled me in his arms. I leaned my head into his shoulder and breathed in the clean scent of Palmolive soap that clung to him.

"How is it possible that you could be married to a lout like Howard? He should treasure you. Marriage is about trust and companionship and understanding, disagreements, a partnership of the good and the bad. Your husband, more than anyone, certainly more than your maid, should comfort you at serious times."

I absorbed this. "Strange, when he's away I'm alive, and when he's home, I feel dead inside. But . . ." I shook myself from Malcolm's arms. "I'm not going to bash him. A friend once said, 'Never despise a bridge over which you've walked.' Howard was good to me when I had heart surgery. I'm grateful for that."

"Wise attitude," he said. "If we allow the past to influence our future, we are not living. One more thing—an important thing for you to know. In my professional opinion, there is no such thing as frigidity. That fraud of a doctor was incorrect on that score, too. There are only inept lovers. But we aren't taught how to be good lovers. Sex isn't talked about in our society, although it seems to be on the minds of most people most of the time. Sex begins in the mind. If you aren't shown kindness, respect, and consideration, how can you have good sex? You said you were sheltered to the point of ignorance regarding the various functions of your body. That's what I call a *real* sin." He raked long fingers through his black hair, causing it to part crookedly. "I can get on a rampage about these subjects. But enough—you should head home before curfew."

The information Malcolm imparted to me was mind-boggling. Never had I heard such opinions before. I saw Malcolm six more times before he was to leave the island. Our sessions gave me insights into my psyche and the reasons I hadn't rebelled against Howard's meanness and dogmatic mindset long ago. It was obvious that my upbringing and society had made me feel it was not only okay to be treated like a second-class citizen, it was expected. It was as if women were born to cook and clean, to flirt and look pretty, have babies and be available anytime day or night for sex, and to use no other talents without a man's consent. But that was baloney! What a revelation.

On one of my next visits, Malcolm and I talked about religion and how the fanatical sermons that thundered in my eardrums throughout my formative years had made me afraid I would go to Hell for the least infractions of his Word. Malcolm called it child abuse. "Patsy, that kind of inculcated fear is child abuse, no different than if you were beaten with a stick. The scars may not show on your body, but they are grooved into your gray matter."

"But, Malcolm, I don't actually believe all that hellfire and brimstone stuff."

"Perhaps not consciously. You say that, but do you really believe it? Those frightening images are probably lodged in your subconscious, ready to leap out and drag you under unless you bring them to the surface and talk about them. Religion is the cause of more dysfunction, including wars, than any other single cause. Religious zealots create paralyzing fears and mental illness by the promulgation of doomsday scenarios!"

"What? Can you say that again? Wow."

Malcolm laughed. "I did get carried away there. Sorry about that string of words."

His erudite words caused a horrifying memory to surface. My ears rang. Fragmentary emotions possessed and released me as a fearsome image floated up from the seemingly bottomless abyss of my child mind. A bulky man, a sermonizer, with a thick head of carbon-like hair, dressed in a shiny black suit, stood at a pulpit and held aloft a black bound Bible as sweat ran down his face, joining the water that seemed forced from under his closed eyelids. Caustic words frothed in a torrent from his gravelly sounding larynx, and spittle collected in the corners of his mouth as he described the Last Days as if he could hardly wait to see us barbecued in Hell while he watched with sanctified feet from atop a white cloud.

"You had better throw yourself on the mercy of Almighty God right now!" he ranted. "Sinner! Sinner! Sinner! Fall down and beg the Almighty Lord to save you before it's too late!" He paused, wiped his brow with a napkin-sized white handkerchief, let out a sob, and continued on. "The great battle of Armageddon, the final battle between good and evil, and the appearance of the Antichrist is upon us. *Amen!* Brothers and sisters, *glory to God*, the Last Days are upon us," he intoned. This he knew, for he avowed to have personally received a message from God. "The Last Days are upon us! Repent, repent, repent! *Hal-le-lu-jah!* The seven signs of the Apocalypse: wars and rumors of wars, plagues, famines, asteroids hitting the earth, earthquakes, volcanic eruptions. *Hal-le-lu-jah! Amen!* Red tides and plagues are rolling toward us right this minute, *glory to God!* Heavenly Father, have mercy on all these sinners." He kept using the giant bandana to mop his sweating brow, and it was bordering on soggy. "You, yes, *you*, my friends, are doomed to burn in a lake of fire unless you beg God for forgiveness . . ."

Then the preacher man beamed his steely gray eyes at nine-year-old me, knowing a sinner when he saw one. "Do you want to be *left behind* during the Rapture? Repent, or you won't see your parents ever again! Repent!"

I was a tender tree in a storm, an aspen in a wicked whirlwind. Spring buds forming on my sensitive soul shriveled and fell to earth unborn. A stuttering howl of terror issued from my throat. Mama bolted from her seat and hauled me onto her ample lap, all the while shouting, "Amen!" and egging on the preacher to continue with his fierce speechifying.

It was at that moment that I figured out how to save myself. I would hang onto Mama's dress tail and fly along with her to paradise. But could I sneak past Saint Peter, who waited with his gigantic Judgment Day book and fat #2 pencil to check off the righteous from the unrighteous? Maybe I could sneak through the Pearly Gates by hiding under Mama's dress! Saint Peter would never see me. But I wasn't sure I could fool Almighty God. Oh, I was doomed, I thought, burrowing into Mama's bosom.

That memory left me as sapped as a maple tree after syrup harvest. I leaned into sofa pillows and gulped as much rosé as I could swallow while I told Malcolm the story.

He said my remembering it in such minute detail showed how much that horrific message impacted me. "A lovely innocent subjected to psychological maltreatment because of religion—that's as cruel as inflicting physical pain on an adult prisoner." He sighed. "But enough, enough! It's time for a musical interlude, and then I'll send you home with chocolate cake Marie, my housekeeper, made."

Malcolm slid a black record from an album and placed it carefully on the turntable. "Get ready for Ludwig van Beethoven's *Moonlight Sonata*. Beethoven will make your anxieties drift away." Setting the player arm, he plopped to the floor and closed his eyes. I followed suit. When the first clear notes reverberated in my ears, it seemed a message from the past, a memorandum of forgotten dreams and hopes. Tight muscles relaxed, and sinew, nerves, bones let go from the bottoms of my feet to the top of my head, reassuring me, validating life as good. In my mind's eye, sparkling illuminations flowed from the ceiling in waves as soft as snowflakes, draping the candlelit room in a crystalline coat, sinking into my skin, making me confident that the music of a genius composer could not be an accident. There must be a benevolent Creator, not one with fierce eyes who wielded swords and condemned people to Hell.

When the music ended, Malcolm replaced the record in its album sleeve and gave it to me. "Patsy girl, when you feel anxious, listen to this music and realize that you have your own special music within you, music to share with the world. Professing beliefs isn't what's important. What matters is appreciating the miracle of life, the mystery, the joy." He lifted my chin and looked directly into my eyes. "A religionist tends toward the excessive, neurotic, controlling, and evil. A religious government is always a cruel government. Questioning and doubting are healthy and should be encouraged, not feared."

I realized how little I knew about anything, having grown up in a linear, black-and-white world where any belief other than ours was considered heathen and therefore without merit. I was an ignoramus. "How do you know all this, Malcolm?"

"Before I woke up to my life, I was studying to become a Jesuit priest, but after I awoke, I became a Buddhist."

"You, a priest? No! You're a doctor. A Buddhist? That sounds far out, too."

"How wonderful it is that you have so much to learn and that I can be one of your teachers, Patsy. There is no limit as to how many careers or interests you can have or how many teachers. You are my teacher, too, you know. As for me, sweet girl, Buddhism agrees with the moral teachings of other religions and provides a long-term purpose within our existence,

294

through wisdom and true understanding.

"I thought Buddhists were heathens and needed missionaries to give them Bibles."

Malcolm sputtered. Covering his mouth with his hands, he burst out laughing and coughing. "As you would say, Patsy,"—*cough, cough*—"Lordy, Lordy, Lordy. No, we don't need missionaries or Bibles. Buddhism isn't concerned with labels like Christian, Moslem, Hindu, or Buddhist. I don't think I've told you that I'll be spending time in Tibet and India after this long military tour." Malcolm yawned while still laughing. "Excuse me, I'm talked out. Anyway, that's enough. I needed that laugh. Next time, I'll take you on a tour of the island so you can laugh, too."

"Good. I'm ready for a change."

Malcolm kissed me lightly on the cheek, said good night, and sent me on my way with Beethoven and a slice of chocolate cake.

~~~

A few weeks later, on an overcast boring day, my friend Bennie and I sat on the floor of my living room cooking up mischief.

"We've gotta get donations for that orphanage in Angra," she said, lifting dark eyebrows to underscore the point, her brown eyes laughing. "Those kids need things, and we can help."

We brainstormed, trying to come up with fun ideas. I thought a musical fashion show would excite people. "We're starved for new fashions," I said, "I can write to stores in the States and ask them to send stuff for a show."

Bennie smiled slyly. "Okay, but that's gonna take time, so while we're waiting, here's what we can do. We'll have booths made by the shop guys and sell kisses." She laughed. "Those horny flyboys piloting fighter planes through here will go crazy. We'll make money."

I giggled and agreed that it was a fun idea. But trying to enlist others to participate in our scheme was not hugely successful. Although the girls tittered at the idea and rolled their eyes, mostly they said no, except for one other wife and Lee Beaumaster, an unmarried nurse who was endowed with astonishing breasts that preceded her like heat-seeking missiles. There were plenty of willing targets, too.

Well, let me tell you right now, our shenanigan became a hit, especially Lee's booth. The line to her stand wound around two buildings and along a cliff before it doubled back. Those guys were so excited that they kept coming back for more. At a dollar a kiss, Lee made 750 bucks in nothing flat. Afterward, we helped put ice chips in the fingers of a rubber glove to go on her swollen lips.

Howard showed up but didn't come to my booth—oh, no. He went to Lee and the young wife of a lieutenant. Bennie and I stared in amazement at the married guys who could hardly wait for our puckered lips—oh, yes—and those rascals would slip us notes asking for more, if you know what I mean. But smacking those boys with lipstick kisses while trying to keep my mouth closed wasn't easy. I made sure to rinse with Listerine between smacks. Those flyboys reminded me of my dates in Waurika and how repulsed I was at the thought of a boy's tongue in my mouth. I also thought of Aileen's kissing lessons at the Dallas Y and wondered what had become of her.

When Malcolm arrived, his velvet brown eyes twinkled as he took in our lipstick-smeared faces. He came right to my booth, and my heart did flip-flops. Bennie gave me the fish eye. "Go for it, Pat," she whispered. "It's clear you're smitten." Well, I took his dollar that turned out to be five, closed my eyes, and kissed him. He kissed me back, and then Bennie interrupted. "Don't get steamy," she said with a laugh. "Although I wouldn't blame you." Malcolm handed Bennie another five, called her a nosy housemother, and bussed her on the cheeks, lips, and forehead. He told her to keep the change and left, whistling a tune.

In four hours, we made almost two thousand dollars by kissing every frog, er, horny toad in the Lages Field pond. "We're in the wrong business,"

Bennie allowed. "Now I get why those Okie girlfriends of ours back home do it."

"Ha! They have to do more than kiss," I said.

I was eager to see Malcolm again, but first I had to think about our imminent return to the States, and was eager to get practical things out of the way. I was anxious to find a way to get my two Siamese cats to California, since there was no possibility of a MATS plane taking them. When a fighter pilot friend said he could take them as far as Westover Air Force Base in Massachusetts and then put them on a train to California, I was elated. I bought a large oval laundry basket with a wicker lid, padded the bottom with layers of paper diapers from the PX, put plastic bowls inside it to hold food and water, and wired a can opener and spoon to the outside, along with a dozen cans of cat food. Then I stitched a square of white sheeting to the top, on which I'd painted in large black letters:

<u>Please</u> Feed Us!

Two Loved Cats Traveling from the Azores to California!

Give Us Water and Food. <u>PLEASE</u>!

Pet us too! THANK YOU!

Twisting a wire to hold the lid in place and still allow for Good Samaritans along the way to have access, I put my two furry pets inside and hoped for the best.

"Are you nuts?" friends asked. "No one will feed those cats."

"They'll die from dehydration or starvation!" said one.

"That's a two-week trip, at least," said another. "Better kiss your animals goodbye, Pat."

My usual nature is to believe, to have faith, and to always expect the best, a trait with which many are uncomfortable. But I was worried, too. Would they make it? The odds were not in their favor, even with nine lives.

Mom Groves met the train the cats were shipped on and said the smell was so ripe she kept the car windows open all the way to the ranch. Once released from their two-week prison, Brother and Sister ran under the huge ranch refrigerator and didn't come out for a week, although when no one was around, they lapped up bowls of water and ate heartily. Later, they became so attached to Mom and Pop that that's where they lived out their long, happy lives, relaxing over a heat register or in a lap.

Throughout the process of getting my "whiskered children" safely to California, I mulled over my intriguing conversations with Malcolm and my feelings for the man. We obviously were attracted to each other, but I was aware that we lived in a hermetically sealed environment on an island. We were both lonely, and we might seem different to each other on terra firma, as I called the US.

One day I drove to a promontory overlooking the ocean, a place full of wild blue hydrangea, red and pink roses, birds, and beauty. Soft breezes caressed my hair and whipped my skirt against my legs as I lay on the perfumed grass, reading Thoreau's *Walden Pond*. "This whole earth which we inhabit is but a point in space," he wrote. "How far apart, think you, dwell the two most distant inhabitants of yonder star, the breadth of whose disk cannot be appreciated by our instruments? Why should I feel lonely? Is not our planet in the Milky Way?"

I was mulling that over when a penciled notation caused me to laugh out loud. "When Thoreau was dying, his sister asked if he'd made peace with God, to which the dying man replied, 'I didn't know we had been quarreling.'"

"Chick-a-lick," Daddy once said, "look at all those stars up there swirling about in the sky. The Milky Way, the Moon, Orion, the Big Dipper, and then look at that cottonwood tree over yonder with its strong trunk and branches and leaves that move in the invisible wind. All of that was created, and so much more, including you and me. No one understands it. No one ever will. They'll make discoveries and claims and awe you with advances, but still, no one will ever be able to break open the true mystery of our beginnings. When you look, Patsy, see, *really* see, nature, the depth of the sky, flowers, weeds, crops, birds, the everyday things. That's God. Life is an unexplained adventure. That blue butterfly over there—that's God, too."

When the day finally arrived that Malcolm and I toured the island together, everything was cast not in blue but in a quixotic golden shade by his presence. Oh, the joy of sharing time with someone intelligent who didn't clear his throat every time he spoke and appreciated beauty, nature, and *me*. We found hidden lakes, volcanic craters, and mystical forests. There was an exhilarating world at my fingertips, one I hadn't known existed. We discovered cheeses and various wines of the region, as well as a seafood café across the island where we gorged on the catch of the day. We danced on the roadway with the static on Voice of America as our music, improvising steps.

The day we planned to go to the beach for a picnic arrived overcast and wintry. Even so, we bundled up in bulky sweaters, coats, and scarves, and headed to the beach. Malcolm carried a wicker picnic basket and blanket to a sand dune in a small cove where clumps of wild grasses grew, an area that afforded shelter from the wind. The beach was deserted. Apparently, we were the only ones adventurous or crazy enough to brave the muscular wind and fit-throwing breakers. We burrowed into our sand bunker, where we nibbled chocolate chip cookies and sipped hot coffee from a thermos. But neither of us felt hungry, nor did we have much to say. We gave up trying to eat and lay down close to each other on the military-issue blanket spread over the soft sand while we listened to the sounds of the overwrought sea.

Malcolm pulled me close to him, and my happy heart thumped hard within my chest. An unknown throbbing sensation thrummed in the lower part of my body, scaring me. What was happening to me *down there*? Involuntarily, I pushed my body as close as possible to Malcolm, wanting to unpeel our heavy layers of clothes and make love. What a delicious sensation.

"Sweet girl," he said softly, "I want so much to make love to you. But after what you've been through, I will only hold you. If we should ever make love, it will be your decision, at a time when you are free to make that choice without guilt." He smiled. "Although, what we're doing now is as much a part of making love as anything else, perhaps more. Except for our bulky clothes, of course. We're bundled up like tractor tires." He laughed. "I couldn't get near you if you were on fire."

"Yes!"

"Yes?"

"Yes, I am on fire!" Erotic stirrings I had never before felt made me bold. Malcolm's words ignited an intensity of feeling already burning inside me. Enveloping him in passionate kisses, I threw off my coat and sweater, oblivious to the chill wind, and helped Malcolm pull his sweater off as sea grasses blew above our heads and feral waves lathered the shore. He responded to my urgency with an urgency of his own. Then, in a courageous move, I unbuckled his belt. He kicked off his trousers, and took his delectable sweet time in doing the rest.

From some deep inner core, I moaned as my body responded to Malcolm's lovemaking. My surprised hormones jittered around in bewildered exhilaration for a few minutes. Hallelujah! I marveled at what was happening to me, enthralled. I was caught up in being loved and caressed and talked to. We talked as we made love, laughing at my lack of knowledge, my innocence, exploring our bodies as my lover sprinkled butterfly kisses along my chilled yet hot body, and then pulled our coats over the top of us. We were cocooned in our own private island on an island in time as sand shifted beneath us and seabirds cawed in a fantasy of desire.

Malcolm's lovemaking was tender and persuasive, not the slam-bam-thank-you-ma'am of my husband's. But still, I worked at feeling what should have been automatic and delicious. I longed for my willing body to be turned into a lover's knot. But I didn't feel the thrill other women talked or wrote about. That wail of forgetfulness and unbridled desire seemed just beyond a border far, far away and receding further with every thrust from my lover like the ocean at low tide.

Even so, a crescendo of self-belief and warmth flowed over me and through me as though pure crystal water cleansed me, filling me with sanity when Malcolm climaxed. At last, I was baptized. There was nothing wrong with me, nothing at all, I told myself. No, I was responsive and loving. Did I have an orgasm? Was that what I experienced? Oh, I hoped so with all my heart.

~~~

Following my yearned for sexual awakening, I expected to feel guilty. After all, I had committed adultery, but instead, the world took on a golden glow. Colors were sharper, nature enhanced, and my self-image soared.

Howard only once indicated he knew about Malcolm and me. His words sent a chill through me. "How's your Armenian friend?" he asked one day as he slammed out the door. "Does that old man wear silk pajamas and feed you grape leaves?"

I was so surprised that I answered with a serious no.

"Don't think you're getting away with anything, Patsy," Howard said, staring hard at me. "I've got you both in my sights, and someday I'll get even. Divorced or not, you'll always be mine."

I couldn't take him seriously.

Malcolm and I spent every minute we could with each other. We laughed together and played together, teased each other and shared secrets as he continued my religious and musical education. My sexual education, too. He pointed out to me that he was twenty years my senior and therefore should have gained a bit of know-how by now.

One Sunday afternoon, he pulled off the road onto a headland overlooking the majestic sea. We embraced, kissing and fondling each other, while avoiding the car's stick shift and steering wheel. I was the teenager I had never been. Later, we sat on the cliff eating cheese and small apples and drinking local wine.

"I'll be leaving soon, you know," Malcolm said. "Come with me. Don't wait for Howard's tour to end."

I shook my head. "I promised Howard I would wait. He says he would be grossly embarrassed if I were to leave ahead of him, and I guess I owe him that much. A few months more won't matter."

"Promise you'll get help if he becomes violent. You don't have to take anything from him."

"He won't get violent."

"My sweet girl, I worry about you living under the same roof with that man. Ever since he crashed his plane on San Miguel, he's acted unhinged. He lashed out at an airman last week because the poor guy reported for duty a few minutes late. The lieutenant who told me about the incident said Howard was rigid with anger and it took two men to control him. It's been hushed up, but his behavior isn't normal."

"No one said anything to me about it!"

"Not many people know, and I don't think they would tell you if they did."

I shook my head. "I'm not afraid of him, sweetheart. He won't hurt me."

"I would be devastated if anything happened to you." He leaned over and kissed me on the forehead and then fell quiet for a long moment. "Patsy, I'm so much older than you that I can't help but think you're still looking for your father . . ."

"No!"

"Think about it, sweet girl." Malcolm held my hand. "It's perfectly natural. You lost your dad when you were fourteen, on the cusp of puberty. You lost the person to whom you looked for protection and trust. That's a huge bereavement. Perhaps that's why you're attracted to men older than yourself, why you are attracted to me."

"I do like older men, but you're different."

"Maybe I'm not so different. Any man would find you alluring, would want to make love to you. The search for your father is something you might want to give a bit of thought to as you go forward. That's another lesson from a man who loves you."

Malcolm was leaving the next day to study the teachings of Buddha in an Indian ashram, and then he would travel to Armenia to visit Spitak, in the land of his parents' birth. It was difficult to say goodbye. Three months later I would be back in the States where I would file for divorce. Afterward, I would head for San Francisco, the city I had fallen in love with during my time at UC Medical Center.

"When I get back from traipsing the earth, will you come to New York? My parents and friends will love you. I just hope you like baklava," he teased. I enjoyed the stories about his family traditions. It was true, he said, that his people loved to dance and eat. They were an exuberant tribe.

I didn't dream, that day in 1958, that in 1988 my future would take me to Soviet Armenia where I would take supplies and Armenian-speaking American children after a devastating earthquake virtually destroyed Spitak, the birthplace of Malcolm's parents.

"Malcolm, darling, I've given lots of thought to what I want to do after my divorce, and . . ." It was hard to get the words out, to express myself.

"And?" He held my hand lightly, as if trying to make what I was going to say easier.

"I want to be on my own after being married forever, it seems. Twelve years! I need to find out who I am separate from a man. Honestly, thanks to you and your teachings, I'm now beginning to think about who I really am without considering anyone else or having a husband tell me what to do and how to think. Can you understand that?"

Looking into my eyes, he said, "Yes, of course I understand. You went from being a daughter to being a wife without getting to know yourself. I admire your thoughtfulness about it. But still, that doesn't preclude our getting together in the future. We don't have to make a decision about that right this minute, do we?"

"No, of course not. I love you, Malcolm. Please don't think otherwise." I kissed him, a long, lingering kiss full of longing and pain and joy and sadness and passion, too.

"Another kiss like that, darling, and I'll pick you up in my arms and run away with you," Malcolm said, holding me close.

I felt his hardness against my thigh, and a throb of desire moved through me, but I moved on with my plan. We agreed that he would come to see me in San Francisco upon his return from Asia. In the meantime, we would write to each other.

Before we parted, my lover put a Judy Garland record on the turntable. Her poignant phrasing left little doubt as to our feelings for each other. As Judy, in her tremulous fashion, belted out "You'll Never Walk Alone," we held each other and cried a little and then laughed at how unabashedly sentimental we were.

"I love you," he said, "and that means I wish all your dreams to come true, and for you to love yourself."

"Oh, Malcolm, I'm scared and nervous at the prospect of being on my own in San Francisco. But I'm excited by it, too."

"Sweet, sweet girl, you are a unique combination of enthusiasm, joyfulness, smarts, creativity, honesty, and silliness. Appreciate yourself. If you follow the herd, you'll get mired in ruts. Be true to who you are, even if it leads to a kissing booth with Bennie." The corners of his eyes flowered with laugh lines. "Do that, and your inner light will blow those San Franciscans away."

"Silly? I'm silly?"

"Yes, of course you are. That's one of the finest things about you, silly," he said, kissing me again.

Just before he hit the tarmac in route to his plane, my amazing teacher and lover handed me an envelope with the first of many notes he would write to me.

> We can't know what the future is.
> Embrace your life, never be afraid,
> When you remove the shroud of fear
> from your life, you can see and
> experience everything in the present.
> I don't have to know what the future
> is. You will always be with me. I will
> always be with you. Every day is the
> day of days.
>
> Malcolm
>
> I love you,
> Sweet Girl.

After Malcolm left, I felt hollow inside. I grieved for the sound of his voice, for his touch, for his tenderness. Had I made a mistake? Should I follow him? But then what? Malcolm was my best friend, teacher, and lover. He awoke in me a yearning to learn and to understand as much as I could about myself and the world. He awoke in me the knowledge of what love could be. He awoke in me a dawning wisdom that said I was valuable and had nothing to fear from the decrees or actions of others, religious or otherwise.

~~~

After we arrived back in California, as I was preparing to leave Howard, I thought that all I had to do was turn around three times in front of my hut and say, "I divorce, I divorce, I divorce," shake a horse's tail or something, and voilà, I would be free. No. When I appeared in front of a judge in Vallejo, California, he said I needed a lawyer and assigned a fellow who arrived on the scene from an interior office, combing his sandy hair and adjusting his pants like he had just been awakened from a nap. When I said I didn't want anything from Howard Groves except a secondhand purple-and-white Chrysler he had already given me, the judge said, "You've got to take *something*." He awarded me one hundred dollars a month for one year, signed my divorce papers, said it would be final in one year, and said goodbye.

"Okay, let's get out of here," I whispered to my thirty-one-year-old self.

I had four hundred dollars saved from my diamond-selling job, the hated purple-and-white secondhand car, and a Belief in Myself.

Which, as it turned out, was enough.

Chapter 14

The Girl from Oklahoma

I felt free at last as I drove toward San Francisco in the purple-and-white Chrysler, singing the "Hallelujah Chorus" as if I could carry a tune. After leaving Marin County, I exited the rainbow tunnel and caught my breath. Tears formed. Ahead of me loomed the iconic Golden Gate Bridge! The bridge towers emerged above wispy fog, gleaming red-orange against the bright blue sky like a welcoming beacon.

"Welcome, Pat Montandon!" they broadcast as if from orange mouths. "Welcome to San Francisco."

Malcolm was right about being true to myself. From the start, my life in San Francisco was touched by magic. I rented an apartment on the famous crooked street of Lombard, even though others said it wasn't possible to find a nice place at an affordable rent in that part of town. Phooey, I said, and found a jewel-like apartment that very day. The weekend before I was to start work at the City of Paris, a sedate old department store, I sauntered into Joseph Magnin, a hugely successful career-girl store buzzing with energy. I got off the elevator in the gown salon and greeted a red-haired woman standing nearby.

"Hi, how are y'all?" I said in my friendly, Oklahoma, just-being-myself way.

"Do I know you?" the woman snapped.

"No, ma'am."

"Then why are you so friendly?"

"Well, my goodness, I'm friendly to everyone, and you were standing right there, and . . ." What kind of crazy question was that?

Her name was Miss Cherry, she said, and she was the manager of the gown salon. She took the liberty of following me into a dressing room, where

I tried on a wool dress. After finding out I was to go to work for the City of Paris in a few days, she said, "You should work for us!" And with that, Miss Cherry stayed late to take me to the personnel manager, who turned out to be Cyril Magnin, the president of the store. After a bit of negotiating, Cyril Magnin—Mr. Cyril—hired me as a junior trainee. Four months later, I was managing a store for Joseph Magnin.

It pays to be friendly.

Okay, now please open your mind and remove the skeptical part of your persona and believe. Are you ready? Let's go.

Friendless when I first arrived in San Francisco, I began giving theme parties as a way of meeting people. I invited anyone who seemed interesting. One of my guests brought Frances Moffat, the society reporter for the *San Francisco Chronicle*, and a photographer to my Mexican fiesta. Before you could shout Jack Robinson, a story and several pictures of my party stared out at me from the newspaper. Wow! Can you imagine that?

By being myself and without a plan, I was soon dubbed Party Girl Pat, a socialite, creative and imaginative. That was the beginning of a serendipitous career: successful store manager, model, buyer for Saks Fifth Avenue, CBS radio personality, teacher of customer service classes for Bank of America and World Airways, and a fashion writer for *Curtain Call* magazine. Years later, I also became a columnist for the *San Francisco Examiner* and often wrote about growing up poor and on welfare. My impoverished background became my strength rather than a negative, as many assumed it would be.

All that publicity opened the door to television. I became the host of a live show on an ABC affiliate, KGO-TV. *Pat's Prize Movie* was the highest-rated show in the Bay Area. If Bennie had been with me, Lord only knows how high the ratings would have soared.

There were romances, heartbreak, more romance, laughter, fun, and tears. When the media dubbed me San Francisco's Golden Girl, I embraced the role. Who would have thought such a thing could happen to a moral young woman who merely liked to throw terrific theme parties? Soon, my photograph at various events appeared in the society section of three different newspapers almost every day and twice on Sunday, like church. McGraw-Hill asked me to write a book about party giving, which became *How to Be a Party Girl*, published in 1968.

But through it all, I was still the girl from Oklahoma, just being my exuberant self, and not realizing that people often believe whatever is printed in magazines and newspapers. It didn't take long for me to experience the flip side of being well known and called a party girl. Some of the fellows I dated expected me to be a heavy drinker and to fall into bed with them after a dinner date. Alcohol didn't sit well with me, so I didn't touch it except for an occasional glass of wine. I slapped down their advances so fast I was accused of being a prude. The jerks! Who did they think they were, Adonis? Well, they weren't, nor I Aphrodite.

I was so put out by all the pawing that I stopped dating altogether. I wanted a guy I could depend on and with whom I could share my life, and maybe have a family. When I complained to a friend about the dearth of appropriate dating material, she said, "Pat, you'll never meet anyone between your bed and the refrigerator." I decided to accept the next date I was invited on.

When coffee heir Reuben Hills called from New York and said he wanted to marry me, I knew he was joking. We had met at a cocktail party and hadn't talked to each other more than five minutes. Reuben had thin-looking skin that appeared burned in a way that made his features seem indistinct. "I want a date with you as soon as I get back to San Francisco," he said.

The evening of my date with Reuben, I wore a chic black wool sheath with turquoise earrings and black high-heel pumps, ready to go out for a glass of something or other. Jittery, I hoped I wouldn't have to fight him off. He told me he was divorced, but other than that, I knew little about him. *Give the guy a chance*, I said to myself, fluffing up my shoulder-length blond hair.

Reuben arrived exactly on time and immediately asked me to hold out my right hand. "I'm going to put something in your hand," he said, "but don't open it until I go in the kitchen and say okay."

"Well, uh, all right," I said, holding out my right hand.

Reuben dropped something into my hand, then bent my fingers closed over it and raced off to the kitchen. *Odd*, I thought, mystified. There I stood, dressed up for a nice evening, with my feet growing numb in three-inch-high pointy-toed heels, waiting for . . . I didn't know what.

"Okay!" Reuben yelled from the kitchen.

When I opened my hand, my eyes almost popped out of their sockets and rolled across the rug. There, nestled in my palm between the mount of Venus and my lifeline, glinting up at me like the all-seeing-eye, was an enormous diamond ring.

"Reuben!" I yelled, sprinting to the kitchen. "What—what is this?" I stared at him, trying to make out his expression, wondering how he could have thought I would accept a diamond ring from him.

"It's my mother's engagement ring," he said. "I want you to have it."

"Good Lord, Reuben Hills, that's ridiculous. I can't accept this ring." I handed the gem back to him.

"You're sure not a gold digger, are you?" he said, grinning.

"What made you think I was?"

"I want to marry you."

"How can you give me your mother's ring and ask me to marry you when you don't even know me? Marriage is not to be taken lightly. I've found that out. Anyway, you can't be serious. You're a jokester, aren't you?"

He didn't deny it. "Let's get to know each other, Pat. I'll cook dinner for you at my place next week. Okay?"

The man was an enigma. I wasn't attracted to him, but I told myself that I had to give guys a chance or I would never find love.

Reuben Hills lived in an attractive apartment on the curve of Telegraph Hill near the famous Coit Tower. He served dinner, one I have no recollection of, on a coffee table in front of his fireplace. As we chatted, he seemed a perfect gentleman. I felt secure. The draperies were open on two large windows, and I could see a woman moving around in the apartment across the street.

"I guess you know your neighbors pretty well." I gestured toward the window.

"Oh, yes, that's Marilyn," he said, "a schoolteacher I once dated."

"Am I on display?" I laughed, not realizing I had scored a bull's-eye.

When I asked directions to the powder room, Reuben pointed me toward his bathroom. What a mistake that was! I emerged a few minutes later, still drying my hands, to see Reuben standing by the bathroom door with only a towel around his waist.

I stared open-mouthed, in shock. "What?"

Without saying a word, the man without features grabbed my arms, yanked them behind my back, took three steps to the bed, and wrestled me roughly onto it.

"Stop! Stop!" I cried. My heart was nearly pounding out of my chest. Was he going to kill me? I screamed, but only a pitiful little cry emerged, lost in the tufts of the brown bedspread. He rolled me to my back, pulled my arms to the front of my body, and twisted them in a throbbing vise across my chest. The soft-bodied viper then plopped his heavy body on top of mine, effectively trapping me. His strong thighs tried to force my legs apart as I fought like a red devil to keep them together. I found my voice at last. "No, no, no," I yelled, "Stop!" We tussled a few minutes because I was also strong, but I was no match for my determined rapist. He pushed my panties off with his foot or knee and then forced himself into my body. The weight of his blubber held me fast. I could hardly breathe. The man came so quickly there was hardly time for the insult to register.

Once done, he released my arms and smiled. A look of triumph shone on his melted face. "Now I own you," he said, and stood up.

I jumped up from the bed, grabbed my panties and my purse and fled, screaming that he did not own me. "You are crazy, crazy, crazy, you ugly old bastard!" I shouted as I slammed the door and raced down the interior stairs.

As I inched my way down Telegraph Hill carrying my shoes, I thought of Malcolm and one of the last songs to which we had danced: *I'll be seeing you in all the old familiar places* . . . Struggling not to fall, I wished I could roll all the way down the steep incline to get away faster. *I'll be looking at the moon, but I'll be seeing you.* I didn't cry. Times were changing, but they hadn't changed enough for me to report the man to the authorities. I was well known and an adult now. If I reported him, my photograph would be splashed on page one of every newspaper in the country and on television, too. I would be blamed, not Reuben Hills. He would look like a stud, and I would be made to look like a slut. I could hear reporters and gossips saying, "Why did she go to his apartment in the first place?" They would say, "She should have known better." They would say, "She was asking for it." No, once again, I could not do a thing about being raped.

I thought about the thousands of women who find themselves in the same predicament. Yes, thousands, I dare say. And while I don't usually pay too much attention to what other people say about me, I didn't want to be branded a slut and throw away a promising career. Even though it was the sixties and San Francisco's Summer of Love, still, I had no illusions about how most people viewed rape. Without fail, it was the woman's fault.

Once down the hill and up two more steep hills, I was home. Trying to catch my breath, I sat down on the cold curb at the bottom of the crooked street and had a mental conversation with Malcolm. The panoramic mist of San Francisco air, redolent with the aroma of flowers, merged with the tears I finally shed and helped ease my pain.

Rudy Noble, a doctor I dated, came over from his apartment on Greenwich Street to comfort me. We'd had fun together, and he had treated me well although we argued a lot over his tendency to stare at himself in mirrors. Now we drank martinis and went through all the stages of drunkenness, from giggly to tears to a hangover, in the space of half an hour. Rudy stayed with me every evening for a week, until one night his little green MG was slathered with catsup and mustard and pushed down the hill where he had parked. When he took his automobile to a car wash, the attendant asked, "Hey, man, you fooling around with someone's girlfriend?"

Malcolm's advice stood me in good stead. I did not blame myself for what that insane man did to me. I was still whole. Thankful that I wasn't pregnant, I moved on with my life. But I had no control over the nightmares that surfaced for several months following that assault. I would awaken at two thirty in the morning night after night, fighting to breathe, being smothered by a man's body and with my vagina on fire.

In time, better days arrived, as usually happens if we have enough faith to allow them to unroll. In 1969, ten years after I crossed the Golden Gate Bridge, Al Wilsey began courting me in a wonderfully genteel way. We fell in love and married. It was only after our wedding that I learned he was wealthy. A year later, at forty-one, I gave birth to a son, Sean Patrick. My happiness knew no bounds. We lived an extravagant lifestyle, commuting by helicopter from our penthouse in San Francisco to our country home in the Napa Valley. It was a heady way to live and a far cry from my life with Howard.

I never took our way of life for granted but thoroughly enjoyed the comfort I found with my husband and child. I couldn't have prepared for the abrupt fall from grace that I experienced when our marriage ended in an explosion of heartbreak and headlines eleven years later. Al was in love with my friend, Dede Traina, a Machiavellian married woman who lusted after Al's money and so gaslighted me by pretending to be my friend. I realized too late that she had also courted my young son, my child, to get to his father. She slithered her way like a serpent into Sean's emotions by buying him forbidden pleasures and giggled and wooed him to such a degree that he only wanted to be with her, even after Dede and Al married. Dede Wilsey alienated my son from me as surely as if she had taken a knife and cut him from my womb. I imagined bloody amniotic fluid gushing from my belly, splattering her designer shoes, and drowning everything I held dear. And Sean's father allowed it to happen.

I was fifty and didn't think I could ever recover from such a blow, or have anything to live for if I did. Like my father, I, too, trusted people, and especially my husband and a best friend. In time I did recover, although the relationship with my son, a connection that I treasure more than life, still to this day bears scars from that brutal ripping apart of my womb by one woman's greed.

I was to learn, however, that what's important in our world most often arises from the wreckage of trauma. And so, as with many painful journeys, my eventual recovery gave birth to something new—something that would transform my life. Strangely enough, I experienced a powerful vision concerning children and nuclear war, which inspired me to create the nonprofit foundation Children As the Peacemakers. In the years to come, I traveled the globe thirty-seven times with young children by my side, meeting with world leaders to plead for peace during the Cold War. One day, somewhere in China, it occurred to me that I was, in my way, carrying on the work of my father but without the religious connotation or belief.

As for love, over the years there have been sweet romances, but alas, I never again met anyone like Malcolm. For years, we wrote to each other. His letters were stacked in a sliding pile tied with blue grosgrain ribbon and stored inside a round black patent-leather hatbox on a closet shelf in my Lombard Street apartment. Malcolm's poetic words to me were consumed by a mysterious fire in that beautiful apartment on the crooked street of

Lombard—a fire that killed my best friend, Mary Lou Ward, a conflagration that left me inconsolable and numb while pregnant with my only child. Sean Patrick was a baby bathed, as I had been, in the fluid of grief.

Was history repeating itself? Fire in several permutations played a huge and horrific role in my life. It wove around my erogenous nerves like the devil serpent Daddy preached about, searing them and padlocking nature's gift of erotic pleasure. Our home burned down, and California wildfires ignited the dry fields and trees and scrub around the ranch, making me fear I was in Hell. But the death of my dear friend Mary Lou Ward in my apartment, in my bed, without a known cause for the conflagration or why she died, was the most shattering of all the ruthless intensities in my life. Five years after the event, I was impelled to write about it. *The Intruders* was the outcome, a best-selling book that was often sprained by critics into a "ghost story."

~~~

I was in the midst of packing to leave my penthouse home in San Francisco and move to a place I called The Enchanted Cottage, a log house I built above San Francisco's Height Street, when the phone rang. Of all the people in the world I didn't expect to be on the line, it was none other than my first husband, Howard Groves. I knew who it was the moment he cleared his throat.

"Harrumph."

"Howard!"

"Hello, Patsy. This is old number one."

"Old number one?" I hoped he was kidding but knew he wasn't.

"Can I come to see you?"

Hmm. Oh, well. "Okay," I said. I was curious to see if he had changed and if he might apologize to me for his boorish behavior when we were married.

Well, I should have known better. Howard walked into that amazing penthouse with its 360-degree view of San Francisco and the bay and didn't even comment on it. This was a spectacular place that caused most people to gasp and run to the windows, disbelieving the jewels laid out in a glittering heap below them: the water, the ships, the Golden Gate Bridge, the Bay Bridge, Coit Tower, the Transamerica Pyramid, and the golden hills of Marin. Howard didn't even notice.

"You're wearing your hair the way I like it, Muggins," he said, commenting on a hairdo I had worn for years and using the nickname I hated.

"Wish I could say the same for you," I joked. Old number one had lost all his hair. His baldness and the heavy, black-framed glasses he wore made him look quite unlike Gregory Peck, as I remembered him. But he was trim, and his erect posture was still that of a military man.

Deciding to be charitable, I led my ex into the living room and indicated an armchair next to the sofa. Ever the hostess, I offered him a glass of Mondavi Cabernet, which he accepted without a thank-you.

"How's Mom?" I asked.

"She died," he said, blinking his eyes behind thick lenses and clearing his throat. "I was driving her from Farmington to the Stockton Hospital when she stopped breathing."

"I'm so sorry," I said, a wash of sadness flowing over me. "I loved your mother."

"Yeah. Harrumph. We saved your life, Patsy. "All those trips to the hospital . . ."

"You probably did, Howard. I appreciate how thoughtful you both were to me when I had heart surgery."

I was sitting in the corner of my large, cushy Michael Taylor sofa in a comfy floor-length Mary McFadden pleated dress, and had slipped off gold sandals and tucked my feet up under the hem of the ivory-colored attire. You will not believe what happened next. No, I guarantee, you won't believe it.

Howard Groves, whom I had not seen in thirty years, untied his Oxford dress shoes and slowly took them off. Then, deliberately, one at a time, he plunked his size-sixteen stocking feet up on my gorgeous travertine coffee table and settled in. Content, with a glass of wine in his big hands, he cleared his throat and launched into mind-numbing stories about the aches and pains of people I didn't remember or had never heard of and never wanted to know. "And, Jack," he said, staring into a space above my coffee table, "Jack, the man up the hill from us, ran his pickup off the road and smashed himself up pretty darn good. Harrumph."

My ex might as well have been alone, so engrossed was he in the unfortunate details of the lives of others. He droned on and on as my mind wandered to more exciting scenarios: a move to Los Angeles and a book optioned by Focus Features for a film, when Howard got my attention by asking a question. Did he want to check out the organization of my canned goods as he had done in Selma?

"Harrumph, Little Okie, do you think we could get back together?"

Rousing, I shook my head. "What? What did you say?"

"I want to marry you again," he said.

Jumping up from the sofa so quickly that wine splashed out of my glass, I was incredulous. "I can't believe you asked me that!"

"You belong to me, honey. I love you," Howard said, draining his glass of wine. "When I saw how you fixed your hair to please me, I knew you felt the same way."

It was all I could do not to throw a lamp at him. I enjoyed the thought of it zinging past his head and crashing through his self-importance while he gaped and cleared his throat. "Howard, please put your shoes on. You don't live here, as much as you might wish to," I announced in a strangled voice. "It was disrespectful of you to remove your shoes in my home."

Old number one flushed with resentment or embarrassment or both, then smiled. He sluggishly removed his black-stockinged feet from my coffee table as if the effort were too great. And then he slowly put on his shoes while I fidgeted. He laboriously tied his shoelaces, double-knotting them as if to make sure they would not blow off should a hurricane pop up out of the clear California sky. Finally he stood up, towering over me.

"Harrumph. Okay, Muggins, what's your answer?"

"Howard, I have a question. Why did you sic a shyster debt collector after me when Sean was born?"

"You owed me for your engagement ring," He leaned back on his heels and put his thumbs in his belt. "You still owe me."

"You are a bargain-basement kind of guy, Howard, and so transparent. You were upset that I had a baby, and when his birth was reported in newspapers, it embarrassed you to be caught in a lie. For years, you told friends that I couldn't have children, when the truth is that you are sterile! How insufferable you are, Howard."

My ex-husband grinned like a dunce. "You're still cute when you pretend to be mad, Patsy. I know you."

"Pretending? You think I'm pretending?" Maybe I *would* throw something at him. No, I was feeding his bloated ego by showing temper. And why was I angry over what was done so many years ago? In a way I realized that Howard represented all the men who had belittled me, raped me, discounted me, and wrote withering and untrue things about me in newspapers and books.

"Howard," I said, in an icy tone, "I would *never* consider marrying you again. I'm a strong woman now. I long ago realized that I do not need a man in my life just to have a husband. I like who I am."

"You mean you're full of yourself." His smirking face glowed crimson.

"You're right. I am full of myself. Who else would I be full of? You? A man who demeaned me and hit me and told me I was ugly? A man who wanted to farm me out? Of all the stupid things to say. Get a grip, Howard. You are not 'old number one.'"

"Yeah? I was the first one to fuck you. You were a virgin and sweeter at eighteen than you are now!"

"You think 'fucking' me makes you number one? No, it does not. The real man, the man who taught me what making love is about, was Malcolm Kerkorian. If a number is attached, then Malcolm is number one."

"Him? Malcolm Kerkorian? That jackass?"

"Yes, Howard Groves, that sweet jackass, Malcolm."

My former husband sputtered and grew even redder, but his thinking capacity didn't afford him enough power to conjure up a fast retort.

"Goodbye," I said. Pulling the heavy double doors open, I ushered my first husband out of my home and my life. He tried to say something, but the beige elevator doors swished open and then closed with the familiar whooshing sound, cutting him off in mid-word.

~~~

Then there's Mama.

Upon returning from the Azores, I patched things up with her, but only after she promised to remove all but two of the wedding pictures of Howard and me that were scattered around her house like chicken feed. There was John Barbour at the CBS microphone while I smiled and my groom appeared shell-shocked, the two of us exiting the "Little Chapman Park Hotel Chapel," the train on my satin gown billowing in a gust of wind, the white-haired minister pronouncing us "man and wife, so long as you both shall live" and on and on. A forest of cardboard-framed photographs of my ex and me veneered every surface in her home. "You let a good man get away," she growled, but took the pictures down after I said I wouldn't come to see her again unless she did.

Mama lived in a tiny, rundown frame house in Modesto, California, to be near Faye and Carlos . . . and maybe me, although I'm not sure. After my financial life stabilized, I refurbished her dreary little house in bright yellows and muted reds—like a McDonald's, Nina said, sniffing at my lack of decorating sophistication. She was probably right, since she was an interior designer. When I offered to buy Mama a new house, she got a set look on her face and declined the offer, so I didn't insist.

Mama loved my modicum of celebrity, especially when she had visitors and got letters from people who watched me on KGO-TV. I frequently talked about my upbringing, seeing the fun in it, the uniqueness of that kind of life, though I got teary-eyed recounting tales of hunger and the Great Depression. According to the mail, my viewers loved my homespun stories.

One day, I asked Mama if she would like to be on the show with me. Well, yes! She surely would!

The studio hairdresser backcombed Mama's silver hair into a high-flown stylish confection that he piled on top of her head. She loved the beautifying but balked when it came to blush or lipstick and insisted on dusting her face with her old standby Rachel #2, the face powder deemed okay by God. Thinking she would look good in my new white mink coat, I draped it over her ice-blue dress. She beamed. My theme music, "Watching All the Girls Go By," came blaring over the loudspeaker, and we sashayed onto the set together as the tech people clapped for Mama. She smiled the biggest smile you ever saw in your life. But my face must have registered consternation when I realized mother's eyebrows and eyelashes, whitened by face powder, caused her features to blend with the silvery hair on top of her head and that ill-advised white fur coat. She looked like a polar bear.

Under the hot lights of television, I saw beads of sweat form on Mama's forehead. But she was a trooper and kept smiling, although she probably longed for her *Herald of Holiness* touchstone with which to fan herself. I couldn't believe how soft-spoken, how grandmotherly, how like Mrs. Santa Claus she was, telling my viewers that Patsy Lou had been the sweetest child ever.

"Mama! You've never said that to me. Was I sweet?"

"Well, I have too said nice things about you, Miss Priss. Now don't

320

you say I haven't!" She smiled through gritted teeth, the real Mama trying to break through the Rachel #2 powder.

The audience must love this mother-daughter exchange, I thought. *I'd better act like I do, too.* I laughed. "Ha-ha-ha. Mama, remember when I refused to take a bath in our old tin tub because I thought you were trying to kill me?"

"Patsy Lou, I never, ever tried to kill you! Why on earth would you say such a thing? Well, I never in all my life . . ."

"No, Mama, no, of course you weren't trying to kill me!" I put my arm across her back to sooth her. "Good heavens, no! Uh, you were making Red Devil Lye soap in our tin washtub that day and cautioned us kids to stay away from it because the lye could kill us. That night, you poured hot water for my bath in the same tub you used for the Red Devil Lye soap, and, well, my kid mind became undone. I thought you were trying to kill me!"

"Jesus help us, Patsy Lou. That's the craziest thing I ever heard tell of! Y'all clung to the bedpost screaming bloody murder, when all I was trying to do was give you a weekly bath. Charles and Poor Little Glendora had to help me pry your fingers off the bedpost. Lord help us, you needed a bath real bad. Why, you had a gray ring around your neck, and your feet were filthy dirty. The three of us plunked you into that tub while you kicked and scratched like a wild chicken. Dunked you, though, scrubbed you, and the whole time you howled like a banshee . . ." Mama lost her train of thought, so I tried to move on to a different subject, but she wasn't ready. "You know, Patsy Lou, I remember right good the time I told y'all not to kiss your little friend because she had the whooping cough. Y'all marched right up to her and kissed her anyway, stubborn as the livelong day."

"Did I catch whooping cough?"

"No, I don't reckon so." Mama covered her mouth with her hand and laughed. The floor manager was giving us a wrap-up, but Mama had one more thing to get off her chest. "Now don't go cutting me off." She sent a stern look to the floor manager, who grinned and continued with the time countdown. "I told Patsy Lou not to be a little weak worm of the dust, and now she's on TV because of me!"

"Amen!" I shouted as the credits rolled. "Mama's right, y'all."

Mama loved TV and got the hang of the studio camera with its glowing red light faster than I had. She was an actress, a born ham just as I was. A preacher's wife and the mother of a gaggle of kids had made Mama a star in the firmament of religious certainty. Lordy!

One wintry day in 1979, my sister Faye called to tell me that Mama was in the hospital. "Patsy," she choked, "Mama had a stroke and may not live. She's asking for you. She thinks you and Little Jimmy are still babies, and she's worried about you."

"Then she's talking?" The last time I had visited Mama, she was in a nursing home and refused to talk to anyone. She hadn't said a word for several weeks. I had pushed her across the lobby in a wheelchair while jabbering away, trying to fill the conversational void. Then I asked Mama if she remembered Sean. Wow—let me tell you right now, I got an Old Time Religion rejoinder. Mama glowered at me, and her crackling voice was contemptuous.

"Of course I remember Sean. Do you think I'm stupid?" Those were her first words in weeks.

"Mama, you can talk!" I said.

"There's nothing I want to say!" she said and clamped her mouth closed.

Faye was still on the phone telling me about Mama. "She's disoriented, and they've had to tie her down to keep her in bed. Can you believe that?"

"I can believe that."

"The rest of the family is here. You'd better come."

~~~

I took a cab directly from the airport to the hospital. It was early morning in a silent world. The medical center filled a city block. The gray exterior of the buildings blended with the steel sky, cement streets, and parking lot. Leafless trees added to the dreariness. I took the elevator to the third floor. It was empty except for one worried-looking man who gazed intently at the lighted numbers over the steel doors.

Mama lay motionless on a metal bed. The side rails were raised. A band of blue webbing stretched across her chest and was knotted to the frame. Once my eyes adjusted to the dimness, I could see Mama's body outlined under a mustard-colored blanket. Her white hair was like finely spun angel hair spread over Christmas tree branches, forming a halo around her head. Her blue eyes stared blankly at the ceiling. My fierce mother was frail and defeated and old.

"Mama, it's Patsy," I said, taking her hand in mine, noting her delicate wrists. "I've come to see you."

Mama turned her head slightly, and her eyes found mine. When I was a child, her startling eyes had pierced my heart, but now they showed no fire or life.

"Patsy?"

"Yes, Mama, it's me. I've come to see you."

"Yes, you've come to see me. Oh, honey." Her eyes brimmed with tears. "What am I going to do about those little children at home? I can't take care of them anymore."

"You don't have any children at home. We're all grown up."

"And your daddy abandoned me. He hasn't even written."

"Mama, you had a stroke, and you're in a hospital in Fresno. Daddy died twenty-five years ago."

"Oh no, don't tell me that. Are you sure?"

"Yes, Mama, I'm sure. He's been dead for a long time."

I looked down at the woman on the bed. This was not my mother, this frail, confused old lady. This was not the woman who reared me, suckled me, the woman who ruled with the iron fist of religious certainty, the woman who was confident her final destination would be a place with a chariot for her to ride in and streets of gold for her to ride upon, a place with "no more tears and no more sorrow."

A forlorn shadow threw a bruised cape of sadness over my shoulders.

Mama repeated, "What about my babies?"

"Mama, there are no babies now."

Suddenly the veil of senescence lifted, and she seemed to comprehend. "I don't have much more time, do I?"

"I don't know, Mama. Are you afraid?"

"No, I'm not afraid, but it grieves me to know your daddy is dead." She started to cry. "Don't leave me . . . don't leave me."

"No, Mama, I won't leave you," I said, wiping her tears with a Kleenex.

Her eyes closed, and soon, gentle snores filled the room. I pushed my black overnight bag against a wall and scooted a heavy recliner up to the bed. I reached for Mama's hand, feeling the thinness of her skin, the warmth still there. The odor of urine permeated the space even though everything was clean. Sitting there in the dimness of my mother's hospital room, holding her hand, I thought about the mother that was and the one lying on the bed, the mother tied down with blue webbing. Her snores faded away, and a hymn began in a high, wobbling voice.

> "Will there be any stars in my crown,
> When at evening the sun goeth down
> When I wake . . . the blessed . . ."

The tune ended and her snores resumed.

On the windowsill of her room stood three bouquets of yellow and orange mums in glass containers, a small black-and-white toy dog with one floppy ear, like Rat-Dog, and Mama and Daddy's wedding photograph. It was the picture that had graced the top of Mr. Steinway until the day our beloved piano was sold. In the picture, Mama is wearing a light-colored dress with a white shawl over her dark hair. She's smiling. Her smile is sweet. She holds an apple in her hands. A generous softness suffuses her face, a gentleness that only now in her dotage reappeared. There is no hint of the harshness I identified with her. At what point had that lovely young girl changed into a stern and inflexible woman, a religious fanatic—a woman who instilled fear and guilt for the slightest infractions of the severe discipline she inflicted?

How many different people are we in a lifetime? What would I be like if I had lived my mother's life: married at sixteen, endured ten pregnancies and eight live births, carried a dead baby within my body for two months, watched a toddler die? My mother, now tied to a hospital bed, had shown the strength of ten. The hardships she endured, the poverty and hunger, the innumerable moves, and the high expectations for her children against huge odds, must have taken a toll on her.

"I want you all to grow up and to be good and educated people," she often said. "You've got to serve the Lord with all your heart and all your soul." Religion was her reason for living. It was her solace in time of trouble and her entertainment as well. Reared in a different milieu and a different time, she might have been a lawyer or a politician or a famous actress, or—who knows—married to a fundamentalist preacher and a religious fanatic. Without a doubt, she was gifted with determination, a gift I inherited.

~~~

Mama gave us religion in the hope that it would make us good and educated people. For me, those moral teachings came bound together with fear and suffering. And years later, at a family reunion, I glimpsed the other tragic effects of our fundamentalist upbringing.

Our family gathering was held in an attractive building on a golf course in Northern California. Relatives I didn't recognize hugged me and introduced themselves. Large pictures of Mama and Daddy were pinned to the walls. After visiting with each other and eating from a bountiful buffet, Carlos, now thin and stooped, said an opening prayer. I recited Mama's favorite poem, "The Touch of the Master's Hand." Nina sang "Shall We Gather at the River?" in her high, quavering soprano. Poor Little Glendora thanked everyone for being there, Faye giggled, and Little Jimmy talked about being diabetic and showed us his glucose monitor. Then Charles, handsome and well educated, a business success in Houston, Texas, stood at the microphone and announced that he wanted to preach a short sermon.

There was a slight stirring in the room as two young girls slipped quietly out the rear door. Through a window I saw them laughing and skipping along in their pretty summer dresses, happy to be free of familial expectations.

Charles quickly reverted to the preacher he once was and began his sermon. "Many of us are strangers to each other, but bound by the same blood and genes," he said. "I think it's important for y'all to know a few things about our family—issues we have never talked about before. I especially want you great-grandkids and great-nieces and nephews to listen to this Bible scripture so you can avoid what happened to my son," he said with a forced smile and a furrowed brow.

"Leviticus 20:13," Charles said, his heavy Texas drawl making each word weighted with doom. "'If there is a man who lies with a male as those who lie with a woman, both of them have committed a detestable act; they shall surely be put to death. Their blood shall be on their own heads..'"

"Amen, tell 'em, brother," Nina said, reminding me of Mama.

Charles smiled at Nina and continued his treatise. "And in 1 Corinthians 6:9-10, the Bible says, 'The unrighteous will not inherit the kingdom of God: Do not be deceived; neither fornicators, nor idolaters, nor adulterers, nor effeminate, nor *homosexuals* . . .'"

I tuned my brother out the way I tuned out all preachers who seemed invested in pouring hate and fear into others. But when Charles launched into a personal story, I gasped for air.

"Most of y'all didn't know James Ray, my firstborn. Well, I need to tell y'all that James Ray decided to be a homosexual after he was married and had two children." There was an audible gasp from attentive relatives eager now to hear what Charles was going to reveal next. "James Ray went so far as to have an operation to try to become a woman. He wore women's dresses. He caroused around and sinned against the Holy Ghost!"

"Amen," Nina said, seeming to relish the hot coals Charles was heaping onto his dead son's body.

"I preached about the sin of homosexuality to James Ray since he was a little boy." Charles wiped his forehead with a blue paper napkin and took a swig of water. "James Ray's wickedness caused him to go crazy and to kill himself!"

A collective gasp rose from the group and hovered over the get-together like a poisonous gray mist. Nina shouted, "Amen." Faye cried. Poor Little Glendora, too vain to wear hearing aids, was blessed by her lack of comprehension. Little Jimmy squeezed his hands tightly together, undoubtedly thinking of Santiago, his recently deceased son who died from the scourge of AIDS. I put my arms around Jimmy and whispered that he shouldn't pay attention to what Charles had said. Because of his many concussions, he couldn't be held responsible for his lack of judgment. Jimmy smiled at me through the film of tears running crookedly down his strong face and into his white beard.

I thought about all those sermons and all that preaching, all that crying and caterwauling at the altar, and being beaten on the back to knock sin out of our bodies, and being assaulted by the Holy Ghost and terrorized by hellfire and brimstone throughout our formative years—now it seemed as if an angry mob of propagandizing devils had been sent from Hell or wherever they hid to exact a pound of flesh from my nephews on behalf of religious zealots.

James Ray was gay, along with two others, a great-nephew and a niece. Little Jimmy's son Santiago was sweet and gentle and openly gay. A delightful free spirit, he traveled to Mexico and South America, sleeping on park benches, in order to see the world.

Another great-great-nephew refuses to leave the closet, although it must be very dark inside. No longer young, he wears a mean and sullen expression. I wonder if that's due to his terror of loving himself, the self he was born to be.

"Charles," I said, not willing to hold myself in check, "it also says in the Bible that we should love one another. 'Love one another. As I have loved you, so you must love one another.' Remember?"

"Patsy, I love y'all, but James Ray was my son, and . . ."

"I love you, too, Charles. Y'all know I do. But you don't seem to have any understanding for . . .

"Now listen, sis . . . just because you've met world leaders . . ."

"Charles, I think you feel sad and guilty about James Ray, and that's why . . ."

"I love you, sis," my brother said, bringing my criticism to an abrupt halt.

"I love you, too," I acknowledged. "But I disagree with you."

Chairs scraped on the wooden floor as relatives made excuses to leave, to get out of firing range. "Got a long drive ahead of us," I heard more than one person say. "Me, too." Before more could be said, I concurred and took off, leaving my siblings to their judgments but recognizing my deep affection and love for them, even so.

~~~

On soft little cat feet, morning arrived in the hospital where Mama slept. Sounds began to penetrate the room. Sick people were awakening to

328

face their day.

Entering the room with a façade of cheer, an African American nurse's aide announced breakfast. "Good morning, Mrs. M, time for breakfast," she sang.

Mama opened her eyes. "Faye," she said, looking at me, "don't leave me."

"No, Mama, I won't leave you."

"My wonderful children," Mama said to the nurse. "What would I do without my family?"

"We're going to get you up for breakfast, Mrs. M."

"No, please, honey, let me sleep."

"You can sleep later." The woman raised the window shade, allowing weak morning light to creep into the room. She spoke loudly, as if to the deaf. "We're going to get you up and into a wheelchair, Mrs. M," she announced.

I introduced myself. "I'm Pat, one of her daughter's."

"Pat, you know what we call your mother? We call her Houdini, that's what we call her, sure do. Why, she can untie herself no matter how many knots we put in that Posey. She sure can."

"Posey?"

"That's the thing we tie her down with," she said, indicating a wide strip of blue webbing.

The nurse was in her midthirties, I guessed. She had lustrous black hair held back from a sunny, round face by two red butterfly barrettes. She wore a smock with images of red birds scattered on the cotton fabric. The smock fit snugly across her hips and was topped by a navy-blue sweater.

"Mrs. M, I'm going to teach your daughter here how to transfer you," she said, untying the Posey. "Now, Pat, I'll pull her arms, and you can help get her up."

My mother shook her head. "Oh no, let me lie here, please, honey."

"You want to go home, don't you?"

329

"Must you do this?" I asked.

"Doctor's orders."

"Well, they're stupid orders, if you ask me."

The nurse continued to explain how to get my mother up and how to transfer her to a wheelchair. Mama sat on the side of the bed with her slender legs dangling down in white elastic stockings, her hair hanging in strings around her face.

"Mama, I'll put my arms around your back. You place your arms around my neck, and on the count of three, come onto your feet and then turn to get into the wheelchair. Understand? I won't let you fall."

"Oh dear Jesus, help us," Mama fretted.

"Okay, ready? Let's go. Put your arms around my neck, Mama." I planted my feet firmly on either side of my mother's feet. My hands were clasped behind her back.

"One, two, three—up, Mama, up." Mother slowly and tentatively rose to her feet. We stood embracing, the only embrace I could remember from her, while we caught our breath. I turned and walked her two steps and into the wheelchair. We were both relieved when the transfer was completed.

"Jesus, help us," Mama complained.

"Very good," the nurse said. "Now undress her and roll her into the shower where you can give her a sponge bath."

After taking Mama's hospital gown off, I quickly covered her with a towel. Never before had I seen my mother nude. Her hips were large, her back narrow, her large breasts resting on her stomach. The telltale signs of pregnancies were evident in stretch marks that striated her abdomen. Mama sat in the wheelchair and stared at the white tile wall of the shower while I discreetly bathed her. After I'd dried her off, I fluffed Blue Grass dusting powder across her back. In a drawer I found a pretty blue flannel nightgown I had sent her five years earlier, one she was saving for "good," and dropped it over her head. I combed her limp white hair, braided it, and pinned it across her head the way she liked it.

"There, don't you feel better now, Mama?"

"Am I going home?"

"Time for breakfast, Mrs. M," said the nurse. "Your daughter can wheel you to the dayroom to eat." She turned to me. "Patients on this floor go to the dayroom for meals. We're trying to rehabilitate them so they can help themselves a little."

"But it seems so hopeless," I whispered. "Why can't I put her back to bed and let her sleep?"

"Your mother has physical and occupational therapy later this morning. She can sleep after that." The nurse was determination personified. She could be related to Mama and me, I thought.

Outdated Halloween decorations hung from the ceiling of the dayroom. Black cats, bats, pumpkins, and skeletons gazed down at the sick. Most patients were in wheelchairs, but one hospital bed showed a tuft of brown hair sticking out from the covers.

I pushed Mama's wheelchair up to a table and sat down next to her. Two patients already sat there, both young women. One wore a neck brace and a cast on her right arm; one leg was covered with a cast and extended out in front of her. Her eyes were blank. A plastic-covered card that hung around her neck read, *Your name is Joan. You have been in an automobile accident. You are in a hospital in Fresno, California. Your husband's name is Steve. Your parents visit you every day. They are from Ohio.*

The other woman at the table was bent like a slender tree caught in a high wind. Gauze circled her head. She sat as silent as death, waiting.

"Here's a towel for you, dear." A woman in a crisp white uniform tucked a flower-sprigged towel into the neck of Mama's gown to catch the food sure to fall there.

"Glendora," Mama said, "is Daddy dead?"

"Mama, yes, Daddy's dead."

Mama played with the mushy food, eating a little but mostly drifting off to sleep.

"Wake up, dear. You need to eat," an attendant said, gently shaking her shoulder.

"I'll try."

"Mama, what's the most fun of anything you ever did?" I asked, trying to distract her.

Mama slumped down in her wheelchair. She cut her eyes sideways at me, not moving her head. "Oh, honey, it was saving souls with Brother Luke in Herman, Texas."

"Brother Luke?"

"Oh dear Jesus, forgive me." Her voice broke.

"Forgive what, Mama?"

Soft tears coursed down Mama's face. I blotted them gently with a tissue.

"Brother Luke and me," Mama said.

What was she talking about? Was she rational? "What do you mean?"

"Oh dear Jesus, forgive me," Mama whispered.

I leaned close and took her hand.

"He was killed." Mama started sobbing.

"Mama, please don't cry. Whatever it was, you're forgiven. It doesn't matter. I'll take you to your room now." I quickly wheeled her across the hall and, with unfamiliar strength, transferred her back to bed without encountering the determined nurse. Enough was enough!

"There, you can sleep now," I murmured.

"Thank you, honey, you're a nice lady," she said, drifting off to sleep.

I sat watching my mother and holding her hand while I tried to comprehend my emotions. I no longer felt anger or bitterness toward the fragile human being who had given me birth. There was only compassion for an eighty-six-year-old woman nearing the end of her life.

How would I face my own demise? Would I be afraid and rail against the fate we all must confront? Or would I go calmly to my rest? I thought of the many sadness's and triumphs of my existence. I thought of Howard Groves and Al Wilsey. They, too, had their ghosts to live and to die with. *We are responsible for all of our experiences,* I thought, *the good and the bad.* The choice is ours to become either bitter and mean-spirited or tolerant and loving. We can choose to be a victim or a hero, or more than likely, just a human being, making the most of things, trying to find humor in life.

A shadow appeared in the hospital doorway. It was Faye. She lived nearby and had been caring for Mama. She and Cecil were the ones our family depended on. I tucked Mama's hand under the sheet and jumped up from the recliner to hug my favorite sister. Before we could say much to each other, our other siblings crowded into the room. They hovered over Mama while I stood back, as usual. A nurse appeared and took Mama's pulse. She said something I couldn't hear. Carlos motioned me over to the bed. "Come say goodbye to Mama, Patsy," he said, taking my hand. "She's dying."

Mama's face was sunken, and her skin was gray. She didn't appear to be breathing. I leaned down and kissed her goodbye. Unexpectedly, the melancholy recognition that I had never before kissed my mother, nor had she kissed me, sent undulations of heartache coursing in shivers throughout my body, triggering a deluge that had been dammed up behind my eyes since birth.

Charles patted me on the back. "It's okay, sis," he said. "Mama's in Heaven now." He handed me a white handkerchief, reminding me of the ones Daddy always carried.

"And riding in a chariot over streets of pure gold, "I said, mopping my tears and smiling at my brother before moving to the outer ring of the family circle. I found a chair and sat down.

Nina began to sing, "Softly and tenderly Jesus is calling, calling for you and for me . . ."

"Oh no, please don't sing that," I said. Tears sprang to my eyes and ran down my face again. "Please . . ."

They didn't hear my soft plea. Carlos and Faye pulled themselves together enough to harmonize, while Poor Little Glendora, Little Jimmy, and Charles sobbed. I tried to sing, but my throat closed, so I hummed. And then, after years of absence, Dead Bettie Ruth appeared beside me. My sister took my hand in hers, tossed her dark curls, and smiled, letting me know that everything would be okay.

Grace

All my siblings are gone now, every one of them. Carlos, the eldest, died first, then Nina Aileen.

Poor Little Glendora and her husband, C. L., were driving from California back to Texas on a narrow road in west Texas, Glendora at the wheel and C. L. asleep on the backseat, when an eighteen-wheeler semi-truck flew across the white line directly in their path. It smashed into them head-on just as C. L. rose from the backseat and pushed Glendora down under the dashboard to safety. C. L. was beheaded, and Glendora was badly injured.

Faye and I flew to a fogged-in airport somewhere in the hinterlands of Texas to be with our injured sister. True to form, Faye got the plane in an uproar while I was in the restroom. Fearful and suspicious of anything and everything, she had told our stewardess that she thought a fellow with a briefcase was carrying a bomb. I was so angry with Faye that I glowered at her all the way to Texas, where more immediate concerns took precedence.

Poor Little Glendora was gravely injured. She had a deep gash on her head, as well as scrapes and cuts on her whole body. I stayed with my injured sister and traveled to her home with her, to La Marque, Texas, to take care of her for two months after attending C. L.'s funeral. Poor Little Glendora was obliged to have shunts placed in her brain, and she never was the same after that tragic accident. Sadly, she was alone when she died several years later in a Houston hospital with Little Jimmy on his way to be with her.

Charles was next. I was with him at a hospital in Houston when he breathed his last. Faye was ninety-three when she passed away sitting in a chair in her living room. Cecil, my sweet brother-in-law, died shortly after Faye passed on. They had been married for seventy-two years! Then, to my shock, Little Jimmy, the baby of the family, died in his sleep a day after we had talked on the phone for two hours.

Suddenly, I was alone the only survivor of a family I thought would be around forever. With so many siblings, it was inconceivable that they were gone and I the memory-keeper.

Now I sit at my computer in Southern California, trying to capture what it was like to grow up in a preacher's family during the Dust Bowl and Great Depression, listening to sermons that would be pulled off children's library shelves if they weren't in the Bible. Looking back on all that petrifying preaching about a fearsome God and hellfire, and my struggles to find my rightful place in a crowded family, I'm nevertheless grateful for an interesting childhood. One of the things engraved on my consciousness is Daddy's motto: "It can be done." I know that whatever I want to do, I can do it. At least, I will try.

Little did I realize when I chose the title *Peeing on Hot Coals* for this book that by writing about that event I would begin to remember the agony I suffered along with a gradual recognition of the horrific and lasting impact being burned on that part of my young body must have had on my life. Nor did I dream that the title would lead me to a consultation with a gynecologist specifically to ask, after so many years and the birth of a child, if she could detect evidence of the burns I suffered from peeing over a bucket of live coals when I was seven. Of course, there have been physicals by gynecologists throughout the years, but not one of the doctors mentioned any abnormality about my vagina or clitoris, and it had never occurred to me to ask them about it. But now I wanted to know. Could the reason for my lack of sexual response—except on rare occasions, and with an exceptional lover like Malcolm—be mapped in those delicate folds of tissue?

I did a Google search for "clitoris nerves," hoping to find out if what I suspected could be true. The Internet with its plethora of information was unlike the Waurika library where I had tried to get information regarding SEX and how to "do it" before marrying Howard. There was so much information to choose from that I felt dizzy. I began reading:

> It's exquisitely sensitive. The clitoris
> contains at least 8,000 sensory nerve endings.
> To put that into perspective, the penis has
> about 4,000. That makes this tiny area the
> most sensitive part of a woman's erogenous
> zone. And while the clitoris is quite small, its
> powerful sensations can spread across a
> woman's pelvic area by affecting 15,000
> other nerve endings!

Oh my God! All those sensitive nerve endings, so vital to my sexual pleasure, had probably been seared away. My heart hurt. I felt sick. That was when I turned off my computer and called my gynecologist, Dr. Collins.

~~~

Dr. Collins is a petite blonde with fine features and a lovely face that radiates kindness. I asked if I could read a paragraph or two from my book to her so she could better understand the reason for my visit.

"Of course," she said. Dr. Collins sat on a corner chair and I on the examining table as I cleared my throat and began to read.

"'I hurried to the bucket,'" I read, "'my hands holding my genitalia as I tried not to wet my underpants before I got there. Trembling from the strain of holding in my urine, I swiftly pulled off my homemade plaid cotton panties and the attached slip. With frenzied swiftness I straddled the bucket, my bare feet on either side of the warm metal, and let go.

"'*Ah, relief,* I thought, discharging a robust stream of urine. As if in slow motion, the liquid from my body rained down in a fall of water that quickly became a torrent hitting the ashes with force and an ominous sound that echoed like bacon fat Mama cooked on the stove—*sssssiiiiizzzzellll*—and released the nether realm of the devil and demons in which the damned suffer everlasting punishment. The earth's crust opened, and a scalding volcanic Hell hit me full force. Magma spewed forth and lye-laced vapor blistered up into the air, where burning rubble penetrated the most delicate tissues of my young body.

"'I was burning in place, unable to move, as I stood there mesmerized, my bare body and my bare feet . . .'"

My voice trembled with unshed tears. I was seven years old again, standing over a bucket of ashes and unnoticed live embers as volcanic steam erupted, burning vital tissue, my undernourished body on fire. Placing my book on the examining table, I leaned over and began to sob, mourning a loss too great for me to comprehend.

Dr. Collins quickly came across the room to comfort me. She put her arms around me and hugged the wounded child inside of me, as we cried together. She acknowledged the suffering I endured when there was no one to talk to about what had happened to me. She recognized the guilt I bore, and as a seven-year-old girl, the humiliation of being savagely burned and exposed *down there*.

After examining me, Dr. Collins told me that she could see evidence, seventy-seven years after it happened, that I had suffered what could be described as a type of genital mutilation from the burns. She said the mucous pouring from my vagina as I began to heal was evidence of a raging infection. She said it was amazing I survived in view of my congenital heart condition. One of the dangers of such a heart problem is that germs collect in that unneeded connection and can cause endocarditis.

At home, my scrambled brain tried to understand all that I had been told by Dr. Collins. I slowly recognized why I was generally indifferent to one of the greatest pleasures women have: a sexual experience that takes one to the moon, I've been told. When I began doing research on the Internet regarding genital mutilation, the photos of female African children with their clitoris removed and their vagina sewn up like a turkey on Thanksgiving horrified me. This torture was inflicted on those poor girls for the sake of making sure a male would know his wife was pure and would not stray. I read accounts of how girls—and even babies—are still subjected to female genital cutting in many African countries. And those tribes often continue this barbaric practice when they immigrate to the United States and Britain, although UNICEF and other organizations are working to stop it. *The New York Times* reported that female genital mutilation refers to a range of procedures performed without a medical purpose. They range from clitoridectomy, the removal of part or all of the clitoris, to infibulation, in which all the outer genitalia are removed and the vagina is sealed, often with stitches, except for a small opening. Despite the risks and the controversy, the cutting is, in many places, grounded in strongly held beliefs about cleanliness, chastity and coming of age.

Those of us living in countries where women and girls have achieved some sort of equality must be vigilant and not allow our gains to erode, as they surely will if we look away. We also need to support our sisters throughout the world, those who have no rights, and are slaves in every sense of the word.

A few weeks ago, ten years after I left San Francisco and moved to Los Angeles, I was invited to ride on the back of a red convertible in San Francisco's Pride Parade. Wearing a flowing blue taffeta robe and a huge hat with multicolored satin ribbons streaming down the back, I waved to the throngs of people lining San Francisco's Market Street. As I rode along—waving, waving, waving—I thought of my birth family and wondered what Mama would say if she could see me now. Charles and Nina and Glendora would be mortified. "Get down from there right this minute, Patsy Lou," Carlos would demand, fully expecting me to obey. That thought caused me to laugh out loud as I rode along, the wind whipping my robe in the air behind me and making the long rainbow ribbons on my chapeau flutter.

Writing about my birth family put me in mind of our last reunion at a rambling summerhouse I rented at Stinson Beach, a romantic site at the foot of Mount Tamaulipas with access to three miles of pristine sand. The house had room enough for all my siblings: Carlos and Marilee; Nina and Harold; Charles and his wife, Corrine; Faye and Cecil; Poor Little Glendora and her new husband, Charlie; Little Jimmy and Jeri; and me. On the last day of our get-together, I handed each of my family members a fat white candle to carry to the beach and scrunch down into the sand near the ocean's edge. With long matches, we lit our candles and then gave voice to our hopes and dreams. And like a litany on a cold night, we wished for Love, Family, Love, Family, Love, Family, Love, Love, Love. The words were uttered through the tears that always welled up and spilled over in our tenderhearted family.

Unaccustomedly silent, we stood on the sand of that pristine white beach on a crisp autumn night with our candles glowing like a morning sunrise after a smothering Oklahoma dust storm. Our lights blazed into the darkness of night as the ocean crashed and receded and crashed on shore again, like the unremitting cycle of birth and death. The incandescent night with dazzling stars wheeling overhead seemed brighter still because of those surrounding me. The distillation of the dreams and hopes of my siblings and of me was an openly expressed need for love, for the wish to be close. There was only love reflected in each of our faces, having let go of childhood angst and forgiven one another for grievances both real and imagined.

Mary McNamara wrote, "Family, in whatever state it finds itself, remains family; without forgiveness there can be no love. And without love, it really is all for naught."

Enduring in spite of treacherous tides, sometimes thrown against sharp rocks, much like the waves that lashed that huge bolder in the Atlantic Ocean that I viewed from the window of an airplane upon my arrival at Lages Air Force Base in the Azores Islands—only a few days ago it seemed—I continue on.

After writing all these pages, bringing up memories that I haven't thought of in forever and a day, I'm feeling good given my age. But I find I need to nap more often than I once did. And sleeping, I often slip into dreams, and when I do, well, there I am, bouncing along in Daddy's old Model A Ford, a kid still. Daddy tells Mama to keep us quiet, to give us soda crackers and rat cheese or something. A wooden slat trailer piled high with broken furniture weaves along on the road behind us. Bossy swishes her tail outside the trailer railings. A black-tailed prairie dog stands on a mound of sand in a lonesome Oklahoma field, causing Rat-Dog to bounce up to the window and let out excited little barks. Charles quiets him with nibbles of cheese.

Poor Little Glendora says to me, "Y'all are as ugly as a mud fence. Go eat worms."

I grab Mama's coffeepot and hit her over the head. "Y'all go eat worms your own stupid self!"

"*Girls!*" Mama shouts. "Y'all are acting like sinners. We're going to sing now." She leads off with "Amazing Grace," a well-worn hymn that is embedded in my brain. We sing loudly, trying to outdo each other and to be heard over the rattling car and bumping trailer.

"Amazing grace, how sweet the sound . . . Through many dangers, toils, and snares . . . we have already come. T'was grace that brought us safe thus far . . . and grace will lead us home."

CPSIA information can be obtained at www.ICGtesting.com
Printed in the USA
BVOW09s0810150914

366788BV00002B/1/P